Code

of

Silence

Ethics of Disasters

Robert Lynn Cook

First Edition

Trojan Publishing Co. • Jefferson City, Missouri

Code of Silence: Ethics of Disasters
by Robert Lynn Cook
Copyright © 2003 by Robert L. Cook

Manufactured and printed in the United States of America. Published by Trojan Publishing Co., PMB #224, 200 Madison St., Suite 380, Jefferson City, MO 65101-3280.

Trojan Publishing is a division of AEC Education Consultants (AEC), a Limited Liability Corporation, LLC, in Jefferson City, Missouri. AEC Education Consultants is an education and publishing business that helps AEC companies excel and helps the public better understand the AEC process. For information on other books by the author, seminars, workshops, and consulting services, please visit the AEC Web site at

http://www.AEC-Education-Consultants.com

Publisher's Cataloging-in-Publication
(Provided by Quality Books, Inc.)

Cook, Robert Lynn
    Code of silence : ethics of disasters / Robert Lynn Cook. -- 1st ed.
    p. cm.
    Includes bibliographical references and index.
    LCCN 2002110265
    ISBN 0-9720984-4-5

    1. Engineering ethics. 2. Disasters--Moral and ethical aspects. 3. Engineering design. 4. Industrial safety. I. Title.

TA157.C66 2002   174'.962
                         QBI02-200647

Dedication

- The 114 men, women, and children who lost their lives at the Kansas City Hyatt Regency Hotel in 1981

- The seven astronauts who died on the space shuttle Challenger in 1986

- The thousands of victims and survivors of the 2001 New York World Trade Center disaster and their rescuers and families

Acknowledgments

This book would not have been completed without the quiet patience and loving support of my wife, Sharron, for over 33 years. She spent countless hours patiently listening to me and editing the many versions of this book, and then gently explaining to me where I was wrong. My family, including Matthew and Susan, kept me focused, and I sincerely thank them publicly for their enduring gift of love.

I thank architect Bob Berkebile and Kansas City police officer Bob Dickerson for allowing me to interview them about their tragic experiences connected with the Kansas City Hyatt Regency Hotel skywalk collapse.

I owe thanks to Thomas M. White, an Omaha attorney and friend, who helped me to realize that every generation must battle injustice wherever it is found—and that our Constitutional freedoms must be secured each generation. And I extend my deepest gratitude to my former students at the University of Nebraska, who learned with me to apply workplace ethics in the present.

I thank the National Society of Professional Engineers and the Accreditation Board for Engineering and Technology, which allowed me to print their codes of ethics in the Appendices.

I express sincere appreciation and gratitude to Denise and Fred Vultee, English and journalism professionals, who tirelessly edited my manuscript. This book reflects their expertise and tolerance of engineers who generally have few writing skills. Any writing mistakes in this book reflect my inability, not theirs, to listen and learn.

Finally, I thank the authors, publishers, and photographers who granted me permission to use their copyrighted material and photographs, as acknowledged in the footnotes, references, and endnotes.

About the Author

Robert L. Cook, an authority on ethics in the workplace, is a licensed Professional Engineer, an author, educator, and business owner with over three decades of experience in engineering, construction, and higher education. His company provides consulting and educational services to private companies, colleges, architectural and engineering groups, construction organizations, and associated professionals.

Until 2001, Cook was a distinguished tenured professor in engineering and technology, and since leaving his academic position, he has continued to teach as a consultant. His company offers regular courses, short courses, workshops, and seminars in business and professional ethics, business methods and operations, construction engineering operations, construction management, project estimating, and project scheduling.

Cook earned a B.S. in Civil Engineering (Structures) in 1970 and an M.S. in Civil Engineering (Construction and Engineering Management) in 1975 from the University of Missouri at Rolla and at Columbia, respectively. He designed bridges for a government agency until 1975, and then, he established a number of successful companies in consulting engineering, building construction, and construction-management in the Midwest during the 1970s and 1980s.

He is a member of the International Network of Engineers & Scientists for Global Responsibility, the American Society of Civil Engineers, and the National Society of Professional Engineers and its affiliated ethics institute. He has served on many professional and higher education committees over the years. You are encouraged to contact him about his ideas in this book and his consulting services. Please visit his website at

<http://www.**AEC-Education-Consultants.com**

Table of Contents

Preface   **x**

List of Illustrations and Photographs   **xvi**

PART 1: THE REALITY OF MAN-MADE DISASTERS

Chapter 1: The Good, the Bad, and the Ugly   **2**

Things We Want to Forget	2
The World Trade Center Disaster	5
The Possibility of the Good	10
The Reality of the Bad	16
The Ugly Truth: Code of Silence	17
The Spectrum of Evil	19
The Ultimate Evil: Industrialized Murder	22
History's Judgment of Technologists	27
Bibliography, Notes & Further Reading	28

Chapter 2: The Well-Traveled Road to Disasters   **30**

Everyday Moral Dilemmas	30
Moral Dilemmas in College	33
Moral Dilemmas in the Workplace	35
Innovative Designs—Human Experiments	40
Dangerous Workplaces	41
Significant Disasters of the 20th Century	44
Galloping Gerdie: A Prelude	56
Bibliography, Notes & Further Reading	60

Chapter 3: The Hyatt Regency Hotel Disaster   **63**

Two Defining Disasters	63
The Terrible Night	65
The Rescuers' Nightmares	68
Technical Reasons for the Failure	72
Gross Negligence by Engineers	75
Bibliography, Notes & Further Reading	78

Chapter 4: The Space Shuttle Challenger Disaster   80

A Cold Morning   80
Origins of the Disaster   81
No Informed Consent   84
Lessons Learned from the Disaster   85
Neglect of Basic Principles   87
Bibliography, Notes & Further Reading   90

PART 2: THE ORIGINS OF THE CODE OF SILENCE

Chapter 5: True Beliefs and Dangerous Myths   92

True Believers in Our Midst   92
The Technical Imperative   95
Emotional Detachment   97
Obedience and Compliance   100
Planned Accidents   107
Fail-Safe Computer Designs   111
The Myth: "You Can't Teach Ethics"   114
Bibliography, Notes & Further Reading   118

Chapter 6: Common Characteristics and Practices   120

Technologists as a Distinct Group   120
Common Backgrounds and Goals   121
Business as Usual   125
Accepted Industry Practices   129
Team Players   132
Personal and Professional Responsibility   134
Bibliography, Notes & Further Reading   139

Chapter 7: Industrial—Military—University Complex   142

The Money Connection	142
Cost-Benefit Analysis	143
Bidding Lowest-Cost Projects	146
Doctrines of Academe	150
Inner Sanctums of the University	152
The Business of Higher Education	157
Bibliography, Notes & Further Reading	160

Chapter 8: Dirty Little Secrets in Universities   163

Dysfunctional University "Families"	163
The Rat Syndrome	165
Poison in the University	167
Mobbing in the Workplace	169
Tunnel Vision in Academe	171
Emphasis on Specialization	174
Bibliography, Notes & Further Reading	178

PART 3: THE SEARCH FOR WORKPLACE ETHICS

Chapter 9: The Great Ideas of Humankind   182

Truth or Consequences	182
Informed Consent	184
The Truth in Great Ideas	188
Repression of the Truth	190
Bibliography, Notes & Further Reading	193

Chapter 10: The Instinct to Be Moral   194

Why Be Moral?	194
Genuine Evil and Interrelatedness	200
The Process of Moral Development	204
The Quest for Truth about Our "Self"	207
Professional Success and Personal Failure	211
The Connection with Ethics	215
Bibliography, Notes & Further Reading	216

Chapter 11: The Journey Toward Ethics   218

The Meaning of Ethics   218
Right and Wrong Actions   220
Codes of Ethics for Professionals   225
Checklists for Ethical Conduct   229
Bibliography, Notes & Further Reading   231

Chapter 12: The Process Toward Ethical Decisions   232

Joe's Moral Dilemma   232
FAIL-SAFE Ethics Checklist for Joe   234
After Joe's Decision: What Next?   247
Applied Ethics: Hyatt and Challenger   249
A Vision for the 21st Century   254
Hope: Possibility of a Fail-Safe Institute   258
Final Reflections on Truth   259
Bibliography, Notes & Further Reading   263

Appendix A: Significant Disasters   265
Appendix B: Characteristics of Technologists   271
Appendix C: Codes of Ethics   277
Index   283

Preface

"Power corrupts the few, while weakness corrupts the many."

Eric Hoffer, The Passionate State of Mind, 1954.

Infamous man-made tragedies in history change everything. December 7, 1941, is one example. The morning of September 11, 2001, is another. Most of us will remember where we were on that day at 8:46 a.m. (Eastern time). Our conceptions about personal safety were forever changed by the events on that warm fall morning, which became known simply as "9-11." This book was ready to publish before 9-11, but I knew this mega-disaster had its place in *Code of Silence.*

I remember walking into a Federal District Court room in Omaha, Nebraska, just as passenger airliners were becoming guided human bombs. In less than two hours, the twin towers of the New York World Trade Center (WTC) collapsed and entombed thousands of people.

We are not as safe as we want to believe.

From the Titanic to the Challenger to the World Trade Center disaster, an unspoken and dangerous scientific orthodoxy has placed a trusting public at risk. A tacit conspiracy began among scientists nearly 400 years ago because of a turf war. Religious leaders drew an implicit line in the sand, and large numbers of engineers and scientists have continued to comply with its boundaries. Today, this unspoken but active agreement continues to mask the truth about the real cause of most man-made disasters. The ethics of creative technologists were, and are, compromised.

The momentous and dangerous system began in the early 17th century, when scientists fought with organized religion during the time of Galileo. Religious leaders declared they would deal with the supernatural issues, and most prominent scientists agreed to work only with the natural world. Science defined itself as value-free in order not to cross the boundaries dictated by the religious authorities. This mind-set became ingrained in our scientific methodology and in the minds of technologists educated at our universities.

In partnership with religious leaders, scientists and other technologists fundamentally shifted personal moral responsibility for their actions away from themselves. Although many technologists would struggle with the inherent moral dilemmas, the engineering and scientific communities usually transferred their moral responsibility to government and corporate authorities. This book is about this denial of accountability, about the origins of preventable disasters, and about the search for workplace ethics.

> **How much is your life worth? Accountants, engineers, and scientists have already decided.**

Corporate businesses worldwide place a dollar value on human life every day. Yet sadly, in contrast, some people place no value on human life, their own or their innocent victims'. In the 20th century, German Nazis and their supporters were the most notorious example of technologists' connections to genuine evil. But in this century, irrational madmen struck again, this time at the very heart of America's military and economic power centers.

A rational human being, for this book's purposes, is defined as one who desires to avoid death, pain, and loss of opportunity, and to acquire the basic needs of life (food, water, shelter, clothing, etc.). While such a definition might omit many acts that are eminently rational—parents' forgoing a better-paying job to keep their children in a preferred school, for example—and leaves aside questions of how one's acts affect others, it covers basics that are widely recognized as logical and reasonable for human beings to desire.[a] And the desire and will to survive are implicit in this concept of rationality.

The WTC terrorists who committed suicide while killing innocent human beings lacked the will to survive. According to my definition, they were not rational. But the Nazis wanted to kill and live. Would this make them rational? Absolutely not. Neither the WTC terrorists nor the Nazis granted the basic need and right of survival to others. Their acts were irrational, as I will explain later when I argue why a person should be moral.

For the first time in recent memory, the word "evil" has become popular again in mainstream America. In the days immediately following 9-11, the president of the United States, George W. Bush, spoke of evil, "evildoers," and those who support evil, directly or indirectly. The terrorists intended to kill as many innocent people as possible.

Much will be written about the disaster on September 11, 2001. Without a doubt, such acts exemplify genuine evil. Within minutes of the collapse, people wanted to know how and why such a man-made disaster could have happened. Initially, the search for answers centered on the inability of the FBI and other law enforcement agencies to intercept the terrorists. But eventually, the design and construction of the twin towers also will be scrutinized.

Whether dangerous technology or lack of law enforcement will carry the brunt of the blame, this alarming fact seems apparent: The WTC terrorists acquired knowledge from someone about structural design and demolition. They used this specialized knowledge to murder more than 3,000 innocent human beings. It is highly unlikely that the terrorists were simply lucky when they flew large, fully fueled passenger airliners full-throttle into the most vulnerable floors of the WTC's twin towers.

Although this book briefly describes the active genuine evil of Nazi engineers and the WTC terrorists, the *Code of Silence*

---

[a] In Part 3, I will expand this definition to include: A rational person neither seeks pain nor gives up food—nor, I believe, does a rational person inflict pain on or deny food to another human being.

is about a type of genuine evil that is more subtle and widespread—and just as dangerous. Technologists participate in passive evil when they abandon personal moral responsibility in the creation of technology. This abandonment can take the form of careless and negligent actions or inaction. Technologists may not intend harm when design flaws cause a building or bridge to collapse, but the result is the same: Innocent people die in preventable tragedies.

> **The technology professions have conspired to hide this participation in passive evil, as I will define it in Chapter 1.**

Author and philosopher Eric Hoffer is right: The weaknesses of the silent majority cause untold suffering. When a person observes an injustice, or an injustice about to happen, and does nothing to stop it, this, too, is genuine, albeit passive, evil. I believe significant numbers of technologists have fallen into this disguised category of evil, as the space shuttle Challenger, the Hyatt Regency Hotel, and other similar disasters demonstrate.

I have given passive evil the name "Code of Silence," or simply "the Code." The Code keeps the "dirty little family secrets" about how technologists abandon their personal moral and social responsibility, allowing active and passive evil to flourish. Many technologists actively suppress troubling thoughts about their direct or indirect roles in preventable man-made tragedies. In Part 2, "Origins of the Code of Silence," this suppression of the truth is shown to be a disease of the mind, the heart, and the soul.

What are the common origins of the Code in today's culture? I first experienced the effects of the Code in my family and in the workplace. But other "families" hide dirty little secrets as well. The origins of preventable disasters and their connections with workplace ethics became clearer when I taught ethics, engineering, and technology for 15 years. Our institutions of higher learning also hide some dirty little secrets.

A university education in technology is often a breeding ground for the Code, and it moves into corporate America mostly unquestioned. The shadowy world of ivory towers conceals a dark side of technologists' higher education that threatens everyone's health and safety. This dark side has played a key role in the thousands of significant disasters during the last 100 years.

> **By presenting the horror and reality of man-made disasters, this book allows readers to examine and judge the act of creation, the creation itself, and the creators.**

I had three objectives in writing about the good, the bad, and the ugliness of technology's creation and application. First, accountants, engineers, scientists, and other technologists should re-evaluate the ways in which they think about their work and professions. Society needs them to feel empathetically, not just think intelligently, about their creative work. So, the first objective was to challenge technologists to reassess their role as faithful agents of their clients and balance that legal role with their moral obligations as protectors of life.

Second, non-technologists and the public need to be informed about the dangers that we all face. An informed public can make wiser choices in a democratic society. I suspect people in the World Trade Center on September 11 believed the structures were safe. People, as users of technology, should understand that they are part of an ongoing experiment. The trial-and-error method of engineering described in this book should require the people's informed consent. The second objective, then, was to inform the public to recognize the risks and to demand changes where they are needed.

My third objective was personal. I wanted to learn why these dangerous behaviors exist and where they originated. I wanted to know whether I had unknowingly participated in the Code. To do this, I discovered that I had to travel a path of self-discovery. Along the way, I have come to believe that a rational human being has an instinct to be moral. If this is true, it has profound implications for our culture of technology. So, the third objective was to practice what I had been teaching.

Perhaps by sharing my experiences as a husband and father, consultant and educator, licensed engineer and business owner, I can help fellow professionals, politicians, and the public to better understand the challenges—opportunities and risks—that all of us face during this third millennium. The future will be what we make it or what, by our weaknesses, we allow it to become.

Robert L. Cook

"Change is one thing, progress is another.

'Change' is scientific, progress is ethical; change is indisputable, whereas progress is a matter of controversy."

Bertrand Russell, Unpopular Essays, 1950, p. 34.

List of Illustrations
and Photographs

Chapter 1

Figure 1: Spectrum of Evil

Chapter 2

Figure 2: Accident Rates by Aircraft

Figure 3: Accident Rates by Year

Figure 4: Tacoma Narrows Bridge Collapse

Chapter 3

Figure 5: Hyatt Regency Hotel Lobby after Failure

Figure 6: Schematic of Skywalks before Failure

Figure 7: Skywalk Box Beam Connection

Chapter 4

Figure 8: Typical NASA Space Shuttle Schematic

Chapter 10

Figure 9: Levels of Moral Development

Chapter 11

Figure 10: The Fail-Safe Checklist for
Ethical Decision-making

Part 1: The Reality of Man-Made Disasters

*****

"Your scientists were so preoccupied with whether or not they could, they didn't stop to think if they should!"

Malcolm in "Jurassic Park," the movie

Chapter 1
The Good, the Bad, & the Ugly

Things We Want to Forget

"I saw children's bodies that couldn't have been more than six or seven years old ... and many bodies were not even recognizable as human beings."[a] Although this may sound like the World Trade Center disaster scene, it has been repeated thousands of times during the last hundred years. The rescuer who said this was not a soldier in a battlefield but a police officer in a city street arranged as a triage area in front of the Kansas City Hyatt Regency Hotel.

On this hot July evening in 1981, elevated pedestrian walkways called skybridges had just collapsed, sending tons of concrete and twisted steel to the floor of the hotel lobby. The tragedy could have—and should have—been prevented. The collapse changed the lives of thousands, and eventually it would be determined that 114 people died because of an engineer's gross negligence.

> **You and I want to believe that we are safe in our buildings, on our bridges, and in our airplanes.**

But sometimes this belief does not reflect reality, nor does it recognize the lessons of history. The collapse of the World

---

[a] In 1998, I interviewed a Kansas City police officer, Bob Dickerson, who was one of the first rescuers to arrive at the Kansas City Hyatt Regency walkways collapse in 1981.

Trade Center twin towers on September 11, 2001, etched this lesson into our collective memories.

As in the World Trade Center disaster that September morning in 2001, rescuers at the Hyatt scene found most victims in the debris unrecognizable as human beings. Though the death toll was far lower, at 114, the Hyatt disaster remains the worst of its kind in the United States.

Most of us will remember where we were at 8:46 on the morning of September 11, 2001. My wife and I were walking into U.S. District Court in Omaha, Nebraska. The worst terrorist attack in the history of the United States occurred during a trial in which I was testifying about freedom of speech issues.[b]

This terrible event in the heart of New York City became known simply as …"9-11."

The tallest structures in America, New York's World Trade Center twin towers, collapsed within hours after passenger airliners slammed into them. Almost 3,000 people died, hundreds more than in the sneak attack at Pearl Harbor on December 7, 1941. The surprise attack and mass murder in Pennsylvania, New York, and Washington, D.C., on September 11 were assaults on Americans' freedoms. The "Code of Silence" described in this book is also an assault on our life, liberty, and pursuit of happiness.

The "Code of Silence" describes a pervasive and dangerous behavior among specially trained technologists. The Code can be understood as an unwritten convention among technologists who exhibit behaviors that foster man-made disasters. It consists of two primary attributes: (1) failure to accept

---

[b] A large number of engineering and technology students at a Midwest state university had been threatened and punished after they wrote a letter to university administrators asking them to investigate some professors, alleging incompetence and unethical actions toward students.

personal moral[c] and social responsibility for the creation and application of technology, and (2) participation in a conspiracy of silence to hide this failure and its connection with man-made disasters.

The Code hides the failure of some technologists to approach the creation and use of technology holistically. As a result, preventable man-made disasters over the last century show a pattern of behavior among designers and creators, many of whom have pretended not to recognize this lack of personal moral responsibility in others. And they certainly prefer not to acknowledge such behavior in themselves. It is an attitude of business as usual.

Who are these professionals called technologists? They are the men and women who create, design, or construct the things of our culture. Some well-known examples are engineers, architects, contractors, scientists, professors, and other groups labeled professionals, who are usually licensed to practice by a government agency. Millions of technologists quietly work in their specialties while most people know little about them and how they think or work.

> **In the pages that follow, I neither condemn nor defend the advance of technology.**

The problem of preventable disasters is not the advance of technology itself. It is human beings' avoidance of personal moral and professional responsibility for their creative work. The underlying reasons for most preventable disasters originate in the human heart, in the dark recesses of minds trained to think

---

[c] In Chapters 9 and 10, I define and explain the concepts of good, right, moral, and ethical. My concept of moral responsibility should not be confused with any particular religious dogma, current trends, or political movements. In this book, I define the concept of good or moral as a rational human being's need, desire, and ability to act in ways that do no harm to one's self and to others. Moral acts promote well being in all life, but evil or immoral acts cause emotional harm, and thus physical harm to life.

rationally—minds trained by scientific orthodoxy to be emotionally uninvolved and free of principled constraints when creating.

This mind-set allows creators to be detached from the potential consequences of the uses of their creations. Technologists who are narrowly focused in their creative work, coupled with business managers overly concerned with immediate business profits, create or allow a work environment favorable to the Code.

Thousands of professionals responsible for advances in technology have created many good things to make life easier and healthier. But these advances also have an ugly side. Most technologists say that the ugliness is the price we must pay for progress. I will argue that it need not—and should not—be this way. In the end, you will have to decide which premise is true, because the price might be life itself.

The World Trade Center Disaster

The World Trade Center disaster has some aspects in common with other man-made disasters. The terrorists' acts were something out of fiction, and orthodox technologists seldom design things to be safe from unthinkable acts. Why? The projects might be too costly to build, or the designers simply could not imagine the unimaginable. Should technologists create with these types of acts in mind? Sometimes, it may be necessary, prudent, and honorable to do so—especially in a post-9-11 era.

> **Most of us feel less safe than before 9-ll, and with good reason.**

President Bush proclaimed on September 11 that America was in a "state of war" with terrorists and their supporters who were responsible for the collapse of the WTC twin towers. Terrorists hijacked four passenger airliners and flew a fuel-laden plane into each of the skyscrapers that had dominated the skyline of New York City and that, for many, had represented the power and economic strength of the United States. Another plane crashed into the Pentagon outside Washington and killed hundreds, including the passengers on the plane.

A fourth hijacked plane, also piloted by terrorists and reportedly headed for the White House, crashed into a Pennsylvania field because passengers heard of the other attacks on their cell phones and apparently tried to overcome the terrorists. There were many heroes on 9-11. But evil was also very real, organized, and effective in the use of advanced technologies to kill.

Investigators of the disaster may never know the roles or the names of professionals who planned and executed the technical side of the terrorist acts. Whether they were active or passive, the result was the same—death and destruction on a scale Americans had not seen since World War II. The fact is that technical expertise and knowledge were needed to bring down the WTC towers.

The WTC had been under attack before 2001. Terrorists exploded a bomb in the parking garage of one of the WTC towers in 1993, but it failed to bring down the structure. Several people died, and many were injured, but the steel columns and beams withstood the powerful blast. Perhaps the terrorists' technical advisors were using a trial-and-error method of demolition. Wherever the truth may lie, we learned that our enemies wanted to bring down a landmark structure. They still do.

Technical data and knowledge openly available on the World Wide Web may have played a passive role in some tragedies, including the WTC. And this possibility raises even more questions: Should technologists place limits on the distribution of sensitive information that could be used by terrorists? I believe we should, within judicial limits and safeguards of our democratic freedoms. It was government policy to do so, even before 9-11.

Our government protects us by classifying specific military information and attempting to keep it from our enemies. It restricts the flow of information about supercomputers, military equipment, nuclear power plants, industrial equipment, and sensitive government buildings. Espionage has managed to circumvent some of these safeguards, but the attempt to protect American citizens is justified. When President Bush proclaimed we were at war after 9-11, protection became even more essential. Sensitive data about power plants, bridges, and other potential terrorist targets should be protected. It is rational to do so.[d]

For a moment, let's consider an alternative to the possibility that published material fell into the hands of the terrorists. Maybe some of the terrorists were trained in American universities as structural engineers or pilots. As an open society, we allow foreign nationals to study with few restrictions, although, for our protection, the government does place some restrictions on any training that involves national security. Should we restrict this training?

Perhaps a national policy review on these issues is warranted. But I do not favor a general restriction, for instance, in structural engineering or in physics. The potential benefits of foreign students' positive exposure to American society outweigh any possible transfer of critical information into the wrong hands. Foreign students who have studied in the United States might return to their homelands better equipped to help raise the standard of living or solve critical social problems. However, this does not mean that we should share existing or future plans of power plants or airplanes or other critical information. A balance of concerns should be found.

Should engineers and other technologists have anticipated the misuse of their creations and done more to prevent disasters? This book addresses this very question. The answer is yes, but it

---

[d] Again, a rational human being will be defined throughout this book as one who desires to avoid death, pain, and loss of opportunity, and to acquire the basic needs of life (food, water, shelter, clothing, etc.). Portions of this concept were taken from my notes during a seminar presented by philosopher Michael Davis. Please see Notes at the end of this chapter.

usually will cost many more dollars. As you will read, engineers, accountants, and other experts use a cost-benefit analysis to place a dollar value on your life and mine. The process can be very misleading.

Some things should not be, or should never have been, created—the efficient crematoriums built by engineers for the Nazi Holocaust, for example. Others should be questioned: The building of taller and taller skyscrapers cannot be justified economically, much less for safety concerns, above about 50 floors.

> **The construction of super-tall buildings usually stems from the need of the buildings' owners, designers, and builders to satisfy their own egos.**

Ask any urban fire chief or fire marshal about the inherent dangers of a super-tall building and you will get the same answer: Occupants are at great risk above levels that fire ladders can reach, about ten floors or less. The "safe" height is much less than the public has been led to believe. Most of the people who died in the WTC towers were above the impact point of the airplanes, above the reach of any rescue attempts. More people might have escaped if the stairwells had been better protected.

The WTC terrorists and their technical advisors must have recognized the inherent weakness of the tallest skyscrapers: The steel columns become smaller as the structure gets taller. Therefore, the area above the midpoint and below the top of the structures became the terrorists' calculated targets.

The most economical design, which corporate owners usually demand and designers usually supply, dominates the way we build things. No doubt this has contributed to tragic results in many disasters. There are straightforward reasons to question the wisdom of the "lowest contract price" method of design and construction. As a general building contractor and a structural engineer, I have seen the problem from both perspectives.[e] The major structural members of the twin towers were designed with fire-retardant coatings,[1] but the terrorists (and their co-conspirators) must have calculated the best size airplane and the correct amount of jet fuel to overcome this design. Advanced technological knowledge about the behavior of steel when it is quickly super-heated probably made possible the progressive collapse of the twin towers.

The structural columns and beams melted at the location of each airplane's entry. Knowledge about the size of the columns and beams at each floor level most likely not only determined the airplanes' entry points but also contributed to the meltdown. The calculated weight of floors above the airplanes' entry points provided the force necessary to collapse all floors, one on top of the other, in a pancake pattern—all the way down into the seven-floor basement.

The terrorists' plans were too well executed for the result to have been a "lucky" guess, as some people have speculated. In fact, without all the available engineering knowledge, the disaster would not have been possible. I am not suggesting that the designers and builders of the WTC were negligent in their original design. It is my understanding that the design actually included the possibility of a Boeing 707 airplane's crashing into the towers. But I am suggesting two things about the role of technology in the disaster.

First, engineering and scientific knowledge were crucial to the terrorists' plans. Even if technologists did not have a direct or active role in "engineering" the disaster, free access to information critical to the collapse mechanism most likely played a key role. Before 9-11, no one in our free society took seriously such a use of technology. Or, if some technologists did, their voices were not loud enough.

---

[e] Chapter 7 presents the good and the bad of various contract methods.

The Internet, not even imagined at the time of the WTC's design, rapidly became the place for anyone with a modem to learn about almost anything. The design of an atomic bomb was reportedly available on the Internet and in published books. Should we have foreseen the possibility that technology would be misused? Maybe. There were precedents. The technologists' roles in the Holocaust are well documented.

Second, a super-tall, cost-effective structure is inherently dangerous, regardless of what some technologists may publicly say. It tests the limits of a team effort and of knowledge about old or new materials under stress. Engineers and designers apparently calculated the design to the best of their abilities and knowledge at the time of construction, but the WTC was vulnerable from the beginning. Most super-tall buildings are.

Structures designed to be safe, and not nearly as tall as the WTC towers, collapsed during earthquakes in the 1990s. They, too, were thought to be fail-safe. And the quick evacuation of thousands of people remains a difficult, if not impossible, task, as the WTC demonstrated. Some days the towers held as many as 100,000 people. If there was any luck at all in the disaster, it was in the precious minutes the buildings stood while most of the people did escape. The good and the bad seem to co-exist with technology's advance.

As you will read in Part 2, we technologists are not very good at introspection and assessing ethical issues, but the process just might prevent another Titanic, Hyatt, Challenger, or WTC disaster. So, before we further explore the darker side of technology's creation and application, I ask you to consider the good things human beings have accomplished. I will return to the reality of the bad caused by the ugliness of the Code of Silence.

The Possibility of the Good

The Taoist's Yin and Yang, or positive and negative traits, apply to the paradox of technology: Freedom to be creative can produce good or evil. Let's think positively for the moment and

 examine the benefits of the things that technologists can create. There are many.

Over the last hundred years, the rate of technological advancement has increased dramatically, and many informed people believe that it will continue to increase at an even faster rate.[2] Unparalleled advances have occurred in medicine, engineering, astronomy, physics, life sciences, and many other scientific areas. This new millennium may take us "where no man has gone before," as Captain Kirk was fond of saying in the *Star Trek* television series and movies.

We creators of technology have produced many benefits for humankind over the centuries. Consider, for instance, medicine and related areas. Scientists in the last century have learned to control or, in some cases, eliminate the most dreaded diseases by using vaccination, surgery, chemicals, and radiation treatments. Smallpox has been eliminated, at least within the human population—though a terrorist could change that overnight.

Physicians and scientists learned to replace human hearts, heart valves, kidneys, livers, and other organs. At the start of the 21st century, gene therapy and animal cloning were hot news. Genetic engineering arrived, and with it a hope for less disease and fewer genetic defects. Scientists may be able to grow human body parts in the near future.

In America and in other industrialized nations, most of us take for granted the availability of medicines and medical services. Medical technologists are exploring the brain with new machines engineered to probe how we think and act. MRI and CAT scans are in our common vocabulary. We use words like "synapse" and "DNA" without thinking how extraordinary this technology really is.

Science and engineering have provided many of us with extended life spans, and it appears that a life expectancy of 110 or 120 years may be possible in the 21st century, at least for those lucky enough to be born in a country like America.

The 20th century gave us atomic fission, quantum theories, subatomic particles called quarks, the Big Bang Theory, and E=mc^2. Physicists have given us the Unified Theory of weak forces and the electrical forces, which are apparently the same. The Chaos and Superstring Theories are new scientific frontiers.[3]

We have power generation plants producing electricity from fossil fuels, from hydro-generation, from the atom, from the wind, from geothermal sources, and from the sun's energy. Humans circle our home planet in space stations and space vehicles. They have walked many times on the moon and returned safely to Earth, and may soon be able to walk on the surface of Mars.

Today we can venture deep inside the Earth or reach the ocean floors to mine for natural resources and to learn the origins of our planet. We can explore the human mind using myriad techniques pioneered by Sigmund Freud and his followers.

Name any scientific field and you will find significant advances in technology. A list of technological achievements of the 20th century could include airplanes, fiber optics, lasers, personal computers, plastics, robotics, satellite technology, and television.[4] Every reader could make his or her own list of advancements in technology that have made life easier in many parts of the world.

Consider the impact of some of the greatest engineering feats during the last century. The Atlantic and Pacific oceans were connected by the Panama Canal. The Sears Tower eclipsed the Empire State Building. Now a building that would be nearly twice the height of the Sears Tower is reportedly on the design tables.

The Golden Gate Bridge in San Francisco is no longer the longest suspension bridge. The Hoover Dam is no longer considered the largest or most impressive power producer in the world. We have indoor sports stadiums larger than small cities and colossal oil-drilling platforms in the oceans. We can ride the train through the tunnel connecting France and England. The Chunnel, as the tunnel under the sea is called, opened in 1994 and is truly a modern marvel of technology and engineering.

The 20th century also spawned the World Wide Web and the Internet. Increasingly, an informed person needs to know how to use that technology. The computer has become one of the most significant advances in technology and continues to revolutionize our world at a very hurried pace. My digital wristwatch is more "intelligent" than my first desktop computer of the early 1980s.

Americans take for granted their washing machines, microwave ovens, e-mail, and other modern marvels. Gadgets, appliances, toys, software, vehicles, and other products seem to have a life of their own. Most of us began using "artificial intelligence" in software over a decade ago without knowing it. Now it's commonplace: Built into our cars, kitchen appliances, children's toys, robots, and many other machines are computer chips that make them seem almost alive. Artificial intelligence is built into computer software to help run efficiently our transportation, industrial, and informational systems.

Computer engineers may specialize in designing, developing, and building the computer systems that guide the space shuttle or developing a better "brain" for a microwave oven. Chemical engineers and chemists may specialize in new compounds for oil synthetics or life-saving medicines.

A team effort makes these things possible. Usually, people think of the scientist as the primary mover, but millions of highly trained engineers who represent many disciplines bring discoveries to life. Scientists and engineers are alike in several ways, but their work domains differ significantly. To understand the Code, you need to know the differences.

Generally, engineers study the knowledge gained by scientists and use it in practical applications that their culture wants. Along the way, engineers may make further discoveries, but their real goal is not knowledge for its own sake. For their companies to make money, they must apply knowledge to current opportunities. Engineers thrive in this business environment.

The Accrediting Board for Engineering and Technology[5] defines engineering as the profession in which a knowledge of the mathematical and natural sciences gained by study, experience and practice is applied with judgment to develop ways to utilize, *economically*, the materials and forces of nature for the benefit of mankind.

Consider the phrase "judgment ... for the benefit of mankind." It indicates clearly the honorable and ethical component that *should be* in engineering. The word *economically* (my emphasis) implies a cost-benefit comparison. This process introduces students and practitioners of technology to the world of business and money.

Scientists share with engineers the restriction of "economical" in private and public work. Most scientists work in cost-sensitive environments. Cost-benefit comparison is one of the *true beliefs* of technologists and others who place a dollar value on your life.[f] In my field of civil engineering, engineers create systems and structures to control water resources for power, for flood control, and for recreation. Civil engineers design and general contractors build highways, railroads, waterways, airports, tunnels, buildings of all sizes and shapes, dams, bridges, and a multitude of other structures and systems that make up our infrastructure. In all these projects, the cost-benefit comparison is hard at work.

Technologists are responsible for many innovations in engineering during the last 150 years. Civil engineers have designed and built longer bridges, taller buildings, larger indoor sports stadiums, better highways, and larger dams. Mechanical engineers have designed and built better automobiles and trucks. We can now fly, ride, or float in machines unimagined even by science fiction writers a century ago. We have perfected the assembly line to mass-produce almost anything, whether we really

---

[f] Philosopher Eric Hoffer first used the term *true beliefs* to describe characteristics of people who are fanatical and irrational in their beliefs about reality. See Hoffer, *The True Believer* (Alexandria, Va.: Time Reading Program Special Ed., Time-Life Books, 1980). Part Two of this book explores these not-so-true "true beliefs" in my profession.

need it or not. These improvements were developed primarily from the work of the scientists who discovered the fundamental building blocks of the nature of things.

Through science and engineering, advancing technologies have changed the face of the Earth, the moon, and the universe beyond. Samuel Florman, a distinguished civil engineer, extolled engineering as an "existential pleasure."[g] According to Florman, before 1850, engineering was more a "craft" than a profession.[6] Between 1850 and 1950—the "Golden Age of Engineering" the number of engineers grew exponentially. And during the race to the moon in the 1960s, enrollments skyrocketed in engineering schools and colleges around the world.

Florman writes that the self-satisfaction of engineers during the last century came from several sources. One is the

simple pleasure of problem solving. But engineers also started "thinking of themselves as saviors of mankind" and "apostle[s] of democracy."[7] They thought their work and way of thinking were improving the world. Probably, the public did, too. I have heard many non-engineers say that engineers and other design technologists think differently from "normal" people.

Yes, technologists can create good things. Within another decade or so, computers may think like humans and eventually learn from their experiences as we do. In a classic science fiction movie, *2001—A Space Odyssey*, a near-human computer named HAL ran the space vehicle. If you are old enough to remember the movie, you probably remember that HAL's personality had a dark

---

[g] Existentialism is a doctrine derived from philosopher Søren Kierkegaard that says man is not part of an ordered metaphysical scheme. Rather, each individual must create his or her own being, each in his own specific situation and environment. Philosophers Sartre, Jaspers, and Heidegger argue the merits of these ideas.

side. HAL began systematically killing its human creators to protect itself. It was just science fiction, right?

The Reality of the Bad

Technologists use creative energy to provide many good things. But every good thing named in the previous section has a corollary that many people would rather forget. Nuclear fission must be examined in light of Hiroshima, Three Mile Island, Chernobyl, and toxic wastes. Genetic engineering must be examined in relation to the Holocaust victims and the Nazi doctors who experimented on them. The Titanic and many other experiments in technology were also considered creative innovations.

Florman argues that after 1950, engineering "entered a dark-age of criticism and self-doubt."[8] Perhaps it is not a coincidence that he chose 1950 as a turning point. Two world wars, the Holocaust, Hiroshima, and numerous high-profile technological failures had occurred by mid-20th century.

The deaths, in some cases of entire families, at the Kansas City Hyatt Regency Hotel in 1981 must be weighed against the passion to create taller and more impressive buildings. The Hyatt disaster was one of many system failures in the 20th century. Why do we need buildings twice the height of the Sears Tower? Could it be that they are only status symbols? Are they worth the risk? Not to those who may perish in these marvels of structural innovation.

Fire suppression systems sometimes do not work as planned. The WTC again was the prime example. To my knowledge, no one has found a way to extend a rescue ladder 1,100 feet, much less 2,300 feet, into the air.

The dichotomy between the good and the bad possibilities for technology's creation and application should give us pause before we condemn or defend technology.

I will argue throughout this book that technologists have a duty to exercise personal moral and social responsibility and accountability. They should accept responsibility and be held accountable for their actions or, in many cases, for their lack of appropriate action. Technologists have a professional and moral duty to create the best possibilities for all life, not just for their own well-being—or their own gratification.

Chapter 2, "The Well-Traveled Road to Disasters," takes you into the reality of the bad by first examining everyday moral dilemmas. These quandaries arise in the education, training, and workplaces of technologists. As you will read, dangerous workplaces and significant disasters over the last century form the reality of the bad in the creation and application of technology. The truth about the cause of these man-made tragedies is ugly.

The Ugly Truth: Code of Silence

The 20th century proved at least two widely accepted beliefs to be myths. First, the creators of technology wanted us to believe that we were safe from catastrophic failures. We were not. Second, technologists wanted us to believe that they were not responsible for the use or misuse of their inventions and discoveries. I believe they were.

Other professionals, such as doctors and attorneys, have also played key roles in man-made disasters, but this book is about technologists who design and build things. These highly trained professionals have printed codes of ethical conduct, which they are supposed to follow; two well-known examples are found in Appendix C.

The code they follow much too often, however, is the unwritten Code of Silence. The creation and use of technology too often center on increasing short-term profits for corporations instead of promoting long-term progress for humankind. The Code of Silence is our "dirty little secret" within the business of technology.[9]

> **The right to create technology without personal responsibility and accountability has become a religion to some professionals.[10]**

Too many technologists believe in a form of "creative manifest destiny," or the right to create anything without regard to the morality of its eventual use. Many prominent scientists have said that they only create, and that others should determine the ideology of technology's practical applications.

Innovation, or pushing the envelope, in science and engineering is considered an ultimate good. "Innovation is the name of the market game," according to Kate Gibney, assistant editor of *Prism* for the American Society for Engineering Education.[11] Simply put, this unwritten Code of technologists says, "We will create whatever we damn well please and let others decide how to use it."

A technologist who rocks the boat and accuses a fellow creator of wrongful acts is frequently labeled a whistle-blower and will likely be isolated and ostracized by fellow technologists.[12] Whistle-blowers face "living nightmares"[13] that can include threats against their lives, but the public is the ultimate victim of such intimidation.[h] Those who try to punish whistle-blowers or to prevent an open discussion of the truth are true practitioners of and believers in the Code.

Dr. Jeffrey Wigand, formerly a tobacco industry chemist, Roger Boisjoly, previously an engineer with Morton Thiokol and NASA, and Joe Carson, an engineer with the U.S. Department of Energy (DOE), learned first-hand about the perils of telling the truth. Wigand was the first tobacco technologist to state publicly that tobacco companies had attempted to hide the truth that

---

[h] The trauma that whistle-blowers experience is well documented; see, for example, Mike W. Martin and Roland Schinzinger, *Ethics in Engineering*. Engineers in the Challenger disaster were ostracized and isolated by their peers. The effects can be worse than those of a car wreck, according to the experts. (See Jim Robbins, "Wired for Sadness," *Discover*, April 2000, pp. 77-81).

nicotine is addictive. Boisjoly tried to stop the launch of the space shuttle Challenger but eventually lost his job. For more than a decade, Carson tried to protect the health and safety of workers at the DOE's nuclear weapons complex in Oak Ridge, Tennessee.

Wigand, Boisjoly, Carson, and others like them deserve our respect and gratitude, because they paid a high price to tell what they knew and when they knew it. They did not receive or ask for any monetary rewards for exposing deadly secrets. They must have felt it was their moral, civic, and professional duty to just tell the truth. Ordinary, everyday ethical decisions confront technologists like these men. How they handle ethical quandaries often determines the outcome of decisions like those Wigand, Boisjoly, and Carson faced.

The ugly truth is that the technologists who follow the Code, consciously or unconsciously, participate in genuine evil. Fellow workers, administrators, and business managers wanted to keep their dirty little family secrets, and Wigand, Boisjoly, and Carson stood in their way. This effort to hide the truth is the most insidious form of genuine evil: passive evil. Is this form of evil equivalent to the evil of those responsible for the WTC disaster or the Holocaust? No: One is passive and submissive, the other active and intentional. Yet the WTC and the Holocaust comprised both active and passive evil. A spectrum of evil encompasses the depth and breadth of the Code of Silence in its active and passive forms.

The Spectrum of Evil

What is evil? Does genuine evil even exist? Questions like these continue to haunt us. To answer them, we need only look at the roles technologists played in Hitler's Final Solution. Some philosophical concepts of evil will help us understand the origin of this ultimate genuine evil.

M. Scott Peck offers three major theological models of evil in *People of the Lie*.[14] Although theological models can be helpful, I prefer a model Peck offers in his own understanding toward a psychology of evil. Peck believes that evil is the "desire to escape legitimate suffering" and that it is a blatant form of "laziness" stemming from "malignant narcissism."[15] This suffering is not the ordinary kind of pain.

The suffering lazy people desire to avoid is the "pain of their own conscience—the pain of the realization of their own imperfections that is caused by self-examination."[16] In Part Three, I call this self-examination the journey toward *genuine self*,[i] and it is this model of evil that I will continue to use in this book.

Beyond a doubt, man-made disasters have caused millions of deaths and untold suffering. Many of the professional technologists directly or indirectly responsible did not stop to think whether they should create some of the things that contributed to those disasters—or at least did not want to think about the possible misuse of those things. Psychologists call this phenomenon suppression and repression of reality, which can be a form of genuine evil.

As I wrote in the Preface, genuine evil takes both passive and active forms and spans a spectrum of values, as illustrated in Figure 1. Hitler's Holocaust certainly represents one end of the spectrum of active evil, but it also represents passive evil. The attacks on the World Trade Center and Pearl Harbor, representing both active and passive forms of evil, *could* be placed closer to the middle of the spectrum. The space shuttle Challenger and the Hyatt Regency Hotel disasters *might* occupy a lower place that represents primarily passive evil, since no intent to harm existed in either tragedy.

Some man-made disasters have characteristics of both passive and active evil, and therefore, are not easily identified in any spectrum of evil. The widespread fire bombing of the city of Dresden, Germany, during WWII remains an infamous example of intent to kill tens of thousands of civilians for purportedly principled reasons. The city contained few significant military

---

[i] The word "self" is the word I prefer in the context of this book. Others may recognize my concept in the religious word "soul," while others may recognize it as "ego, superego, and id" in the Freudian psychological sense.

targets. Yet, the Allies decided to reduce the city to rubble because it *might* shorten the war. Dresden was a prelude to the atomic bombing of Japan because the same reasoning was used to justify the killing of civilians. The bombing of Dresden set a precedent that continues to haunt our modern world.

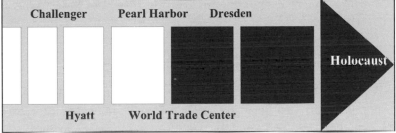

Figure 1: Spectrum of Genuine Evil

The degree of evil in each event is debatable. Even philosophers and theologians have difficulty defining evil, much less measuring it. Most of us intuit that the Holocaust was evil incarnate. In May of 2002, a group of psychiatrists began work on a depravity scale for defining evil.[17] The scale reflects criminals' intents, actions, and attitudes. Criteria for exceptional evil were suggested: intent to emotionally traumatize the victim, prolonging a victim's suffering, and targeting a helpless victim. The WTC terrorists certainly intended to traumatize and target helpless people, and the Nazis were infamous for meeting all three criteria. But a conscious intent to harm is not the only form of genuine evil. The result of active and passive evil is the same: Innocent people die.

Some people might measure evil by comparing the number of deaths in each tragedy, but this measure somehow unjustly diminishes the death of six astronauts when compared with the genocide of millions. A better measure might be the number of people who willingly or apathetically contributed to the horror of each event. This is passive evil, the essence of the Code.

Although people might reasonably disagree on how to rank these tragedies, they are likely to agree that genuine evil existed in each case—and that more than one person contributed to the evil. The passive evil connecting these preventable man-made disasters is the Code of Silence among technologists. This passive evil allows active evil to dominate and can lead to industrialized and government-sanctioned murder.

In the pages that follow, you will read about the roles of engineers, scientists, and other technologists who were both active and passive in their support of the Final Solution during the Holocaust. Many architects, engineers, and contractors planned, designed, and constructed the death camps. Thousands of others who were not actively involved knew what was happening but remained silent—probably to protect themselves and their jobs. Ask today's whistle-blowers about their co-workers' inaction in the face of evil. The rationale of self-preservation is still very much alive.

The Ultimate Evil: Industrialized Murder

Even though genuine evil followed us into the 21st century, the Holocaust remains the clearest example of technologists' roles in mass murder. The Holocaust in Europe represents the definitive example of the Code's potential effect. The creative work of technologists, from Stalinist Russia to Saddam Hussein's Iraq, has contributed to the "efficient" murder of millions of innocent human beings. The debate continues about the moral implications of technologists' responsibility for the development and use of atomic bombs to end World War II. Similarities do exist between the roles of technologists in the Holocaust and in the Trinity Project.[18] Was the use of the bomb morally justified? The answer may depend on who is answering the question.

The women and children in Japan who died and those who survived would answer it differently from the American soldiers who might have died if the United States had invaded Japan. There were alternatives to using the bomb or launching a full-scale invasion; among those discussed were a blockade of Japan, conventional bombing of military targets, a demonstration of an atomic blast, or simply waiting for the Japanese people to overthrow the military regime.

Archived secret information, discovered at the end of the Cold War with the Soviet Union, suggested that the decision to drop two atomic bombs on civilian populations in Japan was more political than military. America was tired of the war after almost four years. And the bomb was designed more to scare Stalinist Russia than to end World War II.

Most designers of the first atomic bombs were enthusiastic in their creative endeavor. Only after the bombing of Japan were some of them remorseful for what they had unleashed. This is my point: Should technologists be more concerned with the good and bad implications in the design and application of the things that are possible to create? Today in the United States, a furious debate rages over the creation and application of the science of cloning human beings. It is about the personal and moral responsibility of the creators: not what they can do, but what they *should* do.

Volumes upon volumes of information cover the Holocaust and the technology that made it possible, but I have yet to find any significant investigations *by technologists* of the roles technologists played in the Holocaust. I expected to find widespread condemnation of Nazi technologists by American technologists during the Holocaust years and the decades following World War II. I did not find any, and I now understand more fully why: Then and now, the Code has enforced their silence.

The roles of scientists, engineers, architects, contractors, lawyers, doctors, and other professionals in the industrialized murder of the Holocaust haunt me, not only because they demonstrate the terrible result when human beings cause or allow a conspiracy of silence to grow—but because I have observed this same type of conspiracy in the higher education of technologists.

The laws of this nation and other civilized nations hold accountable both those who pull the trigger and those who are direct or even indirect accomplices in a crime. If a bank robber during his escape shoots and kills a police officer, the getaway driver in the car outside the bank is also guilty of a felony. Also responsible are those who knew about the impending robbery.

The conspirators are felons because they helped make the robbery and murder possible and should have known about the likelihood of violence. Similarly, the culpability of those who designed and built the Holocaust's technology should be acknowledged so that it will not happen again.

> **The historical facts are clear—the Nazi technologists made the Holocaust physically possible.**

They were morally and physically responsible for the industrialized murder of millions of human beings. Even if they did not contribute directly to the murders, they should have known because of their expertise in areas that made the genocide possible.

To say that the Code among technologists was solely responsible for the Holocaust would be an oversimplification and an affront to those who suffered and died at the hands of the Nazis and other mass murderers. Yet the magnitude of the horror and destruction would not have been possible without the hundreds of thousands of engineers, scientists, and other technologists working diligently and silently in the government, in professional organizations, and in the private industries of Nazi Germany.

> **The Holocaust was industrialized murder made possible by the "Industrial-Military-University Complex."**

I add the university to this familiar phrase of the 20th century because of the intellectual resources it brings to the creation of technology. As Omar Bradley, one of the great

American generals of World War II, said, "The world has achieved brilliance without conscience. Ours is a world of nuclear giants and ethical infants."[19]

According to Robert S. Frey, editor and publisher of *Bridges*, the Holocaust occurred because of the actions of some of the best minds in Western culture—white- and blue-collar workers who personally profited from Auschwitz and other concentration camps. The Final Solution may have been started by Hitler and his psychotic deputies, but it was carried out by professionals in accounting, finance, engineering, and science. As Frey points out, the "pillars" of Western civilization—law, religion, and science—did not prevent the horror of the Holocaust.[20]

Kurt Prufer, the chief Nazi engineer who designed the operations and facilities for the concentration camps, was quoted as saying that he sought work with the Nazis because he "feared for his career and losing his job" at his "advanced age" of about 45. Many German companies were downsizing during the 1930s. But Prufer was also responsible for, and proud of, his new design for the gas chambers and ovens.[21]

Highly trained professionals like Prufer enjoyed skilled creative work and the rewards that accompanied it. Their names appear on the plans, cost reports, production reports, building status reports, estimates, and other documents of mass murder.[22] The Nazi designers of death were not afraid or ashamed to sign their names to their work. They seem to have been proud of their technical accomplishments. Were all the technologists madmen? Or, as I believe, were most of them enjoying their "right" to creative work with the Code in the background?

Gerald Flemming, who wrote a book on war crimes called *Hitler and the Final Solution*, said during a 1995 interview on public television's *Nova*, "There is the beast in man. It can happen again, and whether we can learn from history, I do not know ... but where we have the facts and observe (similar) conditions now, it would be criminal not to expose them."[23]

The fact is this: Without the expert creators and designers, the blue-collar workers and Nazi leaders would have had nothing to build. The Nazis knew they didn't have enough time or bullets to accomplish wide-scale genocide. The trained professionals made efficient industrialized murder possible. The genocide happened because they put their perceived need to earn a living, to keep their jobs, and to be creative above their honorable duty as human beings. Trained professionals remained silent in the face of genuine evil out of pure self-interest. As Flemming said, it can happen again.

Michael Berenbaum of the Holocaust Memorial Museum in Washington said during the *Nova* documentary that the thousands of people physically responsible for the Holocaust were "engaged in inner suppression of difficult knowledge as a way of easing their own conscience." The Code is this "inner suppression of difficult knowledge." They simply chose not to think about their responsibilities as members of the human family.

The Holocaust, like so many lesser-known tragedies, involved a team effort in which no one person believed himself or herself responsible. Hundreds of thousands of people aided and abetted the leaders. This book is not about the Holocaust but about how the pattern of behavior established in everyday business decisions can be a prelude to such horrific events. The Hyatt Regency, the Challenger, and more recent disasters confirm that this pattern of behavior is still operative.

Surely, some designers of death in Nazi Germany questioned the process in which they were intimately involved. Why did they not stop it? Some technologists probably died trying. This book of ideas attempts to explain why everyday man-made disasters happen when the factors that contribute to these disasters remain unexamined from the viewpoint of personal moral, social, and professional accountability. The people who are affected by our decisions on life and death have the right to judge us technologists and demand changes when we act irresponsibly.

History's Judgment of Technologists

Future generations will examine not only our successes but our failures. We should examine them as well, because the process allows the act of creation, the creation itself, and the creators to be understood and judged.

> **The darker side of advancing technology, the negligent and even wanton misuse of technology, will not escape the judgment of history.**

Technologists should use both sides of their brains, the intuitive and the cognitive, the emotional as well as the logical. It is not a well-traveled path for technologists, who typically are dominated by the cognitive left hemisphere of the brain. But a human being who suppresses empathetic feelings moves toward a destructive internal silence. This denial and silence reinforce the deadly effect of the Code on co-workers and others involved in the creation of technology. This "groupthink" spreads to our work and into a trusting society blind to the problem until a disaster occurs.[j]

Unfortunately, this well-traveled road to disasters seems to be growing wider and wider. Along the way, technologists encounter everyday ethical dilemmas, and the choices they make will determine whether the public is safe and healthy.

The 20th century had its share of the good and the bad. The next three chapters chronicle the well-traveled road, with a look at some of the more significant mega-disasters. Part 2 explores the origins of these destructive behaviors, and Part 3 offers solutions for preventing the spread of the disease that I call the Code of Silence.

---

[j] The term "groupthink" has two meanings, one positive and one negative. It can mean the analysis of problems by a group with special talents, which may lead to better decision-making. The meaning that I will use throughout this book—unquestioning acceptance of the views of a leader, group, organization, or government on social, political, and moral matters—represents the darker side of groupthink.

Bibliography, Notes & Further Reading

[1] The building codes at the time of the construction of the WTC mandated the use of fire-retardant material. It was reported on nightly news broadcasts several times that the WTC did have this material.

[2] Alvin Toffler, *The Third Wave* (New York: Bantam Books, 1980), 1-6.

[3] Judy Jones and William Wilson, *An Incomplete Education* (New York: Ballantine Books, 1995), 508-13.

[4] See *Technology Disasters*, exec. producer Nancy Lavin. The Learning Channel, October 2000.

[5] 111 Market Place, Suite 1050, Baltimore, MD 21202.

[6] Samuel C. Florman, *The Existential Pleasures of Engineering*, 2nd ed. (New York: St. Martin's Press, 1994).

[7] Ibid., 7.

[8] Ibid., 6.

[9] The phrase "dirty little secret" comes from Michael Lewis, *Poisoning the Ivy* (New York: M.E. Sharpe, 1997). Lewis refers to secrets within higher education, but I believe the phrase also applies within business.

[10] Harry C. Boyte, "The Struggle Against Positivism," *Academe* 86, no. 4 (2000): 46-51.

[11] Kate Gibney, "Awakening Creativity," *Prism*, March 1998, 19-23.

[12] Mike W. Martin and Roland Schinzinger, *Ethics in Engineering*, 3rd ed. (New York: McGraw-Hill, 1996), 246-57.

[13] See "Federal Safety Engineer Sheds Light on Whistle-blowing Nightmare," *Engineering Times*, June 2000.

[14] M. Scott Peck, *People of the Lie* (New York: A Touchstone Book, Simon & Schuster, 1983). For the three major models of evil, see page 46.

[15] Ibid., 46-47.

[16] Ibid., 76-78.

[17] This information was found on the *Omaha World Herald* website, Omaha.com, on 4 June 2002. The article quoted the *Philadelphia Inquirer* newspaper.

[18] I refer to the atomic bombs developed by the United States during World War II. See articles by Konrad Paul Liessmann ("Hiroshima and the Auschwitz Principle") and by Eric Markusen ("Reflections on the Holocaust and Hiroshima"), in Robert S. Frey, ed., "The Holocaust and Hiroshima: Ethical, Scientific, and Philosophical Explorations," *Bridges: An Interdisciplinary Journal of Theology, Philosophy, History, and Science* 5, no. 1 (1998).

[19] Omar Bradley in Boston took the quote from a speech, "Nor Armistice," 10 November 1948. See Verne E. Henderson, *What's Ethical in Business* (New York: McGraw-Hill, 1992), 33.

[20] Frey, "Holocaust," 3.

[21] Jean-Claude Pressac researched the documents left behind by the Nazis. He uncovered the names, reports, drawings, and other documents that the designers, engineers, architects, and contractors generated for the death camps. Thousands of engineering and construction documents exist to prove the role of technologists and other professionals in the Holocaust. For more details, see Jean-Claude Pressac, *Auschwitz: Technique and Operation of the Gas Chambers* (New York: The Beate Klarsfeld Foundation, 1989).

[22] I learned of this information from a television documentary, *Nazi Designers of Death*, on *NOVA*, Public Broadcasting Service, 1995.

[23] Ibid.

Chapter 2

The Well-Traveled Road to Disasters

Everyday Moral Dilemmas

Moral dilemmas are a prelude to man-made disasters, but they are hardly unusual. Nearly every day, at home or at work, we are forced to make choices between conflicting claims or ideas. I may promise a friend to attend an event but later learn that my family wants me to attend a special event with them. What should I do? We may make one promise to a colleague and another to our employer, but it may seem impossible to keep both. We must choose constantly between competing duties, values, and rights in situations with no apparent correct answer. These quandaries in decision-making are called moral dilemmas.

Several pitfalls exist when we make decisions affecting others. First, we must recognize that we face a dilemma requiring a choice between good and bad. Second, there may be equally strong and competing arguments for each direction. Third, reasonable people may disagree on the right choice. Self-evident truths are hard to recognize if a person wants to remain ignorant, and it is even more difficult for us to act in ways congruent with these clear truths.

For example, a typical ethical dilemma for a college student is deciding whether to use a stolen test to study for an exam. Using the test may give the student the temporary ability to stay in college–at least, she may believe this to be true. Because I taught technical courses in engineering and technology, I was particularly sensitive to this issue of student cheating. I established a no-tolerance policy early in my teaching career, but I also told my students that I assumed they were not cheating.

I explained it this way: Cheat on a test or problem assignment and you may not get caught here, but someday you will run the risk of hurting or killing an innocent person because you don't know how to do your job. Can you live with that? It may not have stopped some students from cheating, but the ensuing discussion about workplace ethics was enthusiastic and worth the time. Most students said they agreed that cheating was wrong and only a short-term gain not worth the risk. It was fascinating to listen to my students explain to other students alternatives to cheating. At least, they were beginning to ask the right questions, which is the beginning of moral autonomy.

 Or consider this dilemma: Should you tell your best friend that his spouse is having an affair? After a while, most students would ask what proof there is about the affair. Excellent question. Before you tell your best friend (or the police, or your boss), you should have as many facts as possible in order to make a good decision. Maybe the spouse is merely confiding in a close friend. Things are not always as they first seem.

The possibilities for dilemmas go on and on. Choices must be made, but the important underlying question is: How do we make a morally justifiable and rational decision?

First, we must recognize that a moral dilemma does indeed exist, and then we must possess the tools to solve it. This process requires both effort and desire. My ethics checklist in Chapters 11 and 12 is designed to help people make these decisions by asking the right questions.

Many professionals, political leaders, and business leaders face tough dilemmas in their careers. News reporters and journalists also have their quandaries. Suppose you are a reporter who observes a U.S. senator using illegal drugs at a dinner party. Should you report it to authorities, run the article in the newspaper, or forget about it? What you do, or do not do, could influence your future and the future of the country.

If you do nothing, and the senator is high while making a key decision about homeland security, everyone could be placed in harm's way. On the other hand, the senator has rights of privacy in his personal life. Right? Perhaps not. He became a public figure when he assumed the office and pledged to protect Americans. And are you sure the drug was illegal, or even a drug?

If not a senator, suppose the drug user (if proven to you satisfactorily) were a design engineer in charge of designing a bridge across the Mississippi River. Would you feel more or less obligated to report the drug use to authorities? In the case of the engineer, I definitely would investigate, not only because I would feel a moral duty, but also because my oath and Code of Ethics as a registered professional engineer requires me to do so. In this way, an adopted code of ethics in a profession can offer a whistle-blower protection and a firm foundation to act. No easy answers await us when we attempt to solve moral dilemmas, but in trying, we are engaged in a very important process that can save lives.

Business leaders and technologists are constantly faced with issues arising from cost-benefit calculations. For example, suppose you are the vice president of a car manufacturing corporation and have to decide between stockholders' demands for a larger dividend and a $100 safety feature that would prevent gas tanks from exploding in a collision. Most of us as individuals would quickly vote for spending the $100 on our new cars, but as part of a corporation, the vice president is pressured from all directions. Deeply held convictions about right and wrong are now in the forefront. Most of my students became flustered when I asked them to decide these issues.

If the vice president ordered you, a design engineer, to ignore the safety defect and not spend the $100, what would you do? What *should* you do? The two questions are very different. I used the Socratic method of teaching ethics (asking the right questions to lead students to autonomous thinking). And the students soon learned to turn the tables on me by asking me what I would do in these cases. I used to tell them that I didn't know for sure what I *would* do—and I only hoped that I would have the courage to do the right thing. It was an honest answer. Of course, the students' very next question was: What is the right thing? You will have to read the entire book to learn what I told them.

Moral dilemmas are ever-present in our world; therefore, we need the desire, the ability, the tools, and the wise counsel and empathetic support of other rational persons to help us make good decisions. Part Three of this book covers this process, but first let's look at some typical situations in college that can be preludes to disasters in the workplace.

Moral Dilemmas in College

Significant moral dilemmas are especially abundant for technologists during their academic careers. The connections between disasters involving the things we create and our moral and social responsibilities can be traced to these everyday dilemmas. The last chapter of this book presents a detailed dilemma of the kind typically faced by college students in engineering and technology who move into the workplace mostly unaware of ethical dilemmas hiding in the shadows. The dilemma will be analyzed using the ethics checklist that I developed while teaching engineering and technology ethics.[1]

 The lead character in the quandary is Joe, a civil engineer in charge of a team effort to design and build a bridge. Many people in workplaces outside technology also face his problem: an incompetent boss—in this case, Joe's departmental manager, a registered professional engineer—who uses fear to stop dissent and investigations into his responsibilities.

Many serious problems like Joe's begin in the classrooms of colleges throughout the United States.[2] A short list of such problems would include emotional abuse of students in the classroom, incompetent professors, and administrators who do not know how to manage.

Conflicts of interest abound within institutions of higher education. Technology professors often moonlight, and in the process they may use government resources—office facilities, laboratories, phones, computers, copiers—illegally. Public funds are sometimes used to support a private business connected indirectly with the university. Undergraduate and graduate students can become entangled in this web of deceit, and they learn from the professionals how the game is played.

> The use of government resources for personal gain appears to be widespread within academia.[3]

The following scenario illustrates one popular method used by some professors to circumvent rules. First, a research professor forms a for-profit corporation and becomes its owner— silent or active in its management. Let's call this professor Doc. Doc's private company, under the leadership of a puppet CEO, contracts for projects with government funding agencies or directly with the university. Doc's university colleagues may funnel work to his corporation, with "appropriate compensation," of course. Doc's CEO may even contract directly for a university research project controlled by Doc himself, who is called the chief investigator for the university project.

You can detect how this process benefits Doc. He receives money two ways: first, from the profit of his company, and second, from the university salary for the same project. If Doc works on the project during the summer, he will draw an additional salary from the same project.[a] University administrators appear to look the other way and let this activity continue. Whether or not this process is illegal, it is certainly unethical, to

---

[a] The normal salary arrangement for tenured professors is based on nine months of teaching, with summers free for pursuing other sources of revenue. For research-oriented professors, this usually means that they "arrange" the project to include summers so they receive extra salary and benefits.

say nothing of the conflict of interest it poses for obtaining accurate research data.

Research projects enhance the image of the professors, the administrators, and the university as a whole. To conduct this research, Doc typically will use students under his direct supervision, who are usually paid minimum wages, if any. So, many students learn to play this game of silence by the time they graduate.

Chapter 7, "Industrial-Military-University Complex," presents insiders' descriptions of the dirty little secrets in universities. For now, let's look at the moral dilemmas created in technologists' workplaces and their relation to man-made disasters.

Moral Dilemmas in the Workplace

The engineering and construction industry is full of ethical quandaries, which, if handled badly, can have disastrous results, for technologists touch all aspects of our lives with their work.

Scientists, as inventors and discoverers, involve themselves in moral quandaries. Engineers, as designers, use the work of scientists, and thus they become involved in moral difficulties. Contractors then build the engineered designs and systems, and they, too, become involved in these moral quandaries. The project owners and their financial backers face many moral dilemmas during the process as well.

Being involved in a moral dilemma is not the same as recognizing or effectively solving it. All too often, technologists shift the responsibility to others, either by default or by intent. We have learned to pass the moral buck, as scientists did in the time of Galileo and as technologists are trained to do in today's universities and professional schools.

In the story that follows, dilemmas abound between good and bad alternatives. If the wrong choice is made in any one of them, disasters become more likely. The footnotes and endnotes expand on some of the intricacies.

Let's suppose you are a scientist who discovers a process that would make possible the manufacture of a new type of high-strength steel. This new process involves highly toxic chemicals, but the new steel could save millions of dollars in the cost of new buildings, bridges, etc.

Should you publish your discovery or remain silent? This is the same dilemma faced by the inventors of the atomic bomb, poisonous gases and chemicals, and other potentially deadly inventions. Let us assume that you patent and publish the details about the process and, by doing so, pass on to others the ethical decisions about the manufacture and final uses of the innovative new steel.[b]

At this point, the "genie in the bottle" has been freed. Corporate interests and venture capitalists will recognize immediately the possible benefits of the low-cost steel. They provide the money to finance the new process, and they reason that others have decided the difficult questions about the toxic materials; that is, if they have even thought or care about the effect on the environment. For the moment, assume that the steel manufactures will not dump the poisons into the rivers or bury them in the ground unprotected and unknown to the public.[c]

---

[b] Not all scientists patent their discoveries in their own names. If the scientist is an employee of a corporation or government agency, that employer usually secures the patent and receives the benefits that go with it. In any event, the employer will no doubt favor the scientist with some benefits, e.g., salary increases, bonuses, or promotions. The point is this: The scientist will receive some type of reward, usually monetary, no matter whose name the patent is in.

[c] I know this assumption may be a big leap of faith for some of us who have seen the opposite behavior that has led to some well-known tragedies. But I want to carry this situation further into the process toward the end users of the new technology—the people for whose safety the original scientist decided not to take personal moral or social responsibility.

After a manufacturer is identified, the new high-strength steel must be approved for use. Let's say that it is certified as acceptable by a laboratory test agency for use by engineers in their designs for long-span bridges and huge indoor arenas for sporting events. Let's also assume the lab engineers did their work correctly and were under no pressure from industry to certify that the new steel meets *appropriate standards of safety*. Who sets these safety standards? Engineers and scientists, of course.

The design engineers in an engineering corporation can now calculate the reduction of costs for a new arena seating 100,000 people to the point where another corporation decides to finance and build the project. This may be the first time the new steel will be used in primary structural members in such a large roof structure. Ever-changing computer software contains design calculations that give "safe" sizes for the new steel girders and beams for the roof. Notice any problems so far if the assumptions should prove unreliable?[4]

The architects and engineers work to complete the design for this fast-track project. In a fast-track project, the entire project design is typically not completed before some key contractors begin work on the initial phases of the project.[d] So, the designers, working for the project owners, solicit bids from contractors to build the structure. The design engineers are required to assure the owner and government officials that the project is safe and meets all government standards and industry building codes.

Government inspectors, at times professionally unqualified,[e] are required to monitor government-funded projects

---

[d] A fast-track project has inherent problems during construction that usually require redesign and rework. The emphasis in such a project is to finish the project as quickly as possible within permissible quality standards. However, the project owners and financial backers typically want the project finished "yesterday."

[e] While acting as a consulting engineer in a small mid-western city, I observed a government construction inspector certifying a multi-story apartment complex. The project did not meet recognized building codes for fire protection. When discussing the issues with him, I learned that he had a degree in chemistry

during critical stages of construction to make sure that the contractors follow the architect's design.[5] On many privately funded projects, government inspectors are not required to inspect if no state or federal funding is used. And the private owner and his designers select the *responsible* and *responsive* general contractor with the *lowest bid amount.* The italicized words represent major pitfalls for a successful project.[6]

After the construction contracts are awarded and signed, the general contractor and various subcontractors will begin to work. They assume that the new steel structure will be safe because it was designed by one of the most respected, albeit very busy, architectural and engineering firms. Of course, the general contractor and subs are responsible for the erection procedures and for the means and methods to complete the construction.[f]

The contractor orders the steel structural roof members from a steel fabricator, who fashions the new type of steel into specific sizes and shapes according to the design plans and specifications. The steel fabricator receives the steel from a steel mill, which produces the raw steel using the process discovered and patented by the scientist.

The contractor receives for review the fabricator's shop drawings for the steel sizes and placement and then certifies to the architect in charge that the plans are okay. The architect and engineers review and certify these same shop drawings for general conformity to the plans and specifications.[g] Then the contractor,

---

with no real experience in inspection. Many situations like this one have lead to tragedies in this and other countries.

[f] Standard construction agreements place the responsibility for construction procedures and techniques (means and methods) on the contractors. It is standard industry practice that stems primarily from potential liability issues for the designers if they tried to interfere with the contractor's work. Most architects and engineers would be unqualified, or at least ill equipped, to perform actual construction.

[g] Shop drawings are crucial documents in the creation of a project. Architects and engineers typically want to leave many of the details of the design to the fabricator, for two reasons: time and money that the designers may not

perhaps for the first time, installs the roof system using the new steel delivered by the fabricator to the project site.

> **Let us assume that the government and private industry inspectors perform their job correctly and honestly.**

The original design engineers are required to certify that their design as manufactured meets all safety requirements. The contractor certifies that the roof system has been properly installed and the rest of the arena has been completed according to accepted, standard industry practices.

After this completion certification, the owner pays the final bill to the contractor and to the engineering design firm for their services. The contractor and the design firm then pay their subcontractors and suppliers, and so on, until everybody receives their final paychecks.

At this point, the public assumes, with little if any thought, that the building is safe to enter. Let's assume that the next Friday night, 100,000 people attend a special event. Their attention is on the performance, not on the creators' sense of moral and social responsibility.

> **You and I have exhibited this blind trust thousands of times as we use technology.**

The people have a good time and return home safely. The arena's owner and the city's leaders are satisfied that the new arena will draw millions of dollars into the local economy. This is the way it should work. Sometimes, it does not, and the Friday night ends in a man-made disaster like Hyatt—and it will probably not be an "accident."

What if the roof had failed while the huge crowd was present? What if the failure resulted from steel that, for any

---

have included in their contract price to the project owner. It is another of those "accepted industry practices."

number of reasons, was defective? What if the designers, under pressure to hurry the design, had missed something critical? What if contractors or inspectors had not done their jobs? Moral quandaries abound in this typical way of doing business in the United States.

At any step along the way, key players in this process can affect the outcome. The trial-and-error or experimental nature of the new steel raises more issues. The steel itself, the design process, and the construction techniques are innovative, but at what cost? The inventor of the steel wanted to believe that the steel would benefit humankind—and probably accepted no moral or social responsibility for its use in commercial applications.

Innovative Designs—Human Experiments

Most construction projects proceed much like this one, but many projects, even years after completion, have ended in tragedy. The Kemper Arena in Kansas City, Missouri, is a classic example of an innovative design that received a design award and collapsed soon thereafter. By sheer luck, no one was present at the time of the collapse on July 4, 1979. The arena was designed using a relatively new space truss concept and a structural steel roof support system. The roof and ceiling structure hung below and from the space trusses with six steel hangers that used high-strength steel.

During a normal Kansas City wind and rain storm, a large part of the roof and ceiling system collapsed onto the convention floor below.[7] The progressive failure began when only two high-strength hanger bolts failed owing to fatigue in the metal after repeated movement. Another hanger connection then failed under the heavy loads shifted to them because of the first failure. One after another, the bolted connections failed, until a large portion of the roof system collapsed. Normal rain and wind proved too much for the innovative system when they were combined with a faulty design and bad construction practices.[8] The complex team effort for building the arena failed to protect the public.

Hundreds of people throughout the process in my fictional story and in the Kemper Arena project had opportunities to prevent disaster. But determining the right thing to do in ethical dilemmas requires clear thinking and empathy for the end users of the things we create. Each moral dilemma represents a choice by professionals who are also very human—a choice that affects their own lives and the lives of those they serve. It is a choice about life and death, every day.

Many times the innovative or "leading edge" technologies are experiments on humans—a type of trial and error. I have heard some non-technologists call this method the "killing edge" technology. If a technology application works as theorized the first few times, the innovative may become an existing technology "worth the risk." The space shuttle Challenger and other significant disasters of the 20th century fell victim to this faulty doctrine.

Like most people, I enjoy beautiful things. But I do not want anyone to be a victim of the Code, as has happened in so many 20th-century man-made disasters. This quest for glory leads to disasters. As philosopher Eric Hoffer puts it:

> We are ready to sacrifice our true, transitory self for the imaginary eternal self we are building up, by our heroic deeds, in the opinion and imagination of others.[9]

Glory is very fleeting. If the motive to be innovative is a craving for status or money at someone else's expense, then the behavior is dysfunctional. If the motive is a quest for immortality in the form of monuments of concrete and steel that put lives at unnecessary risk, it is selfish and immoral.

Dangerous Workplaces

Those of us who live in urban areas are often shocked to see newspaper headlines about murdered convenience store clerks. However, we have become accustomed, and even anesthetized, to everyday death and injury in technological situations like the construction workplace. The creation and use of technology in the construction industry is very dangerous work.

A construction failure in New York in late July 1998, at one of the busiest intersections in the world, illustrates this danger. Forty-eight stories of scaffolding with an elevator collapsed into Times Square and caused major disruptions of businesses. One person was killed and several were injured, but the business disruptions received the most attention. A construction worker nearby, Butch Phillips, had this to say on the television news:

> "When you go onto a construction site, you know it could be your last day. We had a person killed last week on this job. It is part of the game. We go on the job and everybody tries to be careful, but something could happen. It's like crossing the street."[10]

Although many construction workers feel that way, one should not acquiesce in this game. It is not like crossing the street, unless you live in a war zone. The industry's official position is that increased training would help reduce the number of deaths and injuries, but the extra training and time necessary to accomplish it are costly, and trade-offs occur. So, a cost-benefit analysis is applied here as well.

Sadly, as Phillips suggests, most construction workers have learned to play the game of a Code of Silence. It is a game in which death and injury in the workplace are accepted, and it requires this true belief:

"It's the price we must pay for progress."

I do not agree with the game or the true belief, and I do not think the public should, either. Business owners and their agents, creative designers, and builders may discount the significance of work-related deaths and injuries when the bottom line is threatened. I propose that a much higher standard be adopted in the workplace—no deaths or serious injuries are acceptable. At least, the days of the Empire standard of safety are gone. At the time the Empire State Building was constructed, construction industry standards deemed the loss one life per floor during construction acceptable and predictable.

The costs associated with workplace injuries are usually measured in dollars spent litigating and settling a lawsuit after a wrongful death versus protecting lives. The additional costs of intense safety training and the implementation of safety devices and systems to prevent deaths and serious injuries can be substantial. Many times in my career, I heard corporate insiders say that the moral reasons to protect workers were secondary at best, because insurance rates drove the process. The liability, workers' compensation, and other work-related insurance rates needed to be kept low for the company to bid the lowest cost to project owners. If a significant number of claims were made, the construction company's rates would skyrocket, and it would be less competitive in the marketplace.

Sometimes my technology students would try to convince me that this was an acceptable practice—"better than not doing it at all," they would add.[h] But I disagreed, because this type of reasoning can only devalue the life of a human being. It is at the core of the Code of Silence. Moreover, insurance and labor statistics point to enormous problems with work-related deaths and injuries, in spite of the threat of higher insurance rates.

The Bureau of Labor Statistics of the U.S. Department of Labor provides indicators of how technology can kill and injure.[11] Records are kept on the number of deaths and injuries in all categories of work. BLS summaries during the 1990s catalogued thousands of deaths each year in the construction industry. The total yearly fatalities in all industries involving tractors, forklifts, and cranes sometimes exceeded 6,500. And serious injuries exceeded 40,000 in most years.

These are significant numbers by any standards, but many corporations still view the deaths and serious injuries as an acceptable and manageable cost of doing business. The economic

---

[h] This discussion among the students was another sign of moral autonomy starting to bloom.

loss to employers and employees from injuries and deaths is indeed measurable, but the human suffering is incalculable and should be intolerable by any corporation.

Designers and builders like to say that the project owners dictate the cost considerations, but it does not have to be this way. This claim does not excuse the technologists for their acquiescence to unsafe projects or untested innovative structures and systems.

Did this mind-set about the value of the cost-benefit analysis contribute to some of the most significant disasters during the last century? The answer is an unqualified yes. Is a dollar value placed on human life? It is done all the time. Should it be? Whose life is significant or insignificant, and who decides? I wish these questions were more troubling for technologists than the history of man-made disasters indicates. "Remember the Titanic" ought to be printed in large letters across our design tables and computers.

Significant Disasters of the 20th Century

The list of preventable man-made disasters is indeed very long. Where has the Code led in terms of experiments gone wrong? Infamous tragedies like the Fen-Phen drug fiasco, DDT insecticide poisoning, dioxin contamination, and radiation poisoning (to name just a few) harmed millions of people before the truth was revealed. These deadly experiments by technologists, sanctioned by authorities, can appear for a time to be very successful.

It may be unusual to describe an innovative hotel as an experiment on humans, but many times that is exactly what it has been—an experiment to determine the least costly structure. Fire and smoke in structures kill thousands of people worldwide every year. A fire at the MGM Grand Hotel in Las Vegas claimed 85 lives and injured more than 600 people.[12] It was a real "towering inferno," foreshadowed a few years earlier by a Hollywood movie with the same name, in which a similar fire was attributed to the greed of a hotel's owners and designers.

> **The lowest cost or low-bid price for a project can result in the highest cost to the innocent people who use the structures.**

The Harbour Bay Condominiums collapsed in Cocoa Beach, Florida, killing 11 construction workers and injuring many more.[13] Fifty-one workers were killed in a collapse of scaffolding at a power plant in West Virginia.[14] The Vaiont Dam failure in Italy killed as many as 4,000 people in a 330-foot-high wall of water.[15] On August 7, 1975, the Shimantan and Banqian Dams in China failed and killed more than 230,000 people,[i] although China tried to hide the truth from the rest of the world.[16]

One year after the China disaster, the Teton Dam collapse devastated Rexburg, Idaho, and the entire river basin for miles.[17] Fortunately, few people died, because a warning was given promptly. Nevertheless, many residents dismissed the warning as a hoax and refused to evacuate because they thought the dam was safe. The Teton disaster shocked the engineering community, and Teton was the last major dam built in the United States. The records show that the collapse was predictable and could have been prevented had the designers paid attention to known facts and procedures.[18]

The collapse of Silver Bridge in West Virginia crushed or drowned 39 people in the river below.[19] The technical cause was the sudden rupture of a steel link, but the underlying reason was the desire for a low-cost bridge. The bridge had no redundancy in

---

[i] The TLC TV documentary on 20th-century disasters quoted sources to say 85,000 people died within two hours, and 230,000 died within weeks of disease, starvation, etc. The watershed where the two dams were located was in Henan Province in China. Many of the dams' flood-control gates failed to open because of bad designs, lack of testing and monitoring, and the build-up of silt behind the gates.

critical structural members—one steel link failed, and the entire bridge fell into the river. The bridge's designers and builders lacked critical knowledge about new materials. Innovative or under-tested designs have led to countless deaths and injuries.

The Hanford nuclear facility and waste storage reservation in Washington State is widely recognized as a major environmental disaster that has been unfolding for more than 50 years.[20] I know for a fact that it claimed at least one life: My uncle Edwin died of radioactive poisoning trying to protect the secrets at the facility. He was doing his job as a security agent for the government when he entered an unlocked and unmarked "hot" room. A design technologist forgot to lock the door. My uncle's agonizing death made me realize, even as a child, the pain a preventable tragedy could bring.

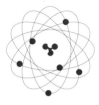

The "unsinkable" Titanic claimed more than 1,500 lives, as a 1999 movie reminded us.[21] Inaccurate steel manufacturing processes, faulty welding techniques and inspection, and inadequate steel bulkheads most likely were the technical reasons for the disaster. The steel bulkheads did not extend to the top of each compartment, and as one otherwise watertight compartment filled, the water spilled over into the next compartment. It was the domino effect, a progressive failure similar to that of the World Trade Center towers. Although the technical reason may have been the faulty low-strength, innovative steel construction, however, many people remain convinced that the "fail-safe" attitude of the ship's captain and designers was the underlying reason why the unthinkable happened.

This attitude, coupled with the great ship's speed through known iceberg fields during its maiden voyage, doomed the passengers and crew. The ship's owner had hoped that future ticket sales would increase if the Titanic could set a new speed record, but instead of winning glory, the ship's captain and chief designer went down with the ship. Some people want to call this type of event an "accident," but it could have been prevented if the ship's designers had not used a faulty cost-benefit analysis.

The list of man-made disasters grows every year. Genetic engineering, biological and chemical agents, cloning, and other high-tech developments require a new assessment of global moral and social responsibility for their creation and use. Preventable man-made disasters have increased in intensity when measured in the number of deaths and in human suffering. Something must change, or the 21st century could be our most disastrous century yet.

New technologies are often oversold to the public as fail-safe systems. At the time of the Challenger disaster, NASA's shuttle program and nuclear energy applications were prime examples of this mind-set about "proven" technology. Most people think of a fail-safe system as one that cannot fail because backup systems would prevent catastrophic failure. The disasters of Three Mile Island and Chernobyl remind us of the fallacy of this true belief. We continue to live in a world haunted by atomic explosions and the potential for world annihilation.

Change is inevitable in the advance of technology, but not all change is progress. The creations of technologists have not always been good for humans, for the planet, or for other forms of life. Thousands of significant disasters occurred during the 20th century, and two books provide extensive lists of these technological failures.

In order to make her 1989 book *From the Titanic to the Challenger* "manageable," Susan Davis Herring defines failures or disasters to exclude fires, floods, earthquakes, hurricanes, and all events that some people call "acts of God." She concentrates on failures caused by poor design, as opposed to what she calls "secondary causes": substandard construction, substandard materials, human error, and natural forces. Even with these restrictions, Herring compiled a list of more than 200 infamous disasters.

Neil Schlager uses similar criteria in his 1994 bibliography of 20th-century disasters, *When Technology Fails.*

He also excludes natural events or "acts of God" but suggests that some cases have overlapping causes. He defines significant disasters as those with heavy press coverage and large losses of life, as well as those that he believes reveal valuable lessons.[22] Schlager also excludes most, but not all, events caused by deliberate actions, such as the terrorist attack on the World Trade Center. He catalogued about 100 disasters.

Herring and Schlager look at very specific categories of disasters. Both tend to downplay human suffering and losses while emphasizing the technical lessons learned from the disasters. Although their work is important, they do not go beneath the scientific causes that they consider primary. This is unfortunate and misleading.

A number of significant disasters have occurred since their books' publications; and most, if not all, man-made disasters are linked by the Code. In addition, the number of injuries and deaths in closed societies like China is unknown but believed by many experts to be in the thousands every year.

Perhaps no list could include all disasters to everyone's satisfaction, but the available lists fail to reflect the effect of the Code. For example, an updated list of the 20 worst disasters of the 20th century labels the collapse of China's Henan Province dams the worst man-made tragedy.[j] Probably, few non-technologists and only a handful of technologists even knew of the dams' existence, much less their catastrophic failures.

A quick check of the literature and the World Wide Web shows hundreds and hundreds of lesser-known failures in many different categories: Ships still sink, airplanes still crash, buildings still burn. It seems that we have been anesthetized to these types of

---

[j] In October 2000, a television documentary on The Learning Channel presented a list of the top ten 20th-century technological disasters. If there was a pattern to TLC's criteria, it was not apparent to me. The documentary's top disasters, in order: China's Henan Province dams; Chernobyl; Exxon Valdez; the Challenger; Bhopal; the Titanic; Tenerife Airport collision; Sampoon Department Store; Estonia ferry; and the Hindenburg. See Notes and references at the end of this chapter.

disasters. In 1994, for example, more than 900 people were killed when the Estonia ferry, carrying cars and passengers across the Baltic Sea, sank within minutes because of the failure of giant steel bow doors. It was not the first time the safety of this type of design had been questioned.[23]

Although Herring and Schlager list airplane disasters, they fail to give the full picture. From 1920 to 2002, 799 passenger airplanes crashed, killing almost 50,000 people.[24] Most of these deaths occurred in the last 25 years. A Boeing 747 SR jet crashed in 1985 in Japan, killing all 520 people aboard, the single most catastrophic crash involving only one plane.[25] The passenger jet TWA Flight 800 exploded in flight in 1996, allegedly because of faulty design of the fuel tanks and electrical wiring.[26] Two hundred thirty people died.

On July 25, 2000, an Air France Concorde supersonic jet crashed on takeoff, killing all 109 people. The apparent cause  was the explosion of a tire, which led to an engine fire and failure.[27] The problem of faulty tires and engine fires had been known for many years: A similar failure in 1979 had almost brought another Concorde down.

One more category of disasters, usually classified as "natural," should be mentioned. Floods, hurricanes, and especially large earthquakes have occurred during the last 100 years. Large human population centers are built close to known earthquake faults, which are often near coastlines.

In January 2001, a severe earthquake in southwest India reportedly killed more than 30,000 people, not including those who died later from disease, exposure to the elements, or starvation.[28] The pictures on the nightly news showed thousands of collapsed, unreinforced or lightly reinforced concrete buildings. Reports immediately surfaced about illegal design and construction practices.

Proven technologies could save thousands of lives in these earthquake-prone areas. What prevents their use? Engineers and builders allow economics or politics to overrule safety. The space shuttle Challenger was a classic example of this problem. It's a common dilemma faced by technologists everywhere.

In the United States, several earthquake-prone regions are well documented. Many existing structures in California have been upgraded during the last two decades, and most new structures have been built using improved building codes to increase safety during these natural events. However, a 1994 Los Angeles earthquake and the 1995 Kobe earthquake in Japan proved that many structures thought to be safer were not.[29]

> **Technologists continue to allow others to determine where structures are built and to allow "cost-effective" safety factors in structures primarily for the benefit of their clients, the project owners.**

Many of these types of natural disasters can be predicted to occur in specific areas with some degree of regularity and intensity. The St. Louis, Missouri, and Memphis, Tennessee, urban areas are at great risk for severe earthquakes, according to the United States Geological Society. These areas have the potential for earthquakes as large and dangerous as any in California, possibly larger. Historically, neither city has enjoyed the kind of design standards that exist in California and in Japan.

Are the consequences of these random natural disasters unavoidable, or are they "man-made accidents" waiting to happen? It is a debatable and controversial issue. The attitude that many of us hold—"it won't happen to me in my lifetime"—can be a dangerous true belief.

Herring and Schlager label the following disasters during the last hundred years significant.[k] The list includes a few notable

---

[k] For a more complete listing, please refer to Appendix A, "Significant Disasters."

foreign disasters, like Bhopal and Chernobyl, but focuses primarily on disasters in the United States.[1]

- Aircraft: McDonnell/Douglas DC-4, 6, 7, 8, 9, and 10; Lockheeds Boeing 747 and 767; Sikorsky, Chinook

- Military Aircraft: B-1, B-52, BAC 111, F-111, F-18, and F-20

- Bridges: Quebec, Tacoma Narrows, Sunshine Skyway, Point Pleasant, Silver Bridge, Lafayette Street

- Buildings & Structures: Bronx Apartments, Skyline Plaza, Hartford Civic Center, Kemper Arena, MGM Grand Hotel, Harbour Bay Condominiums, Hyatt Regency Hotel

- Chemical & Environmental: Love Canal, Hanford nuclear waste facility, Times Beach, Seveso Dioxin, Bhopal toxins

- Dams: Austin, St. Francis, Malpasset, Teton

- Nuclear Plants: Browns Ferry, Three Mile Island, Chernobyl, Fermi

- Ships: Liberty, Andrea Doria, Exxon Valdez, Titanic

- Spacecraft: Apollo 1 and 13, Soyuz 1 and 11, Challenger

- Submarines: Thresher, Scorpion

This list is not prioritized by any single criterion. I include this list and the more complete one in Appendix A to show the sheer number of disasters across all categories of advancing technology. The lists include those disasters that (1) resulted in an unusually high number of deaths and injuries, (2) destroyed a vast amount of property, or (3) achieved general notoriety.

---

[1] The generally accepted Western philosophical and legal values, particularly in the United States, communicate the idea that a single life lost is unacceptable. Therefore, I did not rank the entries in the lists in Appendix A or the following sample, because one death is one too many.

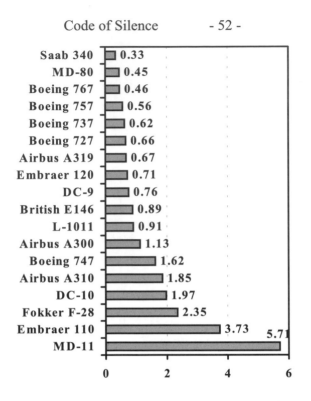

Figure 2: Aircraft Accident Rates by Model

Figures 2 and 3 show aviation accident rates by type of aircraft (Figure 2) and by year (Figure 3). In Figure 2, the fatal accident rates by model are independent of the number of deaths per accident per plane. The rate is defined as "an event in which one passenger was fatally injured solely due to the operation of an aircraft."

Hijackings are excluded from the numbers in both Figures 2 and 3, as is the supersonic Aerospatiale Concorde, because it had only one fatal crash in 80,000 flights, for a rate of 12.5. Omitting the Concorde, the worst record for a model was the McDonnell/Douglas MD-11, with four fatal accidents in 700,000 flights, for a rate of 5.71. Even though the Boeing 727 and 737 aircraft had the highest number of fatal accidents, 46 and 47

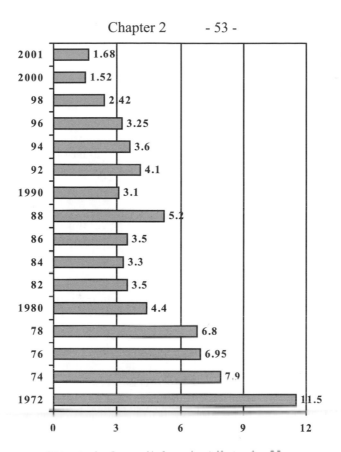

Figure 3: Aircraft Accident Rates by Year

respectively, they had 70 million to 76 million flights each. The DC-9 was not far behind, with 42 accidents and 55.5 million flights.

Figure 3 represents accident rates per year.[m] The data show the number of fatal accidents declining, but the actual number of deaths per year from all aircraft disasters has remained about the same over the years. This may be due to larger passenger loads per aircraft.

---

[m] The rates per year represent the number of fatal accidents, not the total number of deaths per accident. The data cover the period through 31 December 2001. Hijackings are excluded.

The statistics in Figures 2 and 3 are informative, not only because they show a pattern in the aircraft industry as a whole, but also because they suggest a pattern of failure rates for specific models of airplanes. Preventable repetitive failures should not be called accidents. When authorities allow an aircraft to fly time after time with a known and potentially catastrophic flaw, the Code of Silence has taken root.

So, is flying safer than riding in an automobile? If one uses the statistics that the airline industry prefers, deaths per mile traveled, the answer is a qualified "yes." If, on the other hand, one compares the number of deaths per car trip with the number of deaths per aircraft flight, the safety factor changes in favor of the automobile.

The automobile industry in the United States has safety troubles similar to those of the airline industry. For the last 50 years or so, an average of 30,000 to 40,000 people have been killed every year in automobile accidents. Intoxicated drivers and driver errors are certainly major reasons, but a significant portion of the deaths can be attributed to mechanical failures, sometimes from a known defect that was hidden from public scrutiny.

Since Ralph Nader's book about the Chevrolet Corvair and other automobiles' problems, *Unsafe At Any Speed*, thousands of news stories have been written about recalls, product defects, and accidents that involved vehicles and other technology. But most information about the lawsuits from these accidents never became public. Automakers and other manufacturers typically settle cases out of court and admit no guilt. The terms of these settlements have usually required all information about the case, including the cause of the accident, to be kept secret. This type of conspiracy of silence should not be allowed by our justice system.

Because of this legal maneuvering, the public was never alerted to the dangers inherent in some vehicles until many deaths and injuries had drawn news coverage. For instance, it was alleged in lawsuits in 2001 that Ford's popular Explorer SUV was prone to rollover accidents for many years.

Corporate executives may have known or learned of a dangerous defect and determined that the cost of correcting it was greater than that of litigating and settling lawsuits. Bad press coverage will not sell products. Manufacturers of many products, from airplanes to cars to cigarettes, have used this tactic to keep dirty little secrets from a trusting public. You will read in Chapter 6 about the engineer's cost-benefit analysis used to justify this approach. It has its roots in the Code of Silence within colleges of engineering and technology.

Could our automobile trips be made safer? Of course, and large sums of money are not always required. Gas tanks could be located in the chassis, where they are less likely to explode on impact. Bumper heights could be standardized. Speed limits could be set that are more appropriate for various road conditions. Protective barriers between opposing traffic on multilane highways could prevent many head-on crashes. And two-lane rural roads cause more lethal head-on accidents than any other type of situation. At least, the lanes could be widened and obstacles along the roadway removed to a safer distance or protected from impact.

The list of possibilities goes on and on. And from my civil engineering perspective, engineers should be less concerned with determining an "economic" cost-benefit analysis for corporations and government agencies and more concerned with rallying the public to demand safer highways and vehicles. Part of the problem has been that the public is unaware of the alternatives available and the costs associated with them.

How many times have we heard of a possible $10 or $100 modification to a product that would have made it far safer? And if it could not be made safer, why manufacture or use the product? Americans and the world's environment would most likely be better off without some of these products. The point is this: As a consumer in a free society, one should have the right to be informed of the dangers and the alternatives that could reduce them.

The aircraft and automobile industries are highlighted in this chapter because the statistics are more readily available and because most Americans regularly use at least one of these technologies. We want to believe the technologists responsible for these technologies did not intend to harm people, but some of them probably knew—or should have known—of these hidden defects before the major publicity. These types of preventable disasters are not the price we expect to pay when we fly or drive home to see our families. Nor should they be.

Next, we will examine a disaster that caused neither loss of human life nor vast destruction of property but continues to hold an infamous place in history. The bridge collapse discussed in most physics and engineering classrooms should never have happened.

Galloping Gerdie: A Prelude

The Tacoma Narrows Bridge collapse demonstrated the disregard by designers of lessons purportedly learned from similar previous failures. So, before we look closely at the two defining events of the Hyatt and the Challenger, let's look at one of the most photographed disasters of the 20th century.

The Tacoma Narrows Bridge collapse was a conspicuous example of history repeating itself—and it was a prelude to coming tragedies. Figure 4 on the next page shows the Tacoma Bridge collapse as most science and engineering students probably remember it. Luckily, there was time before the collapse to prevent any human deaths, although one dog and a car plunged into the river below. The collapse on November 7, 1940, is one of the classic failures of an engineered structure that was considered innovative at the time of its construction.

Forced resonation from wind oscillations was widely accepted as the cause of the bridge's collapse. At the time, the engineering profession refused to accept that the cause might be an inherently faulty design. Wind was believed to have caused the bridge deck structure to move back and forth, up and down, until it finally fell into the river.

However, this theory is wrong, according to Frederic Schwarz, a writer for the magazine *Invention and Technology*. He is not alone in questioning widely accepted "common knowledge." It took only an hour for the Tacoma Narrows Bridge to collapse, but scientists and engineers have yet to explain exactly why it did.[30]

Figure 4: Tacoma Narrows Bridge Collapse

(Photo courtesy of News Tribune, Tacoma, Washington)

Faulty Doctrine. According to Professor Emeritus Eugene Ferguson at the University of Delaware, it is dangerous to let one chief engineer have final approval on a complex design.[31] He says that another experienced engineer should always check both the implications of the complete design and the details. This was not the first or the last time that a chief engineer's faulty reasoning would lead to disaster. Ferguson, who has studied engineering failures, believes a more insidious problem exists: "The adoption of faulty doctrine by a whole profession."[32] Ferguson goes on to point out that information and data on similar bridge failures were available in American and European professional literature for decades. Without knowing what to call the problem, Ferguson has identified attributes of the Code.

> **Sometimes a whole profession, in this case engineering, makes assumptions about reality that are dead wrong.**

Why didn't the bridge's chief engineer, other bridge designers at the time, or governmental agencies question the design? An individual technologist's arrogance, indifference, and laziness can contribute the final ingredient in man-made disasters.

Some engineers during the early 1900s designed larger, longer, and lighter bridges, which they mistakenly based on other bridge designs believed to be similar.[33] They were not similar enough. The Tacoma engineers used a faulty deduction from work of an earlier engineer, O.H. Ammann, who designed the George Washington Bridge over the Hudson River. Incredibly, the professional engineering organizations at the time defended Ammann and attacked those who spoke out against his design.

David Billington, a professor of civil engineering at Princeton University, pointed out the earlier bridge designs that showed the inherent problems. Billington also uncovered the flaws in Ammann's judgment. Ferguson writes, "The need to justify the way engineers do things is unfortunately often felt even when ill-considered systems lead them to make fatally wrong judgments."[34] It appears from the literature that a form of conspiracy existed to ignore the past. I have called this phenomenon the Code of Silence. It is a conspiracy among groups of technologists to deny responsibility for protecting lives.

It should be noted that Ferguson is a history professor, not a technologist. Perhaps some technologists may protest that "Ferguson doesn't understand" or "He's not an engineer." He understands perfectly. Those outside the creator's narrow domain often have the ability to see through the true beliefs of the specialized group.

Ferguson says that engineers tend to rationalize their wrong judgments and forget past lessons. Is this "forgetfulness" intentional? In most cases, probably not. But callous disregard and negligence lead to failures. It is a passive type of evil. Many technologists want to forget about the failures or ignore history, at least from the viewpoint of the victims in the human tragedies. This "forgetfulness" is a psychological defense mechanism called suppression that helps them sleep at night.

In the example of a preventable disaster in the next chapter, the highly touted use of a team effort and the widespread acceptance of flawed industry standards led to tragic consequences. The Hyatt Regency Hotel tragedy continues to show the power and the dangers of the Code. The evil that led to the disaster may be less obvious to non-technologists, but it has a place on the spectrum of genuine evil as a prime example of passive evil.

Bibliography, Notes & Further Reading

[1] I was privileged to participate in a seven-day national workshop on "Ethics Across the Curriculum" presented by Michael Davis (Center for the Study of Ethics in the Professions, Illinois Institute of Technology, Chicago, Illinois, July 1997). It was sponsored by the National Science Foundation.

[2] Lewis, *Poisoning the Ivy*. For additional sources of information about problems in higher education, see Bruce Wilshire, *The Moral Collapse of the University* (Albany: State University of New York Press, 1990), and Michele A. Paludi, *Ivory Power: Sexual Harassment on Campus* (Albany: State University of New York Press, 1987).

[3] A number of books documenting problems within universities have been written in the last 10 to 15 years. Perhaps a good place to begin is Charles J. Sykes, *ProfScam: Professors and the Demise of Higher Education* (Washington, D.C.: Regnery Gateway, 1988).

[4] A team of experts in both structural design and computer language typically writes the design software and tests it as best they can. Other engineers who later use this software usually will not know the underlying assumptions and internal procedures of the original software. Blind faith in the accuracy, consistency, validity, and specific application of a software package can lead to tragic consequences. Sheer luck, redundancy in structural members, or large safety factors in sizing of members may well keep many structures from failing catastrophically.

[5] Large metropolitan areas (and some counties in a few states) typically have adopted national building codes that architects and engineers must follow in the design and construction of structures. But the vast majority of structures are built in rural areas without any governmental inspection. In addition, most rural areas and smaller cities and towns have no quality inspectors, and these same areas typically do not require a licensed architect or engineer to design the structures. Even the areas that have building codes may have understaffed and unqualified inspectors.

[6] The terms "lowest bid amount" and "responsible" contractor can take on different meanings in variations on accepted bidding practices and typical contracts. Under normal fixed-price or lump-sum construction contracts in the United States, the bidder must be responsible and responsive. A responsible contractor is one who must prove that her company has the experience, the knowledge, the skills, the equipment, the time, etc. to carry out the contract within an established schedule and price. A responsive contractor is one who presents his bid to the owner in a timely fashion and otherwise fulfills the requirements set forth by the designers in pre-bid documents for the bidding process. In fixed-price construction contracts, the

owner, with the help of the designers, has the legal right to declare a low bidder non-responsive and/or not responsible for any one of the requirements previously mentioned. Under these circumstances, a low bidder may not, and should not, be awarded the contract. This situation is especially true where government money is involved. However, the reality of the construction and engineering world is different. The project owners and designers very seldom reject low bidders. To do so would cost the owner more, and the owner and designers fear a lawsuit.

[7] Neil Schlager, ed., *When Technology Fails* (Detroit: Gale Research, 1994), 295-300.

[8] Officials in Kansas City charged the Chicago-based architect-engineering firm C.F. Murphy Associates, Inc., with 22 counts of negligence, including failure to design for appropriate wind forces, water ponding, and drainage. Only eight five-inch roof water drains were used in the entire roof. The city also charged Kansas City Structural Steel Company with four counts of negligence, including improper tightening of the bolts. The proper tightening of high-strength bolts is particularly critical for a safe structure, and the professional literature at the time of the construction of the arena provided ample opportunity for the designers, builders, and inspectors to know this fact. The city's $8.97 million suit and other suits were settled out of court only two days into the trial. See the endnote reference for more details on Kemper Arena.

[9] Eric Hoffer, *The True Believer* (Alexandria, Va., Time Reading Program Special Ed., Time-Life Books, 1980), 71.

[10] *NBC Nightly News*, 23 July 1998.

[11] "Issues," U.S. Department of Labor, Bureau of Labor Statistics, Summary 91-1, January 1996.

[12] Steven S. Ross, *Construction Disasters: Design Failures, Causes, and Prevention* (New York: McGraw-Hill, 1984), 117-25.

[13] Susan D. Herring, *From the Titanic to the Challenger* (New York: Garland Publishing, 1989), 166-67.

[14] Ibid., 184-85.

[15] The sources used are (1) Herring, *From the Titanic*, 210-13, and (2) Ross, *Construction Disasters*, 130-33.

[16] It was a preventable disaster, and it went unreported for many months in China and for years in the rest of the world. The Cold War prevented many disasters' becoming known outside the communist countries in which they occurred. The dams provided the electrical power for the region, and it was days before Chinese authorities knew to respond. See *Technology Disasters*, exec. producer Nancy Lavin, The Learning Channel, October 2000.

[17] Schlager, *When Technology Fails*, 449-54.

[18] The sources used are (1) Herring, *From the Titanic*, 210-13, and (2) Ross, *Construction Disasters*, 130-33.

[19] Alden P. Armagnac, "Our Worst Bridge Disaster: Why Did it Happen? Silver Bridge at Point Pleasant, West Va.," *Popular Science,* March 1968, 102-105.

[20] This information was taken from "A Dangerous Miscalculation," *Omaha World-Herald (*from *The New York Times),* 25 March 1998.

[21] Emory Kemp and Hal Browser, "Calamities of Technology," *Science Digest,* July 1986, 50-59.

[22] Schlager, *When Technology Fails*, 295-300.

[23] The ferry Herald of Free Enterprise sank off Zeebrugge in 1987. See Fiona Courtenay-Thompson and Kate Phelps, eds., *The 20th Century Year by Year* (New York: Barnes & Noble Books, 2000), 333.

[24] David M. Lisk, SkyNet Research, 2000, took this information from a compilation. It can be accessed from <http://www.airdisasters.com>.

[25] Ibid.

[26] Courtenay-Thompson and Phelps, *20th Century*, 339.

[27] I saw these reports on *NBC Nightly News* and *CNN News*, 25 July 2000.

[28] These numbers came from unconfirmed reports on *NBC Nightly News* and *CNN News*, 30 January 2001.

[29] Courtenay-Thompson and Phelps, *20th Century*, 333 & 335.

[30] Frederic D. Schwarz, "Why Theories Fall Down," *Invention & Technology*, Winter 1993, 6-7.

[31] Eugene S. Ferguson, "How Engineers Lose Touch," *Invention & Technology*, Winter 1993, 16-24.

[32] Barbara Moran, "A Bridge that Didn't Collapse," *Invention & Technology*, Fall 1999, 10-18.

[33] See Ferguson, "How Engineers," 16-24.

[34] Ibid., 16-24.

Chapter 3
The Hyatt Regency Hotel Disaster

Two Defining Disasters

Thousands of significant man-made disasters occurred during the last century, but this book will concentrate on two of them to illustrate the underlying reasons for most man-made tragedies. I call them defining events because of their long-lasting and significant impact on humankind. They are the bridge or skywalk failures at the Kansas City Hyatt Regency Hotel and the explosion of the space shuttle Challenger.

Both disasters involved existing technologies, first hailed as innovative in early uses but then believed to be well proven and safe—at least, by the people who used the structures and systems.

> **Technologists' denial and suppression of their responsibilities as trusted professionals contributed to both disasters.**

The Challenger disaster, in particular, illustrates the folly of a fail-safe mentality in "proven" technologists. Systems engineering is a trial-and-error process—always an experiment—but technologists are said to learn from their mistakes. Some lessons were not well learned. The old adage is certainly true in the creation and use of technology: History often repeats itself when we choose to ignore it.

The World Trade Center collapse was a result of terrorists' acts. But the collapse of the elevated walkways at the Kansas City Hyatt Regency Hotel exemplified gross negligence in structural failures during the 20th century and even into this century. The explosion of the space shuttle Challenger also exposed the dark side of technology—the conduct of engineering and science as business as usual.

Innovative new technologies and misused existing ones are human experiments. As you will read in Part Three, human beings should not be subjected to experiments without their informed consent.[a] Yet, when we enter a structure or use technology, we usually put ourselves at risk without being fully informed.

The Kansas City Hyatt Regency Hotel disaster was, and remains, the worst of its kind in the United States.[1] "There was blood everywhere, with some bodies crushed so flat that identification was impossible," according to a veteran rescuer at the scene of one more chaotic man-made disaster.[2] Yes, this scene could have been the WTC. But the Hyatt tragedy was a forerunner of it. The police officer who said this wanted to forget the horror, but decades later he still could not forget the night of July 17, 1981. He also knew we should not forget these tragedies, which are more common than any of us want to believe.

Most adults in the United States remember where they were when the space shuttle Challenger exploded, killing all on board, including the first teacher in space. I heard the news on my car radio when I was a Ph.D. graduate student driving back from an engineering meeting in Rolla, Missouri. Ironically, I was training to become a research-oriented civil and construction engineer.

Most of us remember watching on television, over and over again, the replay of the horrifying explosion. You will read how the technologists put on their "business hats" and allowed NASA to launch in near-freezing weather—in the face of hard

---

[a] The concept of informed consent is widely understood to have two primary attributes: sufficient knowledge and voluntary participation by the subjects of any experiment. The subjects must have all the required information that a rational person would need to make a reasonable and informed decision. The subjects should be neither coerced nor deceived when they make their decision to participate.

evidence that they should not have risked it. These types of events, Hyatt and Challenger, mislabeled as "accidents," are preventable, and they illustrate the basic quandary in the creation and use of technology.

The Terrible Night

It was 7:05 on a hot Friday night, July 17, 1981. Music was playing, people were dancing and talking, and life was fun for almost 2,000 people in the beautiful Hyatt Regency Hotel lobby in Kansas City, Missouri. Without warning, a sharp crack, then a screeching noise, signaled a series of events that changed forever the lives of so many people.[3] For a few long minutes following the collapse of the elevated walkways, there was only silence, except for one sound. The state of disbelief and shock of those still alive was broken by the roar of water as it gushed from broken pipes.

"There wasn't time to scream," according to one of those who survived.[4] Within a fraction of a second, two skybridges collapsed onto the dance floor below, and flying glass and other debris cut people to pieces. Seventy-two tons of concrete and steel crushed and maimed men, women, and children. In some cases, several generations in a single family died. Almost three minutes passed before anyone could call 911 because of the shock of the scene that confronted everyone still alive.[5] Later, it was determined that 114 people died and almost 200 others were severely injured, but that's not the whole story that needs to be told.

Officer Bob Dickerson of the Kansas City Police Department was one of the first rescuers to arrive.[6] He worked beyond his normal shift until almost 3 the next morning. In his first public interview since the disaster, Officer Dickerson told me what he saw as he arrived:

> The first memories that I have after arriving at Hyatt and opening the door to the lobby, was the amount of dust in the air, the blank stares of survivors moving toward me, and the screams. One dazed woman was wandering around looking for her husband, while others seemed to be staring off into

space, including the hotel staff. The screams and moaning of victims seemed to be coming from everywhere. I knew that I couldn't help as much as I wanted to, but I did what I could and was trained to do.

Officer Dickerson was soon assigned to morgue duty, which meant he had to carry the dead to a temporary spot in the hotel. According to Dickerson, "There was blood everywhere, with some bodies so crushed flat that identification was impossible. The children's bodies were the hardest to deal with. I saw children's bodies that couldn't have been more than six or seven years old."

The hotel lobby had a sunken area where most debris had fallen, and it was rapidly filling with water from the broken pipes. As soon as the water was turned off at the street connection, the water-based air conditioning system stopped. The heat and dust quickly became a major problem. The hotel staff, most still in shock, interfered with rescuers when they began breaking the windows to allow fresh air in. Police officers warned them of arrest if they boarded up the broken windows again.[7]

Figure 5 shows the walkways or skywalks shortly after the collapse while looking north.[8] The fourth-floor walkway collapsed onto the second-floor walkway, causing them both to collapse to the lobby below, where people were dancing. The third-floor walkway remained intact, as shown in the middle right of the photo. Notice its steel bar hangers rising to the roof structure. A portion of the fourth-floor walkway rests at an angle to the floor because it is propped against the south wall of the hotel lobby. If you look closely, you can see people who are apparently in shock staring at the scene. The glass façade to the left of the walkways would soon be removed to allow heavy machinery to enter.

The injured were taken outside the lobby into the courtyard and the street to the west of the hotel entrance. Medical teams from a nearby hospital immediately organized a triage area. Volunteer doctors and nurses were arriving. Officer Dickerson described the scene as "well-functioning, but chaotic looking," with rescuers bringing screaming and moaning survivors into the triage area. Doctors were treating the injured as quickly as they could, while police officers were trying to keep the reporters from sneaking in.

Figure 5: Hyatt Regency Hotel Lobby after Failure
(Photo courtesy of Kansas City Star, Kansas City, MO)

Except for the swarm of reporters, the scene looked like the mobile army surgical hospital (MASH) units that function during wartime. Dickerson said, "One man was trapped with his leg under some heavy debris, and in order to save his life, a surgeon came in and amputated the leg right there on the spot." He said the rescuers who were Vietnam War veterans handled their own emotions at the time in the usual manner.[9] They suppressed their feelings, let the adrenaline take over, and did their jobs. The rescuers' training and stamina proved to be crucial in saving so many survivors of the initial collapse.

The Rescuers' Nightmares

Creators of the Hyatt soon began learning of the disaster. The chief architect for the Hyatt project, Bob Berkebile, would soon become one of the rescuers. He and his wife, Libby, had been on their way to a party when they noticed a large number of fire and rescue vehicles headed downtown. When they arrived at the party, a friend led them to a TV to watch the reports of the Hyatt tragedy. Berkebile immediately called the owners and other designers and sped off to the Hyatt, arriving at about 7:30 that evening.

This was not the first time that he had to rush to the Hyatt after a structural collapse. A portion of the roof had collapsed while the Hyatt was still under construction, but unlike that time, Berkebile's fears of a major tragedy would prove to be true. Figure 6 is a schematic of the lobby area before the collapse.[10] As Berkebile and his wife approached the front entrance (to the right in Figure 6) and lobby of the structure, he encountered a surge of people, including police and medical teams. He had to convince the police of who he was and persuade them to let him into the hotel to meet to meet with the emergency management team.

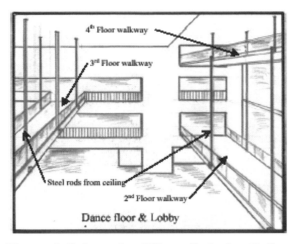

Figure 6: Schematic of Skywalks before Failure

In my interviews with him, I learned that he had never forgotten that night. Only two days before, Berkebile and members of his firm had been celebrating the acquisition of an important project with a major international company. They needed this new project to move forward, but he soon learned that many former clients would not contract with his firm for some time after the disaster.[11] Regular clients and others in the coming days and weeks would label them "too hot" because they were the architects for Hyatt.

The team of rescuers asked Berkebile if he would help in the effort. Although not a structural engineer, he tried to determine which debris could be moved safely. Rescuers needed to know whether the lobby floor would support the weight of the fallen bridges, the rescuers, and their equipment. The engineers, Berkebile's friends for years, were responsible for the structural design and would not arrive from St. Louis for many hours.

> **Chief architect Berkebile continues to remember the night by the smell that remained with him since 1981.**

A police dispatcher, Phillip Wall, went to the Hyatt after his shift was over at 11 the next morning. He recalled the nightmare for reporters: "I couldn't believe the amount of blood everywhere. There were pools of blood down on the hotel floor. You could smell it—a real stagnant kind of pungent smell, just hanging in the air."[12] The lobby area must have been like a scene out of Dante's *Inferno*.

Berkebile assisted the rescuers as best he could, with only one 20-minute rest break all night. He said in his last interview with me that therapists later helped him understand how he managed to function during that night of horror—by *suppressing* fear and emotion.

Bob Berkebile's description of some incidents that night should haunt all creators of technology. He climbed up one of the tilted skywalk slabs to determine whether the heavy equipment beginning to arrive could lift it. He thought he saw a severed head of a friend, collapsed, and was carried back down. The structural engineer for the Hyatt, Jack Gillum, finally arrived and confirmed that the slab could be safely lifted to look for any survivors. At 7:45 the next morning, 31 bodies were found under the last massive walkway slabs to be lifted by the cranes.[13]

After the final uncovering of bodies, most rescuers left the scene and tried to return to a normal life. It would be very difficult for many, including Bob Berkebile. It was apparent to me during the interviews that he had experienced a life-changing event. He is still haunted by that hot night at Hyatt.

> **I asked him how it affected his family and his fellow professionals, and the answer was clear to me when he began weeping. This was 20 years after the event.**

The Hyatt tragedy obviously affected everyone connected with the project, especially his children and partners in his firm. Berkebile agonized over the question of his responsibility for the deaths. His son would ask his dad if he had killed those people. We can hope creators and designers across America began to consider the important question: What is the real impact of what I do on those I serve?

During the days immediately following the Hyatt disaster, the creators, the builders, the rescuers, the survivors, and others connected with the tragedy tried to move on with their lives as best they could. The litigation that followed left little time for work— or family. It was soul-searching time for a lot of people, including the architects and engineers of record.

It would later be decided that Bob Berkebile, as an architect, evidently had asked the right questions before the completion of the hotel. After much personal agony, he and his firm were released from being named co-defendants in the multimillion-dollar lawsuits that followed. However, his friends Jack Gillum and Daniel Duncan, the structural engineers of record, would not be released from accountability.

Most survivors of a tragedy never fully heal from the scars and trauma to their minds and souls. Like the survivors, most observers and rescuers of the Hyatt collapse had similar psychological problems months, and often years, after the event.[14] After the Hyatt collapse, rescuers at subsequent disasters in Kansas City and many other cities were required to seek counseling.

> **Post-Traumatic Stress Disorder (PTSD) is very common among rescuers after such events.**

The painful memories may be suppressed for a while, but they never really go away. Officer Dickerson said, "Whatever I can do to help prevent this from happening again, I want to do. It is something I don't want anyone else to have to go through."[15] Unfortunately, other preventable man-made disasters have occurred since he said this to me.

Why did the Hyatt disaster happen? What could have caused such a disaster? Could it have been prevented? The investigation to determine the technical cause and to assess responsibility for the tragedy took four years. In contrast, it took only a few months for the owners of the Hyatt Hotel to remove the debris and rebuild.

Technical Reasons for the Failure

A brief summary of the technical failure needs to be understood, because only then will the underlying cause of the tragedy become clearer. The official cause was a progressive failure of two pedestrian bridges or skywalks that collapsed owing to gross negligence and a disregard of professional duty by the structural engineers of record.[16] This progressive failure, like that of the World Trade Center twin towers, ended as floors stacked one on top of another.

The National Bureau of Standards (NBS) determined the technical cause after testing models of the skywalks and examining the debris.[17] The steel-to-steel connections of the walkways were able to support only about 27% of the total live load and dead load for which they should have been designed. Live load is the weight of people, carts, etc. on the walkway during the worst case possible. Dead load is the weight of the skywalk itself, i.e., concrete and steel. The weight of the people on the walkways at the time of collapse was about one-tenth of the live load the structure should have been able to carry, according the NBS Report.

The original design called for the single continuous rod to run through the box beam, with a nut and washer on bottom. Figure 7 shows the skywalks' original and the as-built design before the failure.[18] From a practical construction standpoint, the design was flawed because it would be very difficult, at best, to place nuts on such a long threaded rod or to handle the very long rod. But the changed connection showed two rods, with the second-floor skywalk suspended from the fourth-floor skywalk.[19] This essentially doubled the load at the connection with the box beam.

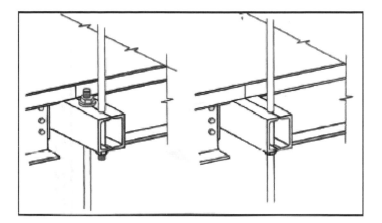

Figure 7: Skywalk Box Beam Connection
(As-built is on the left)

The principle engineers did not check the box beam for web-crippling stresses, and, according to the official report, they blamed the fabricator for not providing the details necessary to check for those stresses.[20] The flanges of the two C-shaped channels forming the box beam crippled, allowing the bars with nuts attached to the rod to pull from the box beam.[21]

According to their official stamps of approval on the drawings, all three firms representing the architect, engineers, and general contractors "reviewed" the shop drawings of the steel fabricator.[22] The shop drawings clearly showed the change from the single rod system to two rods. "The failure started about the center of the 4th floor skywalk at a beam-rod connection and was progressive until complete failure," according to the NBS report. According to NBS's chief investigator, Edward O. Pfrang, the dead load alone stressed the connection to near capacity.[23] "Almost any practicing engineer could easily have seen that the skybridges would not meet the Kansas City building code," according to Pfrang.[24]

Moral responsibility for the deaths and injuries lay with the individual designers who relied upon accepted industry practices that were faulty. It is a common rationalization to shift personal moral responsibility to another person, to a group, or to "accepted practices."

The Code of Silence, as I have defined it in Chapter 1, was operative among many of the Hyatt's creators, especially during the shop drawings review process, in their failure to accept personal responsibility for their work that affected people's lives. Each party—the steel fabricator, the general contractor, city inspectors, and the structural engineers—wanted to blame the other parties or the standard industry practices. The public only heard about the mode of the structural failure during the blame game. The technologists were again sending the message to the public that no one person killed those people—"it was not my fault." This message is the Code.

It seems the engineers and the architects really wanted to believe the disaster resulted from problems outside their control. Did they actively conspire to hide this behavior? We may never know. But the blame game among the players paralleled the strategy of defense attorneys in the Hyatt lawsuits. And a conspiracy need not be overt to be harmful.

A passive, indirect, and unspoken conspiracy can exist when technologists follow a tradition in their profession that allows work to be done in a manner harmful to other human beings—and then continue to operate in the same manner after the disasters. History will repeat itself. As I wrote earlier about the engineers' roles in the Holocaust, inaction in the face of evil can be as devastating as overt murder. Whether passive or active, negligence by professionals is a culpable act.

Gross Negligence by Engineers

The decision of the judge at the administrative hearings found the two principal members with the structural engineering firm GCE, Gillum and Duncan, guilty of gross negligence. The

Missouri Courts defined gross negligence and ordinary negligence the same way: as "an act or course of conduct which demonstrates a conscious indifference to a professional duty."[25] Gillum was also found negligent for placing his stamp on drawings he had not reviewed. Both engineers were found guilty of misconduct in the practice of engineering for misrepresentation to the architects.[26]

Gillum was also found guilty of misconduct for failing to review the atrium design and then misrepresenting that he had done so. The Hyatt atrium roof system had failed during construction, well before the walkways collapsed. Gillum, as the official engineer of record, not Duncan, was found guilty of unprofessional conduct in the practice of engineering. The court said that Gillum did not take responsibility for the project as required by Missouri law.

> **The Missouri Board for Architects and Engineers revoked the Missouri licenses of both engineers on January 22, 1986.[27] No criminal prosecution took place, ostensibly for lack of evidence.**

The Missouri Courts strongly stated their opposition to technologists who want to blame customs and practices, and thus not to be held accountable as individuals.[28] A successful and safe project requires each individual to practice moral responsibility and to ensure that others do their jobs responsibly. The Hyatt disaster raised important questions that remain today, and the tragedy should haunt us creators of technology. The lack of personal moral and social responsibility in these types of disasters seems to have a silence all its own in my profession. The fact that more of us are not outraged by this silence strengthens the case for the existence of the Code.

It had taken only about seven months for the NBS to find the technical cause for the failure. Most failures require much longer. It took much longer before any sense of justice would come from the administrative hearings and numerous lawsuits. Hyatt was, and still is, the worst structural disaster of its kind to occur in the United States, according to the U.S. government.[29]

Nearly everyone involved with the deadly collapse claimed no responsibility for the technical failure of the walkway bridges. During design and construction, the chief architect of Hyatt asked the right questions required by his professional training, but the tragedy still occurred.[b] Common practices were wrong. Yet, blaming others or the system for individual irresponsibility is a typical trait of the Code.

Many members of the team at Hyatt relied upon the specialized structural engineers to do their job honorably. This reliance, without sufficient checks and balances, is an inherent problem in the design and construction of complicated technologies. True beliefs in the "accepted" common practices of the industry failed to protect the very people technologists claim to serve.

Steel beams may crack, rods may fail, or bolts may break, but it is the individual technologist's practice of the Code that allows the technical problems to happen in the first place. Disasters like Hyatt are examples of gross negligence—the conscious disregard for a professional duty—and they illustrate the problems caused by unexamined accepted industry practices. The Tacoma Narrows and the Hyatt Regency disasters had this mind-set in common.

The Hyatt Regency tragedy brings to mind an episode of the long-running anti-war TV series *M*A*S*H*. Colonel Henry Blake tells chief surgeon Hawkeye Pierce, "There are two rules they taught me at command school: rule #1 is young men die ... and rule #2, doctors can't do anything about rule #1." Hawkeye, a medical doctor, would not accept the "true belief" in his profession; nor should I, as a registered professional engineer, accept business as usual in my profession.

---

[b] The architectural firm that designed Hyatt, under the direction of Bob Berkebile, was cleared of any wrongdoing and was dropped from the lawsuits. The engineers of record had assured the architects that the design was safe and that another check of their calculations showed everything was okay.

The next chapter looks at another well-known disaster, the space shuttle Challenger, that demonstrates all the facets of personal and professional irresponsibility and the conspiracy of silence to hide the dirty little secrets in professions and in bureaucratic organizations.

Bibliography, Notes & Further Reading

[1] "Investigation of the Kansas City Hyatt Regency Walkways Collapse," *National Bureau of Standards* (May 1982), 1.

[2] I conducted a personal interview with Bob Dickerson on 9 August 1998, while he was still a police officer with the Kansas City Police Department. More of the interview is presented in this chapter.

[3] Emily D'Aulaire and Per Ola D'Aulaire, "There Wasn't Time to Scream: Anatomy of a Hotel Disaster," *Reader's Digest,* July 1982, 49-56.

[4] Ibid.

[5] "Investigation," 34.

[6] Dickerson, personal interview, 9 August 1998.

[7] Ibid.

[8] "Investigation," 41.

[9] Dickerson, personal interview, 9 August 1998.

[10] This schematic, looking south, shows the two walkways on the right that collapsed. This drawing appeared in "Investigation," 21.

[11] I conducted personal interviews with Bob Berkebile on 6 July 1999 and again on 9 February 2002. He was the chief architect in charge of the Hyatt Regency Hotel project in Kansas City. I will refer to this interview many times.

[12] Robert C. Trussell and Gregory S. Reeves, "Ordeal by Telephone: Sounds of a Calamity," *Kansas City Star*, 19 July 1981.

[13] D'Aulaire and D'Aulaire, "There Wasn't Time," 49-56.

[14] David Rosenham and Martin Seligman, *Abnormal Psychology* (New York: W.W. Norton, 1984), 221-28.

[15] Dickerson, personal interview, 9 August 1998.

[16] The Missouri Courts reached these conclusions. See the lawsuit Missouri Board for Architects, Professional Engineers and Land Surveyors vs. Daniel M. Duncan, Jack Gillum. Case No. AR-84-0239, November 15, 1985. The details of the failure were reached in "Investigation," 253-56.

[17] "Investigation," 253-56.

[18] Figure 7 diagram was included in "Investigation," 251.

[19] Ibid., 25.

[20] Ibid., 77.

[21] Ibid., 77.

[22] This information was noted in "Connection Cited in Hyatt Collapse," *Engineering News Record,* 4 March 1982, 10-12. All charges against the architects were later dropped because they exercised reasonable care and diligence in their contractual and professional duties. They asked the right questions but were assured by the engineers of record that all calculations had been checked and found okay.

[23] Ibid., 10-12.

[24] D'Aulaire and D'Aulaire, "There Wasn't Time," 49-56.

[25] See the lawsuit Missouri Board for Architects, Professional Engineers and Land Surveyors vs. Daniel M. Duncan, Jack Gillum. Case No. AR-84-0239, November 15, 1985, 113-114.

[26] See Daniel M. Duncan, Jack D. Gillum and GCE International, Inc., Appellants, vs. Missouri Board for Architects, Professional Engineers and Land Surveyors. Case No. 52655, January 26, 1988, 41.

[27] Brenda J. Crain, Executive Director, Missouri Board for Architects, Professional Engineers and Land Surveyors, upon my request sent me an official letter on 22 April 1998.

[28] See Missouri Board for Architects, Professional Engineers and Land Surveyors vs. Daniel M. Duncan, Jack Gillum, 157-172.

[29] "Investigation," 1.

Chapter 4
The Space Shuttle Challenger Disaster

A Cold Morning

Nearly everyone at the time believed the National Aeronautics and Space Administration (NASA) to be invincible. The terrible tragedy of Apollo 1 was behind them, and assurances had been made by NASA officials that a deadly fire in the capsule could not happen again. After all, the rocket scientists had landed men on the moon and returned them safely to Earth. NASA

Figure 2: Typical NASA Space Shuttle Schematic

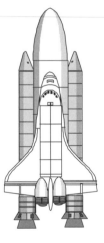

engineers had brought the crippled Apollo 13 spacecraft back safely, and space shuttles had flown 24 successful missions without a disaster.

It was routine technology, or so most of us thought. Christa McAuliffe, the first teacher in space, was on the Challenger and felt it was safe. Most major television networks were not carrying the Challenger's launch live, because the public had lost interest in the routine flights. McAuliffe's presence was designed to change NASA's public image—and influence Congress's opinion about future funding. NASA's image did change, but not in the way it wanted.

On the cold morning of January 28, 1986, the Challenger's booster rockets' joints with rubber O-ring seals leaked shortly after liftoff. This leak fed a fire that caused the explosion of the Challenger.[1] All seven aboard were killed; the entire nation mourned the loss. The explosion of the Challenger shocked Americans and people around the world, and with this shock, our sense of security in "fail-safe" systems was shattered.

Millions of people have watched on television the replay of the explosion of the 25th mission of a space shuttle. The questions on everyone's mind were straightforward: Why did this tragedy happen? What caused the "little leak" that led to the explosion? Who was responsible? The soul-searching at NASA had begun.

Origins of the Disaster

The Challenger decision-making process had much in common with the Tacoma Narrows Bridge and Hyatt Regency Hotel disasters. A callous disregard of a professional duty by some NASA technologists gave the crew of the Challenger a much lower chance of survival than they realized. Important historical data and critical mathematical concepts were ignored.

The constant tension between the safest design and the lowest-cost design, coupled with the adoption of flawed "accepted industry practices" by an entire profession, was a major factor in all three of these disasters. The technical failures of equipment or material were only secondary. The real underlying cause of these disasters was the failure of individuals to exercise moral and social responsibility when confronted with life-and-death decisions.

The Challenger did not have an escape mechanism for the crew, although a losing proposal for the shuttle design did include the safety system. It would have cost more and reduced the payload capability, according to Martin and Schinzinger.[2] All major contractors submitted bids to NASA, including Morton Thiokol, the company that designed and built the infamous rocket boosters.

The O-ring seals of the booster were not designed for the freezing temperatures that morning, according to experts. In many previous flights, the booster seals had shown significant deterioration, but *because they had not failed,* NASA managers did not ask for a recall.[3] It was a crucial decision. A new seal design had been developed, but it was not ready for flights. Richard Feynman, an official investigator, characterized NASA's decision-making process in critical areas (those with no backup systems) as a type of game:[4]

> "a kind of Russian roulette ... the shuttle flies ... and nothing happens. This suggests ... that the risk is no longer so high for the next flights. We can lower our standards a little bit because we got away with it last time."

Some engineers did try to speak out before the launch, but only up to the point where "they felt it only proper to submit to management decisions."[5] In other words, the team effort or, more specifically, the intimidating dynamics of a team effort caused the designers at Morton Thiokol (M-T) to acquiesce to political power.

Many M-T engineers, including Arnold Thompson and Roger Boisjoly, had repeatedly informed NASA managers about serious safety concerns based on past problems with the booster seals. During the hours before the Challenger's early morning launch, they also told M-T's vice president of engineering about these safety concerns in relation to the low temperature at the launch site. M-T vice presidents Bob Lund and Joe Kilminster admitted that safety was a problem.

At one point during the emergency teleconference the night before liftoff, M-T's senior vice president, Jerry Mason, told Bob Lund "to take off [his] engineering hat and put on [his] management hat."[6] The pressure by NASA to launch the morning of the 28th was intense. Congress was already balking at the high cost and "limited benefits" of NASA's space missions. Boisjoly's engineering team still didn't want to launch in the cold weather, and it told NASA managers that "M-T could not endorse the launch" of Challenger. It was at this point that NASA's frustrated project manager for the booster rocket project said, "What do you want to do, wait until April to launch? You ... need to consider the effect of your recommendation." Boisjoly, in a January 2001 interview, said, "Our guys (at M-T) got the message, big time."[7]

M-T's top executives monitored the teleconference. "Their concern was the image of the company, which was in the process of negotiating a renewal of the booster rocket contract with NASA," according to Martin and Schinzinger.[8] The design engineers did not get a chance to vote on the launch, because only the management teams voted to launch. What was management's reasoning? The design engineers "could not prove the seals were NOT safe."[9] The rationale should have been, "Can't prove it safe enough? Stop the launch now." Most Americans were led to believe that this rationale was in place within NASA.

Christa McAuliffe—and most of the public—believed that the space shuttle was fail-safe, or designed with so many backup systems that catastrophic failure was not possible.[a] They were wrong. The number of critical elements identified by NASA rose from about 2,400 before Challenger's explosion to more than 4,600 within a few months after the disaster.

Critical elements were defined as those failures that would cause catastrophic failure and loss of life.[10] There were no backup systems for those 2,400 items in the Challenger, and the failure of

---

[a] An MSNBC television special report (*Challenger: Beyond the Tragedy*, 14 January 2001) showed an interview with McAuliffe in which she talked about her complete confidence in the safety of the Challenger.

any one item, including the booster rocket joint seals, would have been catastrophic. It was not a fail-safe design, and the designers and the managers knew it.

No Informed Consent

It was later discovered that neither the Challenger astronauts nor NASA's launch director were informed of the particular problem of the joint seals as it related to freezing conditions the morning of the launch. They also were not told that experienced engineers at M-T had said it was "suicide" to launch the morning of January 28.[11] Thus, the astronauts were not asked for their "informed consent" to be launched under these circumstances. The experimental nature of the space program did not relieve NASA authorities, who knew the true dangers, from the duty of informing their test pilots.

The concept of informed consent by those who are subjects of an experiment is a fundamental moral and ethical cornerstone of research and medical practice in this country, especially after the horrors of the Holocaust in Nazi Germany. The concept is widely understood to have two primary attributes: sufficient knowledge and voluntary participation by the subjects of any experiment. The subjects must have all the required information that a rational person would need to make a reasonable and informed decision. The subjects should be neither coerced nor deceived when they make their decision to participate.

Federal agencies and universities involved in research use standard agreements to affirm this ethical concept when they use human subjects in experiments. NASA, a federal agency, broke the intent of the written rules. Yes, the trained astronauts were willing to take risks they knew about. But neither the first teacher in space nor the astronauts consented to being deceived.

The engineering and technology professions have never really faced the true nature of their work as "experiments in progress" on human beings. Our innovative buildings, bridges, airplanes, chemicals, and so forth are all experiments. Sometimes, as in the case of the Tacoma Narrows Bridge and the Challenger, lessons about similar failures were not learned in time to stop the disasters. The engineering and technology professions need to reassess the issue of informed consent.

Lessons Learned from the Disaster

Rosa Lynn Pinkus and Norman Hummon at the University of Pittsburgh investigated the disaster from the standpoint of "ethical decision making of its participants."[12] They concluded the Challenger explosion was not caused by "a single event":

> Rather, the decision by Congress to fund the space shuttle program at the "cut-rate" price and the acceptance by NASA to proceed with plans to build the shuttle set the stage for individual engineers continually to struggle to balance safety, cost, and timing.

Many people share their views. To the extent that disasters always have more than one single cause, their argument is valid. However, two subtle themes appear between the lines of their book. First, although Pinkus and Hummon did a good job of investigating, they appear to place the blame on Congress because of low funding levels for NASA, implying that designers must obey the policies and cost constraints of their government and other authorities. Technologists in Germany did the same thing, as you will read in the next section.

The second subtle theme in Pinkus's and Hummon's book also represents the prevailing attitude of technologists in many man-made disasters: engineers' acquiescence to their boss's "persuasion."

> **This persuasion means "take off your engineer's hat" and place business interests above moral and social responsibility.**

Low costs and tight schedules become primary issues during the design process. Selecting contractors by the lowest-bid method is dangerous if safety is to be the highest priority. Since the 1970s, engineering designers have also been subject to the lowest-dollar proposal process. The professional license to practice engineering requires designers to place paramount the safety, health, and welfare of those who are exposed to our creations. The low-bid selection method is not congruent with this requirement.

The dubious process of placing a dollar value on life, coupled with a technologist's sense of obedience to authority, does not promote freedom of speech within organizations. If an employee resists these temptations to conform, the "persuasion" by authorities looks more like intimidation.

This so-called persuasion represents a type of "mobbing in the workplace" that more closely resembles coercion than any real encouragement to exercise moral judgment. Mobbing involves persistent emotional abuse of an employee, usually by a supervisor, designed to coerce the employee to stop what she is doing and/or resign.[13] The connection between this dangerous and pervasive practice and the Code of Silence will be explained in Chapter 6.

A related coercive approach used to stifle open discussion of problems existed at NASA: a disdain for employees who wanted to exercise their freedom of speech and question unethical practices and decisions. Most "whistle-blowers" have brief career expectancies in such an environment, and it does not matter whether the public disclosure is internal or external to the organization.

At the time of the Challenger launch, no policy existed that would have allowed all aerospace workers with safety concerns to report them, anonymously or otherwise. After Challenger, a few vice presidents at Morton Thiokol were demoted, while other outspoken engineers retained token jobs only because Congress protected them for a time.[14] Most of us do not have this political connection, and in the end, it did not matter. Careers and lives were destroyed.

The mobbing of real or perceived whistle-blowers in the workplace has a devastating effect, even on suspected whistle-blowers and their families. Managers or fellow employees use mobbing to isolate those they consider "disloyal" to the company. Company executives and managers can become obsessed with "keeping the secrets" within their "family," which is often a dysfunctional organization. Why? Economic gain and job security are primary motives for preserving the status quo. They are also primary factors in the Code.

Neglect of Basic Principles

Robert S. Ryan, who has studied the Challenger disaster, has concluded "that failure and/or problems in the shuttle generally were not due to undiscovered or missing theory; but to the neglect or oversight of basic principles ... in project management of a program."[15] It is not that engineers were not finding problems in the NASA program; they were. Ryan is describing the classic and common problem for the technologists: how far to take the issues or to remain quiet—in other words, the power of the unwritten Code.

Pinkus and Hummon want their readers to believe that the actions of A.O. Tischler, a NASA chemical engineer for the rocket engines, were "alternatives to whistle-blowing." Yet Tischler's numerous and dedicated internal memos and efforts to change NASA's policies about risk failed to prevent Challenger's explosion.[b] I am not questioning Tischler's dedication to good decision-making or his professional competence, but I do question the wisdom of Pinkus and Hummon's position on whistle-blowing. Although they may not have intend to, they imply that

---

[b] In 1974, according to Pinkus and Hummon, a "frustrated" Tischler "retired" from the space program (p. 180). Tischler wrote countless reports and papers questioning the way NASA conducted business. According to Pinkus and Hummon, he "worked within both the organizational structure of NASA and his professional societies to implement the change he deemed necessary to complete the shuttle project successfully" (p. 172). But their emphasis on "frustrated" and "retired" suggest that something else was happening.

external efforts are not justified even when health and safety are at risk, as they were in the shuttle program.[16]

Tischler spoke out in defense of an alternative to the existing shuttle program, but it is apparent that he "was concerned with the long-term survival and success of the space transportation system so that all persons directly and indirectly associated with it would not suffer adverse consequences."[17] His immediate supervisor refused to "allow" Tischler to publish a paper critical of NASA's project managers and of the "self-serving nature" of everyone's motives at NASA.

> **Tischler failed to exercise his freedom of speech, and in the end, he decided to protect the organization.**

This type of limited action is not an ethical alternative to whistle-blowing. Telling the truth where it may affect change is justified, and this situation warranted it, no matter how high in the chain of command it was necessary to climb. Such action is difficult, but we technologists are paid and licensed to do this very thing.

The National Research Council (NRC) set up a number of committees and panels to study the Challenger disaster. One such panel believed that NASA's process for deciding whether a critical element should have a backup system was fatally flawed. Recall that more than 2,400 such elements existed in the shuttle before the disaster.

The panel noted the following four problems with NASA's waiving of backup systems for critical elements. First, no specific methodology or criteria existed for these decisions. Second, true margins against failure modes were not defined or validated. Third, the probability of the failure mode was never established quantitatively using appropriate statistical methods. And fourth, various design "fixes" were accepted without being analyzed and compared.[18] This process was neither good science nor good engineering by any standard.

The disaster of the space shuttle Challenger did not happen because of a single problem. It happened in large part because past data, current available information, a state-of-the-art statistical analysis, and appropriate "acceptable industry standards" were not used. The Challenger disaster illustrates professional irresponsibility and the conspiracy of silence to hide the truth—before and after the disasters. This quotation from the 19th century describes the Code:

> **"When truth is buried, it grows, it chokes, it gathers such explosive force that on the day it breaks out, it blows everything up with it."[19]**

So, why do highly trained individuals try to shift moral and social responsibility to someone else? Why do groups of professionals and others hide this dirty little secret of a conspiracy of silence? What are the origins of "accepted industry practices" that lead to disasters? The next four chapters of Part Two describe the four primary origins of the Code of Silence: the technologists' true beliefs, their common characteristics, their connection with the "Industrial-Military-University Complex," and their higher education.

Technologists can become so obsessed with earning a living and with being creative that we can forget to live a life worth living—and to give this right to others.

Bibliography, Notes & Further Reading

[1] Martin and Schinzinger, 96-104.

[2] Ibid., 101-102.

[3] Ibid., 101-102.

[4] Michael Collins, *Liftoff* (New York: Grove Press, 1988), 228.

[5] Ibid., 103.

[6] Martin and Schinzinger, 99.

[7] This conversation took place during an MSNBC television special report, *Challenger: Beyond the Tragedy*, 14 January 2001. Correspondent Tom Sawyer interviewed Lawrence Mulloy, NASA's former manager of the booster rocket project, and engineer Roger Boisjoly, Mulloy's former counterpart at Morton Thiokol.

[8] Martin and Schinzinger, 99.

[9] Ibid., 100.

[10] Rosa Lynn B. Pinkus and Norman P. Hummon, *Engineering Ethics: Balancing Cost, Schedule, and Risk—Lessons Learned from the Space Shuttle* (Cambridge: Cambridge University Press, 1997), 259-62.

[11] The "suicide" quote was from Roger Boisjoly during an MSNBC television special report, *Challenger: Beyond the Tragedy*, 14 January 2001. See also Martin and Schinzinger, *Ethics in Engineering*.

[12] Pinkus and Hummon, 17-18.

[13] Noa Davenport, Distler Schwartz and Gail P. Elliott, *Mobbing: Emotional Abuse in the American Workplace* (Ames, Iowa: Civil Society Publishing, 1999).

[14] Martin and Schinzinger, 104.

[15] Pinkus and Hummon, 243. More information about Ryan's work can be found in Robert S. Ryan, "Practices in Adequate Structural Design," NASA Technical Paper 2893, George C. Marshall Space Flight Center, Huntsville, Ala., 1989.

[16] Pinkus and Hummon, 171-181.

[17] Ibid., 178-179.

[18] These conclusions were taken from Pinkus and Hummon, 258. For a more detailed look at the NRC's report, see Committee on Shuttle Criticality Review and Hazard Analysis Audit of the Aeronautics and Space Engineering Board.

[19] Emile Zola, "J'accuse!" *L'Aurore*, 13 January 1898, 405.

Part 2: The Origins of the Code of Silence

*****

"The great enemy of the truth is very often not the lie—deliberate, contrived, and dishonest—but the myth—persistent, persuasive, and unrealistic."

John F. Kennedy, Address, Yale University, 1962

Chapter 5
True Beliefs and Dangerous Myths

True Believers in Our Midst

Reluctantly, I have come to understand that most technologists have a predisposition to think in terms of dangerous myths or "true beliefs." In Chapter 1, true believers were defined as people who tend to exhibit, among other traits, fanatical, irrational, and potentially harmful beliefs about reality. This fanaticism can take the form of passive and/or active evil along the Spectrum of Evil described earlier in Chapter 1.

Over the years, my experiences with engineering and technology students and with corporate America have confirmed my growing awareness of the true belief phenomenon. This predisposition of technologists to be true believers in their traditional, usually unexamined, patterns of thought allows the Code of Silence to continue generation after generation. As much as technologists may want to deny their existence, these true beliefs have a profound effect on the way they create the things of our culture.

True believers have transformed the creation and application of technology into a "mass movement." Philosopher Eric Hoffer describes a mass movement as a revolution with fanatical team players and with disorder at its core. Those who willingly participate in mass movements want to change the world around them.[1] In *The True Believer,* Hoffer describes the influence of inherited attitudes and unexamined beliefs[2] on such people, who hold tenaciously to their myths in spite of any evidence that they might be just plain wrong. This tenacity adversely affects their ability to recognize and solve moral dilemmas.

> This effect blinds us creators to the truth about the real impact that we have on others.

The Code, as well as its connections with disasters, begins deep within each individual technologist and manifests itself both internally and externally.

The internal manifestation of these true beliefs is the individual's conscious attempt to suppress or hide the truth from himself. Consequently, the technologist who is a true believer denies reality before a disaster occurs. Suppression of the truth requires energy and can lead to personal pain and disorders in a rational human being. If we choose not to examine the things that should trouble us at night, what we resist will persist.

The individual's internal suppression also infects the team of creators: A dominant individual, either by her active role in disasters or by her unspoken agreement to remain silent, can convince others in the team that her system of beliefs is valid. Either way, the individual's suppression of reality contributes to "groupthink."[a] This process is a deadly game that technologists play.

The game includes the tendency for associations and organizations of technologists to allow a conspiracy of silence. This unspoken agreement is the external manifestation of the Code. The professional groups will not admit to the underlying reasons for man-made disasters, and the individuals deny their personal accountability as professionals and human beings. Technologists often do not even consciously recognize that a game is being played.

---

[a] In Part One, I defined "groupthink" as the *acceptance without questioning* of the predominant views of a leader, group, organization, or government on social, political, and moral matters.

The true believer effect has its origins in the common heritage and traits of creators.[b] Engineers and scientists have similar family backgrounds, kindred cultural roots and values, and equivalent educational and professional experiences.

True believers hold passionately to their beliefs, even in the face of evidence to the contrary. Hoffer writes that the frustrated and insecure look for something or someone in which to believe. True believers assume this something or someone exists outside themselves. Many technologists and others seem to need a substitute for reality when they feel the world's problems invading their hope for a more secure future. True beliefs become a substitute for insecurity and self-doubt. This phenomenon is not exclusive to technologists, but their effect on our world can be deadly for everyone.

Hoffer, an astute observer of human behavior, believed that we counteract a deep feeling of insecurity about ourselves by becoming part of a group—what he calls a mass movement. The insecurity is a primary trait among technologists, according to the sociological studies presented in the next chapter.

The homogenous mixture of people called technologists constitutes a mass movement, and the insecure often join these mass movements of true believers. Hoffer seems to describe the technologist, although he does not use the term, when he writes,

> It is the true believer's ability to shut his eyes and stop his ears to facts that do not deserve to be either seen or heard which is the source of his unequaled fortitude and constancy. Strength of faith ... manifests itself not in moving mountains, but in not seeing mountains to move. And it is the certitude of his infallible doctrine that renders the true believer impervious to the uncertainties, surprises, and the unpleasant realities of the world around him.[3]

Technologists, in general, want power and control over their environment. We typically enjoy the creative work that is affected by these true beliefs. And none of us like to be insecure.

---

[b] The studies to which I refer will be covered in detail in the section on "Common Backgrounds and Goals" in Chapter Six.

Yet, history has shown us that technologists can become obsessed with the creative urge without regard for the consequences of their actions. This insistence on the right to create blinds many technologists to the moral issues and allows others to use our creations for economic and political gain at the expense of other human beings.

The Technical Imperative

A significant number of technologists subscribe to a common but faulty doctrine about their creative work. This faulty doctrine assumes that the end result of all creations will eventually be good and, therefore, that all intermediate problems along the way can be discounted as "necessary evils" or the price we must pay for progress.

These true believers don't stop to think about whose lives their creations will improve—or maybe they do think about it and simply decide their lives count for more than "those other people's." Thousands or millions of people may be harmed because they are unlucky enough to be in the minority in many cases. Surely, no one will seriously argue that the majority is always right.

The technical imperative, the powerful and urgent desire to create without moral and social responsibility, is one more true belief of technologists who crave innovation at any cost. The technical imperative permeates the narrowly focused university education of technologists and the business world of technology. This true belief could be called the doctrine of *creative manifest destiny*.[c]

Robert Oppenheimer, the director of the Manhattan Project for the development of atomic bombs dropped on Japan, said, "Once you know how to make the bomb it's not your

---

[c] In this country, people believed they had a right to push aside Native Americans during the expansion to the Pacific coast in the 1800s. This faulty belief in a "manifest destiny" proved disastrous for indigenous peoples.

business to figure out how not to use it."[4] This mind-set is the technical imperative, and it allowed true believers to feel that they had no moral responsibility for the deaths of thousands of women, children, and other non-combatants.

> **The people who revere the technical imperative declare: If it can be done, it must be done.**

This attitude is responsible for much of the suffering and death found in modern technology failures and disasters. Innovative technologies for transportation vehicles, for taller buildings, and for longer bridges represent the essence of the true belief in the technical imperative. My profession is only one of many that endorse this concept. In the 21st century, some technologists consider the cloning of animals and now even of human beings to be their creative right.

While attending an international scientific forum in Rome, three medical doctors from Italy, Israel, and the United States who are experts on cloning defied their colleagues and governments by snubbing the idea of submitting to ethical or scientific oversight by any government. The doctors said that "science is ready to move on to cloning humans" despite a disturbing rate of disease and deformities in similarly reproduced animals.[5]

In a *Time* magazine interview, one of these three experts, Dr. Panayiotis Zavos, who was employed at an American university, said this about cloning humans: "Ethics is a wonderful word, but we need to look beyond the ethical issues here. *It's not an ethical issue.* It's a medical issue."[6] The emphasis on his words is mine. Zavos's arrogance is not only disturbing but also alarming.

The world has seen this attitude from medical doctors before. It is, "Get out of my way because I know best." Nazi doctors performed horrible medical procedures, reproduction experiments, and other medical atrocities on humans with the intent to produce the Aryan "superman." I am not claiming that Zavos is a neo-Nazi; he may be an empathetic doctor. But we should remember the role of the Code in man-made tragedies.

Technologists who shift personal moral responsibility for their creations to others practice the Code, and the practice has led to genocide.

The Code feeds on the faulty doctrine I called creative manifest destiny, which is closely connected to the dogma of the technical imperative. It is used as the justification for the shift of their responsibility to others. For the technical imperative to work as it does, another related true belief is necessary so that technologists can sleep at night: emotional detachment—or not feeling or wanting to feel what others feel.

Emotional Detachment

At times, people who are usually rational avoid emotional involvement with other human beings. It is natural to want a break from the noise of modern life. If you are a person like me who loves to fish, you will understand what you are about to read.

I love to fish for largemouth bass in the deep lake in front of my Missouri cabin, but the real enjoyment is not the sport. Nor do I fish because I need the food. That's a good thing, because if I did, I might starve. The real joy for me when fishing in my small boat is the solitude. There are no phones around me, only nature's beauty, and this serenity gives me a new perspective on life—and death. This temporary retreat from others is appropriate and needed to recharge a person's batteries, but when technologists create and build things, aloofness and detachment can be very dangerous.

If a technologist distances herself from feeling what others feel, the result can be life-and-death issues for the rest of us. Creators of technology at times practice emotional indifference toward those affected by their work. The creators of the Hyatt, of the Challenger, and certainly of the Holocaust surely had to distance themselves emotionally from other human beings.

The practice of distancing can be found in technologists, in doctors, in lawyers, and in other professionals responsible for public safety and welfare. For many people, this emotional apathy and/or suppression of feelings about other human beings is a learned behavior. As you will read in the next chapter, it is also one of the common characteristics sociologists have discovered in technologists.

Many professional schools and colleges promote such detachment. Bernie S. Siegel, a physician and writer, admits that he had been "trained to maintain an emotional distance from patients."[7] A number of professional educators, especially in engineering and technology, will not admit that emotional detachment has become a true belief or that it is practiced in the professions and in the application of technology. Most of these same educators and practitioners do not recognize distancing as a problem, while others actually choose to be emotionally detached and aloof from their students—and from the end users of their creations.

> **Engineering students are taught to distrust feelings and to solve problems using logic alone.**

But for many in the profession, distancing begins even earlier. Most males are taught from a very early age not to show emotions. "Don't get emotionally involved," they say. "Use your head," we are told as children. These misguided admonitions only serve to limit our humanity and our empathy with others, leading to more pain and suffering for us as creators and for those affected by our creations.

So, we hide our feelings. The large number of man-made tragedies suggests that real empathy is suppressed. As more women venture into this male-dominated industry, their education and training tends to make many of them emotionally detached, just like their male counterparts. It is a learned behavior that I hope women in technology can begin to recognize and avoid.

When faced with dilemmas about good and bad, scientists and engineers may not consciously consider the enormous impact of their work. Many times technologists have chosen to be silent when confronted by the evil application of their creations. The "flash of a neon light" blinds us, as Paul Simon wrote in his song

"Sounds of Silence." Status, job security, money, an unquestioned creative urge are among the symptoms of emotional detachment and self-gratification.

> **These sounds of silence are cancers, which consume our "self" and allow man-made disasters to happen.**

Technologists in the workplace are similar to soldiers in the military: Their work is usually conducted within authoritarian and bureaucratic organizations that, like the military, are designed to suppress the true, individual self and mold troops who will be obedient, compliant, and ready to abandon personal moral and social responsibility.

It is this suppression of individual responsibility that often leads to a closely bonded team that protects itself from outside influences. Many say that this must happen for the benefit of the mission. Most combat veterans tell us that they fight to stay alive and to help their team members survive—not for country, ideology, or politics. Their small unit becomes family. This process of identity loss starts with recruits in "boot camp" and continues during the careers of those in the military.

The narrowly focused, specialized education of technologists could be compared to soldiers' training in boot camp. Many university professors demand obedience and compliance from their students. And after they graduate from college, technologists continue to submerge their identities in large governmental and private bureaucratic organizations.

Military and civilian design/construction organizations design and build large-scale projects. In addition to its wartime duties, the Army Corps of Engineers is well known for building dams and other large water control systems. These large projects entail specialized and fragmented work assignments and are often far removed from the creators, who may not see their completion. As a result, individual technologists may not feel included in the process or feel any human emotion for the welfare of the people who will occupy their structures or use their systems. They lose a sense of reality about what really happens and how their creations are used.

Sometimes this distancing is intentional, as in the case of the Holocaust designers. But it can be unintentional as well. Many of the technologists who designed Challenger's myriad systems did so from various locations across the United States. They distanced themselves physically and emotionally from the reality of the moment on the cold morning that the space shuttle was launched.

The workload of a technologist is often very demanding, and this can lead to emotional detachment. When too busy and preoccupied with details, human beings are more inclined to use bad judgment and to make mistakes they might not ordinarily make. The Hyatt Regency disaster appears to have been a prime example of the hurried life. Job burnout and the stress that goes with it are real problems in a production-oriented organization.

The engineering design firm for the Hyatt Regency was a large, prosperous, and growing corporation. Perhaps it was growing too fast. NASA management, reacting to pressure from market and funding demands, pressed their employees and contractors to the point that a tragedy was almost certain to occur. The effect of workplace stress on individuals is predictable and well documented.

This tendency of individuals to become almost anonymous in massive bureaucracies often leads them to abandon personal accountability and empathy for those who are affected by the new technology. Such distancing is part of the Code, and its results can be deadly. With emotional detachment firmly entrenched, blind obedience to and compliance with authority become easier for an individual who may want job security over autonomous ethical decision-making.

Obedience and Compliance

"Do what I tell you to do." "Do it because it's the way we've always done it." "Don't make me come down there." Do these statements sound familiar? Most of us as children heard these admonitions from our parents and from other authority figures.

As a child, I reacted as a child; I complied to avoid punishment and pain. As an adult working in an organization, we can feel the same emotion: Obey and escape punishment. But as adults, we have more choices and responsibilities. Yet, if we disobey authority as a whistle-blower might, we may be isolated and harassed. We may even find ourselves unemployed or worse.

If we obey immoral organizational authority in the face of evil, we die the death of a "thousand pinpricks," as an old Chinese proverb says. Specialized, bureaucratic organizations often demand unquestioning obedience to their procedures, which are often devoid of personal emotion or involvement in the final product.[8] This was true of the Holocaust and Hiroshima, but the statements also apply to tragedies like the Hyatt and the Challenger.

Once they have joined the mass movement—in this case, the revolution in technology—one more thing is required of true believers. Hoffer reminds us that "the total surrender of a distinct self ... and the habit of blind obedience [are] necessary ... for one to feel part of the group."[9] The violence in the 20th century demonstrated the existence and perils of blind obedience among the masses of people and among highly educated technologists. It is a road well traveled by true believers in the Code.

> **The pressure for individual technologists to conform, which is first felt within a family unit and then reinforced in a specialized education, continues unabated into the business world.**

An obsession with job security and peer acceptance can easily overshadow sound reasoning and cause individuals to behave in ways incongruent with rational thinking about ethical behavior.

*****

Three academic experiments and one horrible event will illustrate that human beings must resist genuine evil every day on a personal level. The three experiments are the Electric Shock experiments by Stanley Milgram;[10] the Good Samaritan experiment by Darley and Batson;[11] and the Prison experiment by Haney, Banks, and Zimbardo.[12] The horrible event was the My Lai massacre in Vietnam.[13] There are many others, but these three are sufficient evidence of the role that obedience and compliance play in man-made disasters.

The academic psychological experiments illustrate blind obedience to authority and to the Code of Silence. A series of experiments in the 1960s by Stanley Milgram confirmed that, like Germans during the Holocaust, Americans are also capable of following orders to extremes. Milgram set up a deceptive experiment to test obedience to authority and the corresponding lack of personal accountability and responsibility by individuals in a structured environment.

People were hired to act as "learners" and "experimenters." The subjects of the experiment were hired from the street and were told it was a legitimate scientific experiment. The "experimenters" represented the scientific community's authority figures and ran the experiment. They asked the subjects to give electric shocks of 15 to 450 volts to the "learners" when they did not perform the memory tests accurately. The "learners" actually received no shock, but acted as if they had.

The subjects who were inflicting the punishment could see the apparent agony and hear the screams of the "learners," but in the different trials, 50-67% of the subjects still gave the "learners" the full 450 volts. The percentage of subjects who gave the full shock dropped in half when the subject and the "learner" were in the same room together. When subjects hesitated to continue shocking the learners, authority figures encouraged them to continue by saying, "You have no choice, (you're the) teacher, and the experiment must go on."

Milgram explained the results as further proof that even Americans can abandon autonomy when organizational authority figures give immoral orders. His experiment shows the extent to which humans will go in following orders, abdicating personal responsibility, and submitting to authority.

The subjects in the Milgram experiment exhibited active evil: committing with full awareness an act that harms others. Murder and gross negligence are acts of commission. The next example, the "Good Samaritan" experiment, demonstrates passive evil, or the type of immoral behavior that humans commit by omission: that is, by choosing not to act to stop evil when it is possible to do so.

*****

The setting for the "Good Samaritan" experiment was a well-known northeastern theological seminary. A professor instructed 40 students to prepare a lecture on either the Good Samaritan parable from the Bible or job opportunities for seminary graduates. Half of those in each area were told they had plenty of time, but the other half had to hurry to meet the deadline. An actor was placed on the steps outside the hall where the lecture was to be given and told to act hurt and in pain

Of the 40 student subjects, only 16 stopped to inquire. Of those 16, most were from the group that was told they had plenty of time. Some students who chose the Samaritan parable literally stepped over the victim in their hurry to complete the assignment.

> **Sadly, I am reminded of the Protestant minister of 11 years who helped run the killing places during the Holocaust.**

The hurried life in urban centers that most of us lead today makes it easier to see why the students tended to ignore the man. It has become too easy to walk around the homeless and unemployed on the sidewalks of cities these days. The urban environment, in which most people live, places us in a survival mode. When we feel threatened and stressed, as the students did, we react to situations differently. Thomas Lickona of the State University of New York at Cortland, who has studied moral psychology, moral behavior, and moral development, says,

> There is something in human moral behavior that must be given its due, something that may be even more compelling than the best understanding of morality. And that something is: The ecological context of the behavior, the web of situational factors in which the action is enmeshed. Context, to a disturbingly great degree, appears to shape thinking, feeling, and conduct.[14]

Lickona observed immoral behaviors from the context of the person's environment. But the "Prisoner and Guard" experiment provides additional insight into unprincipled human behavior that cannot be easily explained by situational factors. From a pool of 75 college males, 24 subjects were carefully screened and selected for pro-social views, well-developed maturity, good physical health, and mental stability.

Half were assigned as prisoners and the others as guards. Role instructions were given, but were deliberately vague. The mock prison at Stanford University gave a real sense of imprisonment to all the subjects. Guards and prisoners wore typical uniforms, and prisoners were stamped with a number. Guards were to call them by their numbers only. The "warden," a research assistant, established the daily routine: three bland meals per day, three supervised toilet visits, and limited times for reading or writing. Guards were told not to use any form of physical punishment.

How did those college students act? Although there were individual differences, both groups showed "extremely pathological" reactions, and the experiment was stopped after six days. Guards became sadistic and cruel. They used physical punishment, insults, harassment, threats, and other forms of abuse. The most hostile guards became leaders.

Prisoners lost their identities. They first expressed disbelief, then rebelled, then finally tried to work within the system. Early into the experiment, self-deprecation and deprecation of each other became common. Guards would verbally abuse and belittle the prisoners. The prisoners began to believe what the guards said about them and belittled themselves. Half of them became "emotionally disturbed." According to the experimenters,[15]

> Most dramatic and distressing to us was the observation of the ease with which sadistic behavior could be elicited in individuals who were not sadistic types, and the frequency with which acute emotional breakdowns could occur in men selected precisely for their emotional stability.

The guards displayed behavior chillingly close to that found in the concentration camps of Nazi Germany. Prisoners who survived the Nazi death camps told strikingly similar accounts of prisoners who became guards within the camps. If you have not read literature written by Holocaust survivors, I strongly suggest that you read the works of a survivor, a psychiatrist and successor to Freud, Dr. Viktor E. Frankl. He wrote a horrifying, provocative, and illuminating account of his experiences with the interaction of prisoners, prisoner-guards, and Nazi guards.[16]

The similarities between Frankl's experiences and the results of the Stanford experiment are disturbing. Whether the guards were participants in a controlled experiment or Nazis, they should have understood their responsibility to, and accountability toward, other human beings. In the final analysis, the situational factors that Thomas Lickona believes led to immoral behaviors should not be the scapegoat. These horrible actions come from individual choices, as you will read in the next example.

Vietnam

On the morning of March 16, 1968, a task force of American troops moved into a small South Vietnamese village known as My Lai. It was a typical search-and-destroy mission for the troops—to find and kill Vietcong soldiers. The Vietnam War was the first war in which American forces found it difficult to tell the combatants from the non-combatants in battle areas. Thus, troops tended to hate and distrust all Vietnamese in an area where known Vietcong operated.

> **The My Lai massacre exemplifies genuine evil and the power of the Code.**

Company C, 1st Battalion, 20th Infantry of the 11th Light Infantry Brigade moved into My Lai, where the troops found not a single typical combatant. There was no resistance and only unarmed women, children, and old men. American troops of C Company proceeded to kill between 500 and 600 unarmed villagers. Troops opened fire in huts and killed children as they ran. Under the direction of Lieutenant William L. Calley Jr., villagers were herded into groups of 20 to 40 and slaughtered by rifle fire, machine gun fire, or grenades.[17] However, Calley's platoon was not the only platoon killing civilians that day.

The killing continued all morning, and only three people attempted to stop the atrocities. Three soldiers in a combat helicopter were flying over the area trying to draw fire from the enemy ground troops. Hugh Thompson Jr., Lawrence Colburn, and Glenn Andreotta noticed piles of bodies of non-combatants in ditches the first time they flew over. On another pass, they noticed women and children in a ditch being sprayed with machine gun fire.

They now understood what was happening and set the helicopter down between their fellow Americans and the people in the ditch. The three men provided cover to protect the villagers from their fellow troops and called in another helicopter to evacuate the wounded and survivors in the ditch. Thompson reported what they saw to his commanding officer, who then called off all action in the sector.

> **Another crime then started: the cover-up, or the conspiracy to hide the truth.**

It took over a year for news of the massacre to reach civilian and political authorities. Until the late 1990s, the official U.S. Army documents showed that the Viet Cong killed the civilians. On March 6, 1998, the Army corrected the documents and issued medals to the three men in the helicopter (one posthumously) for their heroic actions that day.[18] As many as 50 soldiers actually pulled triggers, but about 200 directly witnessed the killings. Eventually, charges were considered against 25 soldiers, but only six were brought to trial. Of these, only Calley was convicted.

According to M. Scott Peck in *People of the Lie*, the Army General Staff rejected studying the massacre for political reasons because it might prove a further embarrassment to the administration.[19] Peck was one of three committee members who were Army psychiatrists in 1972, and he recommended that the Army study the nature of evil. The Army rejected his recommendations, and he has a theory on why it did. Peck writes, "If we are to study the nature of human evil, it is doubtful how clearly we will be able to separate *them* from *us*; it will most likely be our own natures we are examining."[20]

> Peck defines evil as "the use of political power to destroy others for the purpose of defending or preserving the integrity of one's sick self."[21]

He defines political power as subjective, biased, and prejudiced power. His definition of evil is closely connected to the true believer syndrome described by Hoffer. An important connection exists between the creative good that is possible and our ability to look inside our "selves," an ability that Part Three explores. It is no accident that where evil exists, the Code of Silence has been allowed to grow.

Planned Accidents

Misuse of technology because of the Code is not an accident. It is a common mistake to think of accidents as inevitable—and acceptable. In our technology professions, however, the harm we cause to others without their informed consent is no accident, but rather a form of passive evil.

Rational people neither seek pain nor inflict evil in the form of pain, as I defined evil in Chapter 1.[d] Most technologists do not like to think about the potential for genuine evil in the creation and application of technology. As a result, when something bad happens, it is rationalized as a mistake in judgment.

When engineers refer to a mistake in judgment, most mean simply a wrong choice among alternatives using accepted industry practices. The assumption is that these alternatives have been investigated to the best of the designer's ability. The reliance upon acceptable industry practices suggests that a wrong choice is considered acceptable professional behavior.

> **This concept is essentially the myth, "It is the price we must pay for progress."**

A belief in an excusable "mistake" corresponds with technologists' acceptance of trial and error in a new technology's application.

The word "accident" is defined as a chance event commonly involving catastrophe. The idea of acceptable accidents and mistakes appeals to technologists who prefer not to look beyond the technical reasons for man-made disasters. "Accident" and "mistake" are sometimes used in the same context.

To make a mistake is "to form an incorrect estimate of, or have a wrong opinion of, or to think wrongly of ... some person or thing." It may seem incongruent with moral responsibility, but in my profession and others, it is sometimes legally acceptable to make a mistake even when deaths occur.

Over the last 20 years, U.S. courts' acceptance of mistakes, accidents, or "errors in judgment" as a relief from

---

[d] In Chapter 1, evil was defined in terms used by M. Scott Peck in *People of the Lie*. Peck believes that evil is the "desire to escape legitimate suffering" and that it is a blatant form of "laziness" stemming from "malignant narcissism." The suffering the evil people desire to avoid is the "pain of their own conscience, the pain of the realization of their own imperfections that is caused by self-examination."

liability has declined. According to construction industry experts and authors, Clough and Sears, professionals including doctors and lawyers only "have a duty to exercise *ordinary* skill and competency in carrying out their function."[22] They go on to write, "Learning, skill, and experience are expected *to the degree customarily regarded as being necessary and sufficient for the usual practice of that profession.*" (The emphasis is mine.) This industry accepted model leaves a lot of wiggle room for the technologist. Although this wiggle room might have declined because of the courts' actions, most engineers and contractors that I know still endorse the "ordinary skill and competency" position taken by Clough and Sears. It is still found in most college textbooks in engineering and technology.

I suspect that most of the public does not understand this concept, but it clearly affects their safety. "Ordinary skill and competency" translates in many cases to the public receiving standards generated by "C minus" students instead of "A plus" students who later become our designers and builders. Designers of buildings, bridges, power plants, and so forth are not required to produce perfect sets of plans, nor are they required to guarantee satisfactory results.[23] When the safety, welfare, and health of human beings are at stake, the standards for creators are generally believed by the public to be higher than they really are.

Many technologists want to believe that the Hyatt Regency collapse, the Challenger tragedy, and other man-made disasters were accidents. This classification is somehow supposed to ease their consciences. Perhaps the Hyatt Regency and the Challenger disasters should have been called accidents waiting to happen, because a series of conscious human decisions and actions led to the deaths and injuries. By anyone's definition, mistakes in judgment were made.

Eugene Ferguson, professor emeritus of history at the University of Delaware, has researched engineering failures from a different perspective.[24] Ferguson argues convincingly that engineers trained since the 1960s do not develop an intuitive feel for their work. He points to the use of computer models and software that try to break reality into a large number of areas for a higher degree of accuracy.

Cray supercomputers can model portions of reality, but the models always remain limited in their ability to connect to the real world. There are simply too many variables, even for a Cray. In addition, the designers of our technology rely on models of reality that only a few experts may understand. According to Ferguson, "Bad design results from errors in engineering judgment which is not reducible to science or mathematics."[25] I agree; it is more fundamental than that.

Technologists continue to want others to believe that mistakes result from undiscovered laws of science and mathematics—in other words, that an accident implies no personal moral responsibility. This is rarely the case. Yes, humans are fallible. However, overly ambitious designers of leading-edge technologies and negligent designers who use existing technology fail to adequately consider the ethical aspects of the technology they design.

Zealous creators, when at their rational best, probably sense at some level that they put lives at risk with innovative technologies, but they continue anyway, consciously disregarding their professional duty and violating basic human rights. Again, Ferguson believes engineers should be reminded, "nearly all engineering failures result from faulty judgments rather than faulty calculations." [26]

> **The optimistic enthusiasm that accompanies the impulse to create obscures the moral judgment of many technologists.**

The experimental nature of our work as engineers and scientists does not give us the right to place at risk non-consenting human beings or our planet's existence. If Ferguson is right, faulty and self-serving judgments about reality contribute to most, if not all, man-made disasters. I argue that these bad judgments can be conscious decisions, but more often, they result from a suppression of feelings that should trouble technologists at night. The passive evil of the Code is very real.

Two more related true beliefs lie at the origins of the Code: reliance upon computers said to be infallible, and the mind-set that ethics cannot be taught—and should not be taught in university classrooms. These beliefs are dead wrong.

Fail-Safe Computer Designs

The true belief in the infallibility of computers begins in the higher education of technologists. It is often claimed that the power of today's computers ensures safety in design—in other words, that the public does not have to worry, because a "fail-safe" design is possible. It will not fail because of the safety factors built into the system. The significant disasters of the 20th century contradict this assertion.

When I was trained as a civil engineer in the late 1960s, slide rules were used. I still own my POST Versalog Slide Rule, and from time to time, I show the antique to students. I receive a few laughs and taunts about my age, but at least I get their attention to make a point about our over-reliance on technology to solve our human-based problems.

The degree of accuracy in most of our calculations with the slide rule was, at best, only about three significant figures. Pocket calculators were beginning to appear, but I still was required to use a slide rule on tests. It seemed illogical to continue using old technology. The calculator would have been faster and more accurate—at least, I thought so.

Our professors gave us two primary reasons to continue with slide rules. First, the precision of calculations with the slide rule was the same as the real world behavior of our materials in our structures. Second, the accuracy of the data from the field measurements, on which the calculations depended, limited our need for higher accuracy. I was not sure my teachers were right at the time, but today I better understand their reasoning—and concerns. The hand calculator's ability to carry calculations to 14 significant figures did not help our ability to design safely.

The hand-held calculator replaced the slide rule, and it soon gave way to the computer. The trend has grown among many technologists and most of the public to accept computer solutions as nearly infallible. Ferguson addresses this subject in an article in *Invention & Technology*.[27] Until the 1960s, engineering students were expected to have hands-on experience with the things they designed—and an intuitive feel for the real world. Ferguson believes a paradox exists because more computing power has not stopped the string of flawed designs and horrible disasters. It is not a paradox; it is the Code at work.

 Ferguson goes on to say that these failures are really failures of human beings to operate in a chaotic environment. In other words, by relying on the judgment of computer programmers in their modeling of reality, the engineer can shift responsibility for critical design elements from herself to another. He writes, "[A] computer model is just a set of arbitrary rules, chosen by programmers"[28]—a model most engineering students assume to be fail-safe.

The designer who uses the available analytical software must either accept the program's results on faith or check them using the old-fashioned methods of experiments, graphics, and longhand calculations. This manual checking is problematic, because much of the time it is not possible. The problem of checking software's reliability becomes one of time and money, and the business of technology declares this testing impractical.

The impracticality may be true. For instance, where should the checking stop to avoid disaster? This rhetorical question was examined in the movie *Fail-Safe,* which was released in 1964 and starred Henry Fonda as the president of the United States.

The plot was simple: What do you do when the use of technology drives your moral decisions?

In the movie, a group of nuclear bombers goes beyond their fail-safe point by "mechanical accident." The fail-safe point represents the geographical place near the old Soviet Union's border where our bombers would circle and return home if no order to attack were received via the fail-safe system in the cockpit.

Predictably, in the movie the fail-safe system fails; the bombers cannot be recalled or stopped, and they drop two 20-megaton bombs on Moscow. The American president and the Soviet premier can find only one solution to this dilemma to prevent an all-out nuclear exchange: Our president agrees to drop similar bombs on New York City, using our own bombers. Technology—or, to be precise, a technology's failure—drives the decision that leads to the death of 20 million to 30 million people unlucky enough to be in cities.

The fail-safe mentality of the technologists in the movie turns out to be wrong. Their trust in the equations, mathematics, and computers is misplaced. At the time of its release, *Fail Safe* was seen as an anti-war movie. I now view it as a prophecy of sorts to warn us about technological failures that can lead to mega-disasters. Many failures have occurred with similar scenarios, including the Hartford Civic Center's roof collapse under a load of snow in 1978. The design had used extensive, but faulty, computer modeling.[29]

Henry Petroski, a civil engineer and author, might understand the Code of Silence in the context of the fail-safe syndrome. In his book *To Engineer is Human: The Role of Failure in Successful Design*, Petroski writes that structural "analysts" do much of the design using computer programs. But he believes, and I agree, that structural designers should be doing the work:

> [M]ore than ever before, the challenge to the profession and to educators is to develop designers who will be able to stand up to and reject or modify the results of a computer aided analysis and design.[30]

The reliance on more and more sophisticated and inadequately tested software presents humankind with a new, misplaced fail-safe mentality. Our math and computers are not perfect, and the technologist must make judgments, ethical as well as rational. Computers cannot now think and act ethically, and I predict they never will.

The infallibility of computers is one of the true beliefs that remain a major obstacle to true progress. Another inhabits the ivory towers where engineers and other technologists can learn good and bad things from their professors.

The Myth: "You Can't Teach Ethics"

"Engineering and technology students cannot be taught ethics; they either have it or they don't when they arrive at the university." I cannot remember the number of times I have heard this true belief expressed in academic circles. Those who hold it contended that ethics courses in the engineering and technology curricula are a waste of the professor's time, and thus the student's time. This true belief is one of the primary myths that I have encountered at the university, and it needs to change.

If this argument against teaching ethics were true, then this question would be relevant: Should we test students to see whether they are ethical enough to design for life-and-death situations? And should we test students before they enter college? Logically, the test would be needed, because if you did not test, then you would be condoning the acts of dangerous and dysfunctional creators.

> **This argument that "they either have it or they don't" should be rejected as illogical and irrational.**

Given the disasters of the last 100 years, we cannot afford *not* to teach ethics. Educators are negligent if they ignore teaching personal moral and social responsibility—and if they themselves do not practice what they teach. Perhaps someday, a personal injury attorney representing a victim of a disaster may want to connect the training of engineers to the disaster. She may have a case for contributory negligence by professors and even possibly the institution. At least, there is moral culpability.

Teaching dogma is not the solution, of course; but teaching autonomy to decide between right and wrong begins the process toward acceptance of personal responsibility. Students must be allowed and encouraged to think critically and rationally, so that they will then be able to question myths and true beliefs presented in the classroom and during their careers. Students who are informed of the arguments for accountability are more likely to act ethically than those who are not informed.

The second argument for and against teaching ethics focuses on the validity and necessity of using a scientific method and rationale to justify the ethics courses. The case for teaching ethics in the classroom does not require a traditional scientific proof—it should be a self-evident truth for a rational person. Our Declaration of Independence says life and liberty are among the unalienable rights whose truth is self-evident. Therefore, given the life-and-death decisions inherent in the creation of technology, the need should be obvious, because engineers and other professionals are licensed to protect the public.

Even in science and mathematics, assumptions about reality are often made because they are self-evident, and because making them facilitates continued progress. For instance, Albert Einstein, in his famous calculations on relativity, used an assumed mathematical constant because he could not account for a missing component. The search continues for the missing matter and for a way "to unify ... quantum mechanics with the vast cosmic one of general relativity."[31] Technology took a quantum leap without Einstein's complete scientific proof.

So, for those technologists and others who still cling to the need for a scientific rationale to teach ethics, I offer two reasons. First, my survey research, my years of classroom experience, and my 30 years of industry experience in engineering and technology have convinced me that students need, and most desire, a strong ethics component in their education.

I conducted survey research on engineering and technology students in the early 1990s. The survey and my conclusions were based on 3,000 students in the Midwest from all engineering disciplines.[32] The response rate was considered higher than normal. A significant portion of the engineering students— roughly 1 out of 3—admitted to cheating on tests and homework.[e] And of those who admitted to cheating in the anonymous survey, most believed it was all right to do so. This alone was quite alarming, but there is more to the story.

The majority of those engineering and technology students who said they did not cheat responded that it would be wrong for them to rat on or report to authorities their colleagues who they knew cheated. Appallingly, many of the students reported that professors did not seem to care when cheating was reported. This mind-set is the Code of Silence at work in a technologist's education, and it moves into the workplace mostly unquestioned as "the way it is."

Second, a 1998 study by Self and Ellison at Texas A&M University concludes that a "scientific rationale" now exists for teaching ethics.[33] They administered a test called the "Defining Issues Test" before and after a course on engineering ethics, and the results reportedly showed an increase in moral reasoning. Self and Ellison argue that these "results support the inclusion of an engineering ethics course in the required curriculum of all engineering students." A highly regarded engineering publication printed this *revolutionary discovery*.

Flaws exist in the scientific methodology of Self and Ellison's study design. First, the sample of students was small, non-random, and confined to one course. It is possible the researchers found what they wanted to find in a select audience.[f]

---

[e] At the time of the survey, this result was generally lower than national averages in all colleges across the United States.

[f] I know from experience in teaching ethics courses for a decade that students who elect to take a course not required for their degree are different in many respects from a cross-section of students from the entire program. These

Second, their test instrument had not, to my knowledge, been proven reliable across a wider population of students in other schools or classroom situations. The test may be measuring, if anything, areas of comprehension, such as the ability to memorize information.[g] But I certainly agree with their basic conclusion that we should give more attention to issues of social justice and the role of values in professional development. Higher education is supposed to do this.

Technologists' true beliefs about right and wrong and our long-held collective myths are embedded in our thought processes, and they have their origins in our deepest self—the individual psyche. We can begin our continuing process of self-awareness of true beliefs by understanding our common characteristics and accepted practices. To what extent is a technologist programmed by genetics, by his family of origin, by his educational environment, and by his workplace to think in distinct ways and to believe in specific ideas? This is the subject of the next chapter.

The tragedies that occur because of unexamined myths are not mere mistakes or accidents. The real reasons can be found in the Spectrum of Evil. A journey to remove these dangerous beliefs from our psyche will eventually lead us technologists to continue on a path to "know thyself." Part 3 of this book begins the process of this journey.

---

select groups have more motivation to achieve and a heightened awareness of the issues, particularly in an ethics course. If the entire population of engineering students had been sampled according to accepted statistical standards, or if a random sample of students from other colleges were tested, Self and Ellison's survey results might have been significantly different.

[g] There is a lot of pure memorization in traditional engineering and technology higher education. When I taught engineering and technology, I wanted the students to recall not just facts and formulas, but where and how to research for the data needed. And I wanted them to recall the personal moral and social implications of their work. Memory can be faulty, as we all know; and old data may be misleading or simply wrong. I would not want to cross a bridge if I knew the bridge designer had relied upon only her memory of a crucial set of formulas.

Bibliography, Notes & Further Reading

[1] Eric Hoffer, *The True Believer* (Alexandria, Va.: Time Reading Program Special Ed., Time-Life Books, 1980).

[2] Ibid.

[3] Ibid., 83.

[4] Darrell J. Fasching, *Bridges: An Interdisciplinary Journal of Theology, Philosophy, History, and Science*, Spring/Summer 1998, 7-8.

[5] The information was taken from an article in the *Omaha World-Herald* ("Doctors Defy Critics of Human Cloning," 10 March 2001, 10).

[6] Nancy Gibbs, "Baby, It's You! And You, and You," *Time*, 19 February 2001, 50.

[7] Bernie S. Siegel, *Prescriptions for Living*. The quotation was taken from *Reader's Digest*, July 1999, 158.

[8] Fasching, 7-8.

[9] Hoffer, *True Believer*, 121.

[10] Martin and Schinzinger, 94. The actual study referenced is by Stanley Milgram, *Obedience to Authority* (New York: Harper & Row, 1974).

[11] J. Darley and C. Batson, "From Jerusalem to Jericho: A Study of Situational and Dispositional Variables in Helping Behavior," *Journal of Personality and Social Psychology*, 27 (1973): 100-108.

[12] C. Banks, Haney, and P. Zimbardo, "Interpersonal Dynamics in a Simulated Prison," *International Journal of Criminology and Penology*, 1 (1973): 69-97.

[13] Peck, *People of the Lie*, 213.

[14] Thomas Lickona, "What Does Moral Psychology Have to Say to the Teacher of Ethics." In *Ethics Teaching in Higher Education*, edited by Callahan and Bok (Plenum, 1980), 125.

[15] Ibid., 127. Lickona quotes Haney and Zimbardo, 69-97.

[16] Viktor E. Frankl, *Man's Search for Meaning* (New York: Washington Square Press, Simon & Schuster, Inc., 1969).

[17] Peck, 214.

[18] "Army Admits My Lai Mistakes," *Omaha World-Herald (Washington Post)*, 7 March 1998. For a more complete story about the heroes of My Lai, see Trent Angers, *The Forgotten Hero of My Lai: The Hugh Thompson Story* (Lafayette, La.: Acadian House Publishing, 1999).

[19] Peck, 213-253.

[20] Ibid., 215.

[21] Ibid., 241.

[22] Richard Clough and Glenn A. Sears, *Construction Contracting,* 6th ed. (New York: John Wiley & Sons, 1994), 61-63.

[23] Ibid., 62.

[24] Eugene S. Ferguson was quoted in "How Engineers Lose Touch," *Invention & Technology*, Winter 1993, pp. 16-24. The quote is from Ferguson's book, *Engineering and the Mind's Eye.*

[25] Ibid., 18.

[26] Ibid., 18-20.

[27] Ferguson, "How Engineers Lose Touch," *Invention & Technology*, Winter 1993, pp. 16-24.

[28] Ibid., 18.

[29] Ibid., 18-20. In addition to the Hartford Civic Center collapse, a large number of articles were written about the 1979 failure of the prize-winning arena in Kansas City, Missouri. Examples: (1) "Why All Those Buildings Are Collapsing," *Fortune*, 19 November 1979; and (2)"Rocking that Fatigued Bolts Failed Arena Roof," *Engineering News Record*, 15 August 1979.

[30] Ferguson, "How Engineers." See Henry Petroski, *To Engineer is Human* (New York: Barnes & Noble Books, St. Martin's Press, 1994), 189-227.

[31] If you wish to pursue these thoughts see (1) "The Search for Missing Matter," *Discover Magazine*, August 2000, 36-39, and (2) "From Here to Eternity," *Discover Magazine*, December 2000, 54-61.

[32] Robert L. Cook, "Ethical Dilemmas in the Classroom and in Construction: A Classroom Case Study with Survey Results," American Society for Engineering Education Annual Conference, Toronto, Ontario, June 24-28, 1990.

[33] All of the quotes about this study were taken from "Now a Scientific Rationale for Teaching Ethics," *Engineering Times*, April 1998. The magazine-newsletter is a regular publication of the American Society of Civil Engineers, a professional engineering organization.

Chapter 6

Common Characteristics and Practices

Technologists as a Distinct Group

If any large group has a homogenous membership, it is engineers and scientists, who represent by far the largest portion of the technology professions.[a] As the last chapter described, technologists are engaged in a revolution, a mass movement designed to create technology as fast as they can. Their common characteristics and backgrounds reinforce the Code of Silence and bind them together into a community of true believers engaged in business as usual.

The intent of this chapter is not to describe *all* technologists or *predict* their behavior. Rather, it is to show why some technologists behave dysfunctionally and illogically, and why such behavior has led to a Code of Silence in their professions.

The engineer is neither a technician nor a scientist, nor is technology merely applied science, as many claim. Most engineers think of themselves as users of knowledge, whereas scientists—if they stop to consider the philosophy of engineering[1]—generally think of themselves as discoverers of new knowledge.

---

[a] In this chapter, the word "technologist" refers chiefly to engineers and scientists.

The lines of distinction have blurred between the practice of science and the practice of technology, between the scientist and the engineer.[2] Engineers and scientists have similar interests and passions, innate talents and skills, economic and social histories, work and family values, education and work cultures, and other influential characteristics.

"Science and technology refer to comparable concepts," according to Michael Davis,[3] a philosopher with the Center for the Study of Ethics in the Professions, who has studied engineers as a group for over a decade.[4] Few would dispute his claim that engineers are a large group central to the development and implementation of modern technology,[b] but Davis adds this problematic statement: "The primary commitment of engineers is not to knowledge, theoretical or applied, as one would expect of scientists, but to human welfare."[5] The history of disasters contradicts this view.

Common Backgrounds and Goals

Two important sociological studies conducted in the 1960s combine engineers and scientists into one group to investigate their common traits.[c] Lee Danielson, in *Characteristics of Engineers and Scientists*,[6] shows that both engineers themselves and their supervisors consider engineers to have distinct characteristics that differentiate them from other

---

[b] According to Davis, the number of engineers employed today in the U.S. stands at over 2 million; with the exception of teachers, they constitute the largest group of professionals (p. 8). While Davis treats engineers and scientists as distinct groups, I will not make a clear distinction between the two, because they are similar enough in many respects to be considered the primary group responsible for the creation and application of technology.

[c] To my knowledge, these two studies, Danielson (1960) and Perucci and Gerstl (1969), are the only extensive sociological studies of engineers and scientists.

employees, especially blue-collar workers.[d] The specific differences mentioned most often are (1) their total involvement in their work; (2) their need for recognition by their organizations; (3) their ambitious and creative mind-set; (4) their need for self-esteem; and, later in their careers, (5) their considerable need for job security and money.

Danielson recognizes that each profession tends to attract people with different degrees of given personal characteristics.[7] But he predicted that the characteristics of future engineers and scientists would depend more on the training they receive than on natural selection.[8] This prediction provides little comfort. In 16 years of teaching, I have observed little change in many of these common attributes among university students.

> **When I ask students why they chose engineering and technology as a career, an overwhelming majority of the students in my surveys say, "Because of the money."**

A more detailed study of the two groups of professionals by two sociologists, Robert Perrucci and Joel Gerstl,[9] reveals characteristics similar to those Danielson found. Incoming engineering students are single-minded in their career interests. They are (1) more likely to be good at math and science; (2) bearers of family values that differ from other groups'; (3) very interested in money and security; (4) disinterested in people; (5) innovative and creative; and (6) uninterested in creative outlets outside of the job. Among 18 professions, engineers were thirteenth from the top in their faith in people and seventeenth from the top in being people-oriented.[10] And, according to Perrucci and Gerstl, the narrow education of engineers only

---

[d] The study was conducted by the Bureau of Industrial Relations at the University of Michigan in response to the tremendous growth in technology in the United States and the important contributions professionals were making to economic progress and national security. Ten companies and a sample of 412 engineering or research personnel participated.

reinforces the already restricted interests they bring to the university.[11] Two separate but smaller studies published in scientific journals during the late 1960s and early 1970s[12] support Danielson's and Perrucci and Gerstl's conclusions.[e]

These observations and studies contradict Davis's view that engineers hold human welfare paramount. Engineers and scientists, as a group, prefer to deal with things, not people. The sociological studies also show practicing engineers and scientists to be more authoritarian and prejudiced in their attitudes than their younger counterparts, particularly when they become university faculty members.[13] This observation will come as no surprise to engineering and technology students.

> **According to these studies, the personal goals and objectives of engineers are closely interrelated with the goals and objectives of the organizations to which they belong.**

Technologists are good team players. Their passion for their companies' survival, and thus their own security, is one of their defining common characteristics. It reflects their increasing concern with company profits, especially as they age, and provides an avenue for the Code to become engrained in their work culture.

In another study of a specific group of technologists in 1973, Richard L. Schott analyzed the characteristics and education of engineers in Federal executive positions. His study provides further evidence to support my view that the Code reflects technologists' lack of empathy for those affected by their creative work. Schott writes, "The industrial and federal groups ranked higher in agreeing that work is essentially a way of making a living; in putting greater emphasis on status; and in rating lower the kind of work in which one could help other people."[14] In addition, the engineers in Schott's study cited security in their

---

[e] See Tables 1-5 in Appendix B, "Characteristics of Technologists."

government jobs as a primary reason for choosing Federal service in the United States.

The technologists who worked for the governments of Nazi Germany and the Soviet Union under Stalin reflected similar attitudes. Schott's findings, unlike Davis's opinions, are not reassuring for those who rely on government officials to protect human welfare.

Nina Brown and Ernest Cross, Jr., researchers at Old Dominion University, used a revised California Psychological Inventory System (CPIS), a measure of specific psychological characteristics, in their 1987 analysis of the personalities of engineers and engineering students.[15] They found that engineering students and practicing engineers have the same patterns on the CPIS: both groups (1) "adhere to norms," (2) are "action oriented," and (3) "carry out the sanctioned mandates of the culture."[16]

> **Their analysis shows these technologists to be ambitious, boastful, conceited, ingenious, opportunistic, shrewd, and concerned with boosting their egos.**

According to Brown and Cross, these past studies may not accurately assess current students. More recently, they have suggested that "today's [1993] engineering students are more outgoing, aggressive, exhibitionistic, interdependent, and global in their thinking."[17] They admit, however, that much more research into the personalities of engineers and engineering students would be needed to confirm their opinions. If Brown and Cross were to conduct a study in 2001, I would not be surprised to find them revising their hypothesis about most current engineering students. Global markets are expanding, but personal moral responsibility on a global scale is a different matter.

My observations in the classroom over 15-plus years show that a significant majority of engineering students are opportunistic and motivated overwhelmingly by the prospect of good salaries. Only a small minority of technology students tries to understand the moral and ethical implications of their professional work while they are undergraduates.[18] How can they, when their teachers will not or cannot teach ethics in the classroom?[f]

All the studies that I found reveal that engineers and scientists have a high need for recognition, status, respect, prestige, job security, and money—especially money. These traits give management and other authority figures over technologists a big stick. If they want, they can control engineers and scientists by withholding or by offering to provide these needs. And, of course, if the technologists' immediate supervisors are also engineers or scientists, they will tend to be obedient and compliant as well.

> The 20th-century disasters illustrate that many technologists fear the big stick, and consequently, many of them comply with business interests more than they should.

Instead of emphasizing personal moral and social responsibility, these professions exhibit a palpable attitude of "business as usual," which has led to preventable disasters.

Business as Usual

Products created by scientists, designed by engineers, and manufactured by others continue to harm people.[19] Buildings and other structures believed to be fail-safe continue to fail when they should not. In the late 1990s, an earthquake in Kobe, Japan, killed hundreds and left thousands homeless. What was unusual about this particular earthquake was that it destroyed buildings and bridges thought safe from this type of quake. Japan's preparation for earthquakes was also thought to be the best in the world. The

---

[f] I have observed this unwillingness or inability of professors to teach ethics in their technology courses both in my experience as a university professor and in my research on ethics in the classroom.

disaster sent engineers from all over the world scurrying back to the drawing boards. Trial and error is the method of choice.

Moral and social irresponsibility maintains a strong presence in the business of technology. As former U.S. Treasury Secretary William E. Simon observes,

"The real question facing the American business community today is not whether it can afford stronger ethical standards, but how much longer it can go on without them. Our entire way of life is held together by voluntary, society-wide bonds of mutual trust and respect." [20]

In *Friends in High Places, The Bechtel Story*, Laton McCartney exposes the questionable business practices of a major international corporation based in the United States. [21] The company is not a typical public business found on the New York Stock Exchange, but an example of engineering and construction interests run as a private business—a very private business.

The Bechtel Corporation, later known as the Bechtel Group, is one of the largest and most powerful engineering and construction companies in the world. It has engineered and built some of the largest engineering projects for almost a century, with interests and political connections stretching around the world. Bechtel built pipelines in Peru, copper mines in South Africa, nuclear power stations in India, subway systems in Washington, factories in California, and hospitals, hotels, airports, and industrial structures the world over. [22] While Bechtel has accomplished many good things, McCartney tells the public and private inside story of this corporation "with the family character" as its image.

Bechtel managed the Alaskan oil pipeline and built the majority of the world's nuclear power plants and much of the Middle East's infrastructure. According to McCartney, Bechtel's refineries and pipelines made possible the rise of OPEC, the regime of Moammar Qaddafi, and the modernization of Saudi Arabia. Bechtel built roads, airports, bridges, and dams that benefited many politicians' agendas, including the Nixon and Reagan administrations' foreign policies, with secret help from presidential and other U.S. governmental connections. Bechtel was a very private company that operated for years with little public scrutiny.[23]

McCartney describes the inner workings of Bechtel as sometimes unethical—and "corrupt." He writes that in foreign operations, Bechtel allowed violence and drunkenness on job sites, participated in the Arab boycott of companies that employed Jews, and paid bribes to government officials.

> **His book documents what he sees as the unethical and illegal activities of technologists and others who worked for Bechtel in the United States.**

These unethical and illegal actions include sex and race discrimination, anti-Semitism, bribery, war profiteering, falsification of technical reports, and harassment of whistle-blowers. Many of these accusations were later substantiated by U.S. Congressional hearings and became public knowledge.

McCartney paints a disturbing picture of the power Bechtel exercised over the U.S. government and some foreign governments as well. Steve Bechtel once told his senior executives,

> **"We are not in the construction and engineering business—we are in the business of making money."[24]**

If McCartney is accurate, and I believe he is, his book provides a rare look at the inner workings of one of the largest international corporations in construction and engineering. Bechtel's apparent political manipulations and disregard of human rights were dirty little secrets. If it had not been for McCartney's investigative reporting, the Code probably would have continued to grow within the mega-corporation.

Friends in High Places forces us to look at the business of technology and examine our rationalizations for creating things. It can be the economic gain, and not the creative urge, that sets the pace of technological advances. But aren't profit incentives the essence of capitalism and free enterprise? Isn't profit good? It can be, if others are not harmed in the process.

McCartney's book about "business as usual" exemplifies the ethos of the 1980s and 1990s. Movies and the corporate world characterized greed as "healthy and good." Ivan Boesky, Wall Street's infamous inside trader, said in a speech in 1985, "You can be greedy and still feel good about yourself."[25] He spent only 22 months in prison and reportedly retained much of his huge fortune.

McCartney would probably understand, in the context of Bechtel Corporation's history, the following quotation from an inside trader executive: "I've always thought of myself as an honorable citizen. We didn't do these things for our own behalf ... but for the betterment of the company."[26] Over the years, this rationalization has been used time and again to justify team efforts gone awry.

This business attitude, never very far from the surface, appeared again in 2001 and 2002 with the bankruptcy of one of the largest corporations in the world, Enron. Officers of Enron, an international energy technology company based in Houston, Texas, allegedly perpetrated fraud that cost investors $30-$60 billion. In contrast, the FBI reportedly estimated the value of real property stolen in the U.S. in 2000 to be $16 billion.[27] It would be difficult to deny the existence of a double standard in justice.

In the competitive world of business, poor and greedy decisions are more likely to occur. Ken Dayton, former CEO of Dayton Hudson Companies, proposes a departure from business as usual:

> "I maintain that business must change its priorities. We are not in business to make maximum profit for our shareholders. We are in business for only one reason—to serve society. Profit is our reward for doing it well. If business does not serve society, society will not tolerate our profits or even our existence."[28]

Dayton's view is evidently not yet widespread within the business community. A number of other companies in engineering and construction would probably fare no better than Bechtel if they were subjected to the scrutiny of aggressive reporters. And Dayton is wrong on one point: our society tolerates greed better than common theft of property, as the Enron crash and the Boesky scandal demonstrate. Corporate misconduct and white-collar crime are widely recognized as worldwide phenomena.[29] Unacceptable industry practices have become business as usual for many in the creation and application of technology.

Accepted Industry Practices

To understand the ethics of disasters, you need to understand the process of design and construction for a typical building project. The professionals have been trained to use accepted industry practices that introduce many pitfalls along the way.

> The following scenario illustrates the typical precarious process used in the business of architecture, engineering, and construction.

Typically, a client who wants to build a structure hires a design professional, usually an architect, to prepare conceptual drawings and preliminary cost estimates. The architect, in turn, hires engineers to help him. The client wants to become a project owner if she can justify the initial cost.

For her business to be competitive in selling her product or service, she first has to know the costs for the building project. She then can predict the total cost to produce and to market the intended product or service.

Her cost to produce and market the product or service is directly related to the buildings, equipment, and systems for the project under design. If the total cost of these things in dollars per unit of product is too high, the owner may decide that her product cannot be competitive in the marketplace. If this happens, and she decides not to continue, the architect and his engineers will not be awarded a contract to continue.

For example, if the product is a personal computer, the owner, after consulting with her designers, may predict the total unit price for the product to be $10,000. The competition may be selling essentially the same computer for $5,000. So the owner will ask the designers what can be done to lower the project cost. The answer depends on the criteria for acceptable cost, which of course raises more questions. Who decides what is acceptable? How is this acceptable cost determined?

The project owner, a businessperson, usually makes the determination after consultation with the designers. The designers have a professional duty, usually in their codes of ethics or in their government licenses to practice, to inform their clients when a project is not feasible based on the owner's criteria. These criteria, including the cost, can be negotiated lower and lower between the owner and the designers. This negotiated cost usually turns out to be the "acceptable cost" for the project.

If the designers need work to pay their bills or to achieve a corporate income goal, they may be tempted to accept work at an amount insufficient to perform a professional service for the project owner. This does not happen frequently, but it happens often enough to make a few of us who know about these practices very nervous at times when we encounter buildings, bridges, medical procedures, chemicals, airplanes, etc.

What changes could be made to lower the project cost? Let us assume, first, that the designers have done a competent job and used appropriate "accepted industry practices" in the original design.[g] Accepted industry design practices require designers to calculate the least-cost acceptable design and to use standard

---

[g] This assumption also raises other questions about the phrase "accepted industry practices." As you may recall from Part One, the Missouri Courts in the Hyatt Regency disaster recognized that the accepted practices at the time were inappropriate and were used in an attempt to justify the defendants' actions.

safety factors in each of the project elements. To charge a client for unneeded services and systems that only raise the owner's cost and the designer's fees would be unethical and deceptive.

In addition, building codes and other published standards for safe designs dictate the use of a multiplication factor for safety. This "safety" factor is an industry-accepted amount that increases the exact theoretical calculated size.[30] For example, specific accepted design methods for sizing a steel beam might require the designer to use a safety factor of 1.6.[h] This essentially means that the mathematical theoretical calculation for the size of the beam must be increased by 60%, according to professional standards. This explanation is a simplification of the process, but it provides a basis for non-technologists to understand the inexactness of the methods used.

If safety were the controlling design parameter without cost considerations, the designers could use a steel beam 5, 10, or 100 times as big as the exact size was calculated to be. Would it cost more? Of course it would, but that is the point. Someone always wants to place a dollar value on the lives of other human beings. In order to save costs for the owner's project, the designers could simply lower the safety standards below the 1.6 factor. Is it done? The number of man-made disasters speaks to this issue. I am not advocating the general use of such large safety factors; however, I am suggesting this:

> **It is time to re-examine the use of the least-cost, low-bid paradigm in the creation and application of technology.**

---

[h] The exact factor may be difficult to determine because of the different layers of calculations that may have individual factors added for different features of the overall structure.

A better way to lower the predicted costs of a project is to re-evaluate the project's parameters, with safety and quality foremost in everyone's minds. Designers and the owner could re-evaluate the criteria for the entire project and suggest a smaller physical size or a focus on the owner's most important criterion. This does not or should not mean a cheaper project, only lower total costs, and thus a lower unit cost for the owner's final product.

The re-evaluation process, or "value engineering," as it is known in the profession, might show the owner that less storage area is required, or that the entire building could be constructed using a less expensive structural system. For example, a prefabricated metal building could be used instead of a reinforced concrete and brick structure.

Many different types of construction materials and processes could meet the project's needs without any change to the margin of safety. The aesthetics of the structure may change, but if value engineering and cost estimating are done correctly, the changes will not affect the quality or safety of the project—just the total cost. If you just need water to flow, you don't need solid gold faucets.

The design and construction process should work this way—and most of time, it does. But the built-in safety multiplication factors may not be large enough to prevent catastrophic failures as in the cases of the Hyatt Regency Hotel, the space shuttle Challenger, and the World Trade Center.

If safety were paramount, some projects would not be built at all because of their high cost and high risk. But perhaps not every project *should* be built. At least, we should not place a company's short-term profits above the lives of innocent people and the health of the environment by building projects as cheaply as possible. These accepted industry practices have led to thousands of tragedies and man-made disasters. It is business as usual for technologists, who are usually very loyal, obedient, and compliant team players in corporate America.

Team Players

In Part One, I defined "groupthink" as the "acceptance without questioning" of the predominant views of a leader, group, organization, or government on social, political, and moral matters. An honest and open groupthink process is harmless enough, and it can often result in a good decision. At times, it can even persuade an unethical team member to conform to the ideals of the group—a lot like the effect of an organized religion. I have seen teams in education and in industry function well in accepting moral responsibility. Usually, the old adage that two heads are better than one is a good one—depending on the specific heads. But the Hyatt Regency and Challenger disasters are irrefutable evidence of the dark side of groupthink.

Bad things can happen when individuals in an organized, homogeneous, self-protective team accept the opinions of others without questioning their ethical implications. Technologists engaged in a team effort can play a deadly game of denial about significant problems. As we have seen, the Challenger disaster was a public manifestation of this problem. The groupthink of technologists in the Holocaust demonstrated the worst that can happen.

The team approach can make it difficult for co-workers to report problems within an organization, whether it is a business corporation, a government agency, or a university.[31] Well-meaning team members can be drawn into this deadly groupthink trend, which impairs their ability to recognize the moral dilemmas present in their work.[32] Members of a team may obey authority for protection from personal attack or simply to remain part of the team. Not to be part of the team or "family" would be unthinkable for their careers, or so they generally believe.

Many work environments, not just technology, promote a deep-seated fear among their employees. If someone is seen as a troublemaker, the other team members and quite possibly the organization's managers may isolate and harass him. Often this employee's fear of speaking out has dire personal consequences.

> **This emotional abuse by other team members and management has a name: *mobbing* in the workplace.**

We see this phenomenon frequently in the workplace, because the work "family" can provide monetary and psychological benefits.

One person in any group can make a difference and stop the disorder from spreading, but it takes courage and determination—and possibly self-sacrifice. The sanctioned ability to practice our professions provides many existential and monetary benefits—and a duty to protect life above all else. This duty includes autonomous ethical decision-making while part of a team.

The groupthink problem is well entrenched within colleges of engineering and technology. Rational human beings will acknowledge the virtues of teamwork that are important to successful projects.[i] These virtues include collegiality, cooperativeness, and respect for and loyalty to legitimate authority.[33] Technologists can and should choose not to carry out the "sanctioned mandates of a culture," as sociologists have said, when those mandates are harmful to human beings and to the environment. The dark side of a team effort places narcissistic interests above personal moral and social responsibility. Technologists appear to be in a league by themselves when it comes to common characteristics and backgrounds that reinforce team effort thinking.

Personal and Professional Responsibility

Engineers seem to worry about their status more than most professionals. I first wrote about this strange phenomenon while a graduate student in 1974.[34] The sociological studies confirm my

---

[i] In Chapter One, a rational human being was defined as one who desires to avoid death, pain, and loss of opportunity, and to acquire the basic needs of life (food, water, shelter, clothing, etc.). These things are widely recognized to be logical and reasonable for human beings to desire.

observations of status-conscious technologists while I was a young engineer. I was not immune to this disorder early in my own career.

In Chapter 1, I introduced author Samuel Florman as a prominent civil engineer concerned about technologists' images.[35] He writes that the image of engineers in his day (1994) appears to agree with the studies about them: An engineer is someone who belongs to the middle class and has self-centered, materialistic, and conformist ideas.

Florman's views parallel the studies that reveal engineers have narrow interests and a relative indifference to human relations. He writes that engineers avoid introspection, dislike ambiguity, and would rather deal with things than with human beings. These critical opinions come from a civil engineer who also loves his profession, as many of us do.

Florman wants society to respect engineers, and he wants engineers to enjoy the "existential" pleasures of engineering.[36] From his perspective, at least three groups are responsible for the "decline and fall" of engineers from prominence as a profession: (1) government and politicians, (2) universities and college educators, and (3) the engineering students attracted to the profession. It seems to me that he fails to recognize the absence of personal moral responsibility in many technologists.

Florman writes that part of the problem is not the engineering profession but democracy itself.[37] He apparently thinks politicians are lazy and pander to corporate interests; few would dispute his assessment. But he implies that engineers must follow orders—in other words, acquiesce to the authority of politicians— apparently even in life-and-death situations. He downplays engineers' obligations to follow their codes of ethics, which mandate placing the public's health, safety, and welfare first.[j]

---

[j] Appendix C includes two codes of ethics that contain similar language regarding an engineer's paramount duty to protect life.

His view of higher education for engineers closely parallels my view of the Code of Silence in universities. But while Florman recognizes that the curricula in our colleges of technology lack "imagination, social concern, ... or cultural interest"—and that they contain too many technical subjects[38]—he seems to avoid discussing the lack of ethics in the curricula. He wants to blame "those type of students" who enter the schools. Florman thinks the type of person who chooses engineering is intelligent but insipid.[39] He writes, "It is time for the engineering profession to grow up. Its problem is not lack of morality, but rather lack of maturity."[40]

Florman, as "literate a polemicist as any profession can claim,"[k] appears to have experienced a pleasurable career in engineering for many years, and he is a well-intentioned engineer. However, the engineering and technology professions *are* on trial each time a man-made disaster occurs. And I fail to see the difference between a lack of morality and what he calls immaturity in engineers.

Florman and I agree more than we disagree. We agree that engineering and technology schools and colleges are part of the problem. We agree that we must get to know our "inner-self" and be honest with ourselves. (Unfortunately, Florman offers little insight into what he means by this.) And we agree that emotion plays an important role in our inward search for truth. But we seriously disagree about the source of the problems in technology's creation and use.

Florman blames not the engineers themselves, but rather our democracy and its selfish and lazy citizens. At other times, he blames those "sort" of persons who choose engineering as a career. I understand Florman to say that engineering students are

---

[k] Davis says this about Florman (p. ix) when making the point that society does not appreciate engineers as much as it does scientists, lawyers, architects, etc. Davis adds that engineers do not seem to make a good case for their profession, and he says that Florman writes to "please engineers instead of informing non-engineers." I agree.

lazy, selfish, immature, and products of a "troubled system" of government. It sounds as if he has become disillusioned with democracy, college professors and administrators, and technology students.

These types of rationalizations are forms of denial and of transference. They are scapegoating at its worst. We deny that we are the problem, and then transfer the responsibility for our behavior to others. It is the government's fault, or it is the corporate president's fault, or it is the fault of those "sort" of students, or ....

> **When someone says, "I was only obeying orders," she is practicing the Code—the underlying reason for most man-made disasters.**

These dangerous rationalizations obscure the real reason for the dark side of technology's creation and application. Cartoon character Pogo was right when he said, "We have met the enemy and he is us."[41] Apologists for the Code miss this point when they use Florman's types of excuses for unprofessional conduct, laziness, apathy, etc.

Although I want to believe that Florman is not referring to races of people, other technologists have done this very thing in trying to exclude "those sort of persons." A large number of technologists in the engineering and scientific community wanted to exclude "those sort of persons" from the professions during one dark period of the 20th century. Thousands of members of professional societies sympathetic to the Nazis (and to the Stalinists) excluded Jews and others they believed to be inferior. German and Hungarian technologists and other professionals, including lawyers, doctors, and professors, aggressively purged Jews from the professions.[42]

The purge of "those sort of persons" was a worldwide phenomenon during the first half of the 20th century. European technologists were not alone in this crime against humanity. A significant number of American engineers and scientists tried to exclude Jews and others during the 1930s and 1940s.[43] It is very dangerous and simply wrong to label groups of people as "the problem," whether the engineers are Jews or simply sons and daughters of the working middle class. The real problem begins with the individual and his or her everyday choices.

In man-made disasters from the Titanic to the Holocaust and beyond, teams and organizations of technologists worked on projects that harmed human beings and the environment. But it was the individuals in a dysfunctional team effort who allowed each tragedy to happen. The moral and social responsibility for disasters does not reside primarily with any government or organization that may hold temporal political power. The analogy of the direct connection between the bank robber and his getaway driver applies in these disasters, as I argued earlier. Governments and professional organizations are composed of individuals with free will.

"Remember the Challenger" ought to be the rallying cry of today's engineers and scientists. NASA's technologists used available government resources to build a dangerous system. They were not forced at gunpoint to do it. They chose to do it. Each individual could have refused to be an accomplice in the Holocaust, the Hyatt, or the Challenger disasters. We should not overlook or forget this simple fact: the problem is not he—*it is I.*

Bibliography, Notes & Further Reading

[1] Davis, 5-17. Davis presents a more detailed discussion of the similarities and differences in the practice of science, technology, and engineering in *Thinking Like an Engineer* (New York: Oxford University Press, 1998). Although I also believe that philosophical differences do exist between the two groups, they sometimes form an unholy alliance, tacitly agreeing to bring new technologies to life without questioning the moral implications of those technologies or whether they *should* create and build the things that could harm other human beings and the planet. Therefore, I consider them as one group for the objectives of this book.

[2] The Accrediting Board for Engineering and Technology (111 Market Place, Suite 1050, Baltimore, MD 21202) uses the following definition for engineering: "Engineering is the profession in which a knowledge of the mathematical and natural sciences gained by study, experience and practice is applied with judgment to develop ways to utilize, economically, the materials and forces of nature for the benefit of mankind."

[3] Davis, *Thinking Like an Engineer*, 7.

[4] Ibid., ix. The Center is on the campus of the Illinois Institute of Technology in Chicago, Illinois.

[5] Ibid., 16.

[6] Lee E. Danielson, *Characteristics of Engineers and Scientists* (Ann Arbor, Mich.: Bureau of Industrial Relations, University of Michigan, 1960).

[7] Ibid., 16-18.

[8] Ibid., 29.

[9] Robert Perrucci and Joel Gerstl, *Profession Without Community: Engineers in American Society* (New York: Random House, 1969).

[10] Ibid., 146.

[11] Ibid., 142-146.

[12] I used the following two studies in my work as partial fulfillment of my requirements as a graduate student at the University of Missouri at Columbia in 1974: (1) F. Landis, "What Makes Technical Men Happy and Productive," *Research Management*, May 1971, 22-42; and (2) Eugene Raudsepp, *Managing Creative Scientists and Engineers* (New York: Macmillan, 1969).

[13] Perrucci and Gerstl, 189.

[14] Elinor Ostrom, et al., "Professionals in Public Service: The Characteristics and Education of Engineer Federal Executives" (Beverly Hills and London: Sage Publications, Vol. 1, No. 03-005, 1973), 13.

[15] H. Gough, *The California Psychological Inventory: Administrator's Guide* (Palo Alto, Calif.: Consulting Psychologist Press, 1987).

[16] Nina Brown and Ernest Cross, Jr., "Retention in Engineering and Personality," *Educational and Psychological Measurement, Inc.*, 1993, 661-71.

[17] Ibid., 669-70.

[18] Cook, "Ethical Dilemmas."

[19] For example, in 2000 and 2001, Ford Motor Company and Firestone Tire Company were accused of hiding from the public information about millions of faulty tires and unsafe vehicles that allegedly have killed people. See "Tire Woes Threaten Top-Selling Explorer," *Omaha World-Herald* (Associated Press), 10 September 2000.

[20] Verne E. Henderson, *What's Ethical in Business* (New York: McGraw-Hill, 1992), 14.

[21] Laton McCartney, *Friends in High Places* (New York: Simon & Schuster, 1988).

[22] Ibid., 12.

[23] Ibid., 12.

[24] Ibid., 80.

[25] "Payback Time?" *U.S. News & World Report*, 11 March 2002, 38

[26] Henderson, *What's Ethical*, 18.

[27] "Payback Time?" 36.

[28] Henderson, *What's Ethical*, 155-56.

[29] One book that documents unethical business practices in all areas, not just technology, is Maurice Punch, *Dirty Business: Exploring Corporate Misconduct* (London: Sage Publications, 1996).

[30] Determining the "exact" size of structural elements is not an exact science. The computers of today can give us "near-perfect" sizes, but they are based on the human assumptions that are included in the software of a fallible computer. Also, the near-perfect design is based on the lowest "practical cost." Earthquake design is a primary example of design criteria that change after each disaster. When designers use the lowest-cost criteria, the safety factor is smaller, and thus the project design is not as safe as it could be. A number of structural design engineers have noted a smaller margin of error in safety factors over the last several decades. Revised design criteria, new design methods, and computer software have evolved to allow designs to become closer to the "exact" theoretical size—translated, this means to a lower cost. There is every reason to think that this trend will continue in the 21st century.

[31] Stephanie Armour, "Office Ethics: Teams Make it Hard to Tattle," *USA Today*, 17 February 1998, 6B. A second source of detailed information is

Davenport, Schwartz, and Elliott, *Mobbing*.

[32] Armour, "Office Ethics," 6B.

[33] Martin and Schinzinger, 43.

[34] Robert L. Cook, "Incentives for Professional Employees," in partial fulfillment of Master of Science, Civil Engineering, University of Missouri—Columbia, December, 1974. When I wrote this paper, I found engineers to be very concerned, almost obsessively, with their status, image, etc. And late in their careers, engineers become very concerned with job security and money. The situation has not changed much since 1974. Thomas Foley (engineer for 44 years in New Bern, N.C.) writes in a National Society of Professional Engineers publication called *Engineering Times* (March 1998), "If we remain silent and inarticulate, we (engineers) will continue to be regarded as mechanics, and janitors." He goes on to say that the public's attitude that engineering is a "lowly trade" is as "firmly rooted today as it ever was."

[35] Florman, *Existential Pleasures*. I first wrote about Florman in Chapters 1 and 2.

[36] Existentialism is a doctrine derived from philosopher Søren Kierkegaard that says man is not part of an ordered metaphysical scheme. Rather, each individual must create his or her own being, each in his own specific situation and environment. Philosophers Sartre, Jaspers, and Heidegger argue the merits of these thoughts and ideas.

[37] Florman, 34.

[38] Ibid., 92.

[39] Ibid., 91-93

[40] Ibid., 28.

[41] This quote is from a cartoon strip in 1971 by Walt Kelly. Source: Wesley D. Camp, *Camp's Unfamiliar Quotations* (Paramus: Prentice Hall, 1990), 85.

[42] Maria M. Kovacs, "The Ideology of Illiberalism in the Professions: Leftist and Rightist Radicalism among Hungarian Doctors, Lawyers, and Engineers, 1918-1945," *European History Quarterly* 21 (1991): 185.

[43] Frey, "The Holocaust and Contemporary American Business Ethics: Values, Management Decision Making, and Architectures of Knowledge," *Bridges: An Interdisciplinary Journal of Theology, Philosophy, History, and Science*, Spring/Summer 1998.

Chapter 7

Industrial—Military—University Complex

The Money Connection

Some powerful people play a game with their words, with our money, and with our lives. It was thought that the well-known "industrial-military" alliance of the 20th century was one primary reason for America's victory in two world wars. But the Industrial-Military-University Complex has always been active, though mostly hidden from public view. It remains very active in placing a dollar value on human life.

The silent partners in today's rapid growth of technology are the universities. This chapter and the next explain why the primary origin of the Code of Silence rests with academic doctrines and practices. Despite the denial of academics, the money connection begins in the classroom. Its connection to man-made disasters could be called another true belief, and it is known by many names, including greed.

> In the creation of technology, the money connection has a very subtle and misleading name: the "cost-benefit analysis."

The word "analysis" is used to legitimize a process that can be manipulated just as much as a politician's opinion poll. The primary reason for these manipulations is the power that money promises. To understand the origins of the Code, technologists need to be honest with themselves and the public about the pitfalls of the cost-benefit analysis.

 A business-as-usual mind-set about the use of the cost-benefit analysis is fraught with unethical, and sometimes illegal, methods to achieve more profit at the expense of others. It is the Achilles' heel of a free enterprise economic system. The true belief in the sanctity of the cost-benefit analysis is inherent in the beliefs that make the Code shadowy for most non-technologists in modern society.

It is said that "money talks," but very few technologists will admit that this axiom often becomes the dominant partner in the creation of technology. It is an indisputable fact that our structures and systems could be much safer if a low-dollar value were not placed on human life.

Cost-Benefit Analysis

Greed is widely recognized as a common problem within corporate America.[1] The obsession to accumulate more money, and to obtain the power it brings, reveals itself in this process called the cost-benefit analysis. The technical process has two inherent problems: it provides the user of the analysis with (1) a convenient scapegoat and rationalization to discriminate against persons and groups, and (2) an illusion of more accuracy and credibility than the analysis is capable of providing.

> **This illusion of credibility permeates the engineering world and spreads to the trusting public.**

First, consider the scapegoat and rationalization that the analysis provides technologists. The cost-benefit analysis is a by-product of the Utilitarian Theory of morality, which many of the founding fathers of this country endorsed.[2] As it is usually practiced, the theory declares that we ought to "give equal consideration" to everyone affected by our decisions, but in the final analysis, the theory says that we should create the most good for the most people. In other words, the majority rules—assuming, of course, that a dictator is not in control. As we have learned from history, the majority may not have liberty and justice in mind for all people.

The Utilitarian Theory is the foundation for the reasons generally used to endorse the cost-benefit analysis. The theory has many pitfalls, one of which is: Who decides what is good and bad? In practice, the group with the most political power usually decides. The theory also raises the question: Who is "affected?" Does "everyone affected" mean only the neighborhood in which a structure is located, the people on the "other" side of town, all Americans, or all human beings on Earth?

The analysis can become a tool to justify prejudices. Although it can also become a tool for including minorities in the decision-making process, usually it is used only to the point of protecting them from the decisions of the majority. Environmental concerns are often given low priority; for example, other countries must contend with air and water pollution that originated in the United States. Usually, the final decision depends on political power, not on what is just or good for the "most people"—and even less likely, what is good for all life. Thus, the cost-benefit analysis provides misleading justifications so that a project can be done without too much acrimony.

Clearly, the worst pitfall of the Utilitarian Theory is its placement of a dollar value on human life, where one life is valued more than another. This ethical theory was the subtle foundation in the decision to drop the atomic bombs on Japan. The most good for the American people was accomplished, so the reasoning went, by ending the war sooner with fewer American lives lost.

If I had been a soldier on an American ship waiting to invade Japan in 1945, I probably would have welcomed the news about the bomb and Japan's unconditional surrender. Yet, the fact remains that hundreds of thousands of innocent civilians died in seconds. Many more died of complications from the blast, including radiation sickness and plain starvation. The blast and the radiation that remained made food production impossible for some time.

The bomb continues to haunt humankind. Other countries seeking nuclear weapons, purportedly for their own defense, remind us of our incongruent position. They call us hypocrites for denying them the technology on the grounds that they might use the weapons offensively. After all, we used the bomb offensively and told everyone we did it for the defense of our troops.

> **The Utilitarian Theory and philosophy provides a rationalization for deciding the fate of another less powerful person or group.**

Most Americans ignore another of the pitfalls of the Utilitarian Theory: its social implications. Technologists can say to their critics that they are following written guidelines when they decide to place a new six-lane expressway through the poor neighborhoods instead of the wealthy ones. And the politicians can say that the technologists made the "scientific" analysis, which tied their hands in the decision. Actually, it is a way to place a dollar value on the lives of people in various social and economic classes.

The "scientific" answer is in the numbers: the purchase cost of the small homes is much lower than that of the large mansions. And the middle-class or poor people in the affected areas will file very few lawsuits. Technologists and politicians place responsibility for the decision on an "approved, technical, unbiased, scientific method." It is a game with high stakes. However, the results of the analysis can be manipulated like any statistical data for the benefit of one party over that of another.

> **The cost-benefit analysis provides an illusion of accuracy and credibility.**

Day-to-day business decisions using the cost-benefit theory in the creation and application of technology promote the use of the lowest costs and the highest benefits, usually called net profit after tax. This process often makes the anticipated outcome appear far better than it really is.

Consider, for instance, the dollar benefits for the public of a dam with a recreation area near a large city. The benefits can be subjective and exaggerated, while at the same time, the cost of construction and the long-term impact on the environment can be deliberately set too low. Sometimes, the anticipated benefits and actual costs are simply not known well enough, and the project then becomes an experiment. Both the deliberate lie and the experiment on an uninformed public are wrong by any standard of ethics.

The Army Corps of Engineers has used a "skewed" cost-benefit ratio analysis on a number of river and dam projects. In December 2000, a study by the Pentagon concluded that the Corps used "rigged data," with the value of benefits set artificially high and the value of predicted costs set artificially low,[3] making the cost-benefit ratio look more attractive than it really was.

Rigged data does not lead to safe structures, safe transportation systems, or safe medical procedures—but the money connection appears to be a fact of life in our technology-driven culture. Many projects could be made safer by using well-known, existing technologies, if the lowest cost were not the dominant factor. Moreover, the cost-benefit analysis is directly connected to another dangerous tradition: the low-bid selection process.

Bidding Lowest-Cost Projects

The United States continues to use the fixed-price or lump-sum contract method for the selection of contractors. It is the dominant method, and we are one of the few industrialized countries that continue to use it.

In theory, this method provides high-quality construction at the lowest cost when open bidding competition is allowed among competent companies. The method is also used in manufacturing, defense contracts, and most transactions that involve services and products in a competitive economy. The wisdom of this method depends on how quality is defined and implemented in the project, and on the competence and skill of those who perform the contracts.

Of course, before contractors bid, the designers have the task of designing a cost-effective model for the project's owner. Since the late 1970s, project owners have often selected the designers of engineered projects on the basis of the lowest-price agreement, in one form or another.[a] If not selected this way, the design firms, like all competitive companies, operate on the basis of low-cost criteria. Owners and stockholders of corporations typically want the highest return possible, and if they do not get it, they demand new corporate decision-makers. If a prospective project owner cannot predict a good profit for the company, the project may not be undertaken, and the designers will not receive a contract.

Potential project designers estimate and submit to the project owner two costs: their own design fees and the probable cost of the proposed project. Project owners issue a Request for Proposals (RFP) to design firms for this purpose. The design firms may be tempted to submit a low estimate for the two costs so that the owner will fund the project. The project owner selects the designers on the basis of a combination of price, qualifications, and other factors in the owner's best interests. This selection process assumes a morally and socially responsible project owner.

Design and construction firms have learned to play this game of marketing themselves, and so they may quote a "low-ball" price in order to get the work. In doing so, the designers believe that changes during the design phase will increase their fees to a desired level of profit.[4] Generally, the more a project costs, the more the designers will earn. If the prospect for adequate

---

[a] The U.S. Supreme Court ruled on April 25, 1978, that designers of projects could participate in the low-bid process for their professional services to owners of projects if the owners desire it. This ruling was a result of years of litigation, because many designers believed that a low-bid process for their services would lower the quality of the design. This is interesting logic, since designers typically solicit low bids from the contractors who build the project.

profit is not apparent, design firms may be tempted to lower the amount and/or quality of their services for design plans and construction administration. This behavior is not rampant in technology design firms, but it does exist in many businesses that directly affect public safety.

Low-balling is the more common practice among construction contractors. By doing this, they hope to win the low bid, and thus the project award from the owner.[b] As a former general building contractor and structural design engineer, I have experienced both sides of the argument about bidding. I have seen many projects bid too low for contractors to make a reasonable profit. In many of these cases, the contractors for the project will rely on good luck or, worse, try to cut costs by using inferior methods and materials in the project's construction. Obviously, the quality of the project will suffer if the designers and owners of the project allow this to happen.

The cost-benefit analysis by the designers, formal or informal, initially determines the margin of safety for the project—whether the project is a bridge, a power plant, or an airplane. But the construction contractors do their own cost-benefit and risk analysis, and they then give the fixed price or bid to the project owners and their representatives, the designers. It seems incongruent for designers to force contractors to bid at the lowest cost and then not accept the same procedure for themselves, but that is not the central issue here. The crucial question is: Does the lowest-cost, fixed-price project give the owner and the public the

---

[b] The term "low-ball" is commonly used in the construction industry for contractors' bids in lump-sum contracts with the project owner. Other types of contract delivery systems are also open to this deceptive device to get the job, e.g., cost plus a fee, cost plus a percentage, and unit price contracts. To low-ball means to give a price that is lower than the real or expected total cost to the owner and the designer (agent of owner in most types of contracts in the United States). Once the contract is awarded to the low-ball bidder, the contractor will try to find ways to increase the company's profit, usually at the expense of quality and safety.

best quality and safest project? I think the answer is: Usually not, and other contract delivery systems are possible.[c]

In addition, a fixed-price contract implies a maximum price that the project owner will incur. This is a myth. Both designers and contractors can increase their profits by the use of change orders, legal documents between parties after the project has been started that allow for an increase or decrease in the original contract amount and/or project time.

Even ethical designers and contractors will encounter change orders that often substantially raise the final price for the project owner. It is common for change orders to add 20% to 60% to the cost of a project, depending on the type and size of the project. In some instances, with construction and defense contracts involving Federal governmental agencies, change orders have amounted to more than the original contract price, effectively doubling the cost of the project.

> **Setting aside the issue that the lowest bid is sometimes the highest cost for a project owner, the safety issue remains a serious problem.**

These accepted industry practices are often incongruent with the best quality and safest project, regardless of the nature of the business. The cost-benefit analysis, when coupled with a low-bid, fixed-price contract delivery system, can be a very dangerous accepted industry practice. The business may be construction, manufacturing, medicine, or engineering, but the result is the same. If the safety, health, and welfare of human beings are to be the most important criteria, these practices are fatally flawed.

---

[c] Other forms of contract delivery systems have begun to make inroads into the traditional low-bid, fixed-price agreements in construction and engineering. One of the more popular forms is the Design-Build (DB) contract with negotiated contract amounts. The owner solicits RFPs from DB firms and then contracts with one firm. This firm then provides both services, with the owner hoping to eliminate omissions and errors in plans and to eliminate change orders during construction.

On the other hand, could society sustain the economic growth necessary in some cases to pay substantially higher costs for goods, services, products, and structures? This rhetorical question, often presented as a definitive truism to justify placing a dollar value on human lives, is the wrong question to ask in many situations.

The questions should be: Can we afford not to? Should the thing be created at all? Do alternatives exist to the more costly plan that would accomplish essentially the same goal? The answers to these three questions would be very different in the case of constructing a new medical device and that of building the tallest skyscraper in the world. As I have written, skyscrapers primarily serve the egos of the participants in the financing, design, and construction of super-tall buildings.

So, where did these accepted industry practices and true beliefs come from? They are cultivated in the minds of students within our educational institutions, where the search for truth can be an illusion. The dogma and policies of science, engineering, and technology colleges set the stage for the acceptance of the cost-benefit analysis and lowest-cost projects. The money connection begins in higher education—in the hallowed halls and classrooms of our universities.

Doctrines of Academe

Our universities and colleges are indispensable to our economy and to our society. It is within these universities that knowledge and our culture are conveyed to the next generation. Many of us have enjoyed the good salaries and job security found in an academic environment. However, some of what is learned in these environments can be categorized as true beliefs or myths, unacceptable industry practices, and faulty team efforts. These things sustain the Code and promote the ugly side of the business of technology.

The following discussion on higher education is directed primarily toward engineering and technology programs and curricula. However, many authors have confirmed the existence of the deteriorating and hostile environment found in most university systems and colleges in the United States.[5]

Destructive and common industry practices originate from doctrines found within institutions of higher education. Many of these doctrines are unspoken, while others are written into the official rules. The university system was originally designed to enlighten individuals and to foster autonomy, but at the same time, it hides dirty little secrets that contribute to the Code's impact on society.

Before I describe some of the most common problems, you need to understand, to the extent that it is possible, how the academic world works. As long as I have been in the system, I still do not fully comprehend the bureaucratic business of education. Hoffer's description of the doctrine of true believers helps explain the conflicting doctrines in academe:

> Doctrine, if not unintelligible, must be vague or at least unverifiable. And if some part of the doctrine is simple, there is a tendency among the faithful to complicate and obscure it. There is thus an illiterate air about the most literate true believer. He seems to use words as if he were ignorant of their true meaning. Hence, too, his taste for quibbling, hairsplitting and scholastic torturousness.[6]

Many academics learn to be very good at this "quibbling, hairsplitting, and scholastic torturousness." I have been a member of a system that seems to enjoy these activities, which consume enormous amounts of time and money. The phrase "ivory tower" reflects the tendency of many academics to withdraw from the practical world where time is money. Sometimes it can be a good thing to avoid business as usual.

However, the ivory tower also has a dark side, which becomes apparent in a myth about the goals of the university. The same academics create and sustain a widely accepted threefold mission of public universities, dating back to government land-grant policies. The mission was for the public good: to teach, to conduct research, and to provide community services.

Many authors have written about the problems with this dubious trinity of missions in academia.[7] I will try to limit my observations to facts and ideas that give rise to true beliefs. The public needs to know the rite of passage young technologists must suffer in order to practice their professions.

Inner Sanctums of the University

The research game is the money connection that dominates the administration of a university. A college or university is not what it appears to be to most parents of prospective students, because quality teaching is not the first priority. The research component of a professor's job description drives the business of universities.[8]

> **If most parents who work hard to send their children to college really knew the system, they would be appalled at the use of their tax dollars.**

Perhaps enough people are learning the truth, because a number of state universities are finding it difficult to fund their myriad programs and research projects. The ongoing debate over teaching versus research is only the tip of the iceberg. Even the type of research that is considered best—"pure" versus the "applied"—remains a source of tension within academe. Scientists are said to conduct pure research, which is usually described in non-technical language as the discovery of knowledge for knowledge's sake. According to this argument, pure knowledge does not need to have immediate or any commercial applications.

On the other side of the argument is applied research, which is usually performed by engineers and other technologists. It is described as the application of pure research to immediate human health, safety, and welfare problems within the society. Industry, government, and the university typically "partner" in applied research activities, with industry expecting immediate commercial gain. When hard economic times arrive, pure research often receives less attention and limited funding.

The old school of thought within universities says that industry must keep out of the research business that is conducted within higher education.[9] This traditional school of thinking says that industry's motives are impure and that this can somehow taint the results of pure research. Of course, their position assumes that professors might be unethical—an implication that the traditional thinkers may not have pondered. However, the purpose here is not to settle the debate, but to show the deeply engrained beliefs within the institutions of higher education that affect technologists' education and practices.

University administrators, particularly presidents, chancellors, deans, and department chairpersons, constantly prowl in corporate America for more money for their institutions. So, these business managers of universities have devised a scheme to  raise money outside state funding sources, which they always view as inadequate.[10]

These university business managers seek research grant money from industry and government agencies in order to pull additional resources into the university, and these additional resources are often outside the regular scrutiny of the public and the state legislatures. The business managers "encourage" professors to conduct funded research, but it is often more like coercion than encouragement.

This outside money brings a professor status, recognition, promotions, extra income, and other perks from the university system. The research grant money also brings the institution status and recognition, which the university administrators hope will bring more research dollars and endowments into the system. Of course, university administrators want the recognition from the research conducted by their subordinates.

If university administrators can push professors to bring in more research dollars, the administrators and the University will look better—at least, they believe that a good research image attracts more money. Image and reality, of course, can be quite different.

Many, if not all, state universities follow this pattern to acquire outside sources of funds. University administrators often use the improved status in national rankings to move to a higher-paying job. As a result, the turnover rate among top administrators is high. Chancellors' and deans' positions have been revolving doors.[d] The public and politicians have begun to notice the transient nature of administrators in many institutions.

Like coaches in high-profile sports programs, administrators "resigning" from one institution are snapped up by another institution that hopes to increase its revenues. It is a game—one with few benefits for the students. It is quite common for chancellors to earn nearly a quarter of a million dollars or more in one year when perks are added into the pot. And engineering deans command almost as high a salary, while other deans—for example, in physics or in English—earn far less, sometimes only a third as much.

The reason for this disparity in deans' salaries boils down to the amount of research money and the prestige the money commands in the business community. The chancellors and deans are always putting the pinch on contributors to increase the pot of discretionary money. This research money and prestige bestow more status on the chancellor and the institution. All of it helps the deans and the chancellors find better-paying positions—the revolving door policy at its worst.

> **Administrators also pressure professors to conduct research because it makes extra money available for other uses through a kind of slush fund—the game of "soft" money.**

This slush fund money, which administrators skim off the top of each researcher's grant, is used to create a cash account under their sole control. Top administrators typically will use the soft money to fund pet projects or to reward professors who play

---

[d] A university chancellor might be the equivalent of a CEO of a corporation, and a university dean might be like a department head.

the game well as loyal team members—or to punish a dissenting professor who believes effective teaching is more important. The university offers tenure and promotions as positive reinforcement, primarily on the basis of the number of these research dollars a professor brings into the institution.[e] The god of research rules a lot of hallowed hallways and ivory towers.[11]

Quality teaching as the university's primary goal is only for the public image. Few real rewards exist for professors who are good teachers, and some of the best teachers are often pushed to resign. Administrators often give lip service to the importance of teaching quality to lessen the public's awareness of the reality of the business of higher education. Good teaching will not secure tenure or a lifetime job guarantee in most engineering and technology colleges.[12]

Tenure and promotion concerns can become a trap for professors who wish to excel at teaching. The pressure to research and to publish is intense, and a new professor soon learns to play the game so she can remain employed by the university. To be denied tenure is to be an outcast.

> Insiders know that good teaching has become quite secondary to the operation and growth of large public universities.[13]

Unfortunately, instructional skills are not required for professors in technological fields like engineering and the sciences. College professors usually hold a Ph.D. degree in specialized fields of engineering and technology, but they are taught to be researchers, not good teachers in the way most parents and students expect. As a result, many professors are very

---

[e] Tenure is a lifetime job appointment beginning after a 5- to7-year probationary period. Tenure is ultimate job security, or at least that is the predominant view among professors. During the probationary period, the business managers of a university apply intense pressure on professors to acquire grant money for research projects.

authoritarian in the classroom, where they have no real credentials or rewards for being a good teacher.

Most professors who are active in research use graduate students to conduct most of their research projects. These same graduate students are then often paid a nominal amount to teach the undergraduate courses that the research professors say they do not have time to teach. Graduate students often become virtual slaves to their professors-advisors, for whom they perform most of the actual day-to-day research.[14]

Tenured technology professors who conduct a lot of research will typically teach only one or two courses per year and may "supervise" dozens of graduate students in research projects. The so-called leading-edge knowledge gained by research may be so specialized that only a few graduate students may benefit from it.

> **Undergraduate teaching is not a priority for research-oriented professors or university administrators. There is no money in it.**

The graduate student's advisor may be uninterested in the student's needs or too busy, and thus he often reviews the student's work only minimally as it progresses. This is especially true if the advisor's research interests do not coincide with the graduate student's work—that is, if the student is lucky enough to be able to pick her own project. So, students learn this game of minimal review of work, which they take to their industry jobs.

When the student finishes the research project, the professor "reviews" her work and usually signs his name as the primary investigator. Some students also learn that the authority figure may take unfair credit for students' work, even at the undergraduate level. Students are not the only ones accused of plagiarism. Graduate and undergraduate students learn to comply with authority early in their careers.[f]

---

[f] Undergraduates have many of the same problems with their advisors. Good advisors and caring professors should visit frequently with the student

Finally, the graduate student's research results are published using academic guidelines controlled by the student's advisor. In return, the student hopes to receive his or her graduate degree. The power the professor-advisor holds over the student's career at this point is almost absolute. Acquiring a graduate degree in technology can resemble a hazing process in a secret fraternity.[15] It is a rite of passage into the practice of technology—and the Code.

> **This practice of the Code among professors is a prelude to the same behavior in the business of technology.**

A professor with a dictatorial approach promotes obedient and compliant behavior that becomes part of the practice of engineering and technology. This is the inner sanctum of the university where academic doctrines become accepted industry practices.

The Business of Higher Education

College professors and university administrators have become salespersons in the business of education. As you have read, the business interests of the university dictate a research game to pursue government and private funding. Higher education, when linked in the Industrial-Military-University Complex, becomes a business that has dramatically changed curricula for technology students.

This change was beginning to take hold when I was an undergraduate in the late 1960s. The race to the Moon allowed little time for Great Books and the humanities in an engineer's studies. It is not difficult for the university to attract students to technology because of the common characteristics and goals that these students bring with them.

---

about his or her career goals, courses to take, workloads during the semester, any problems, etc. Most students will tell you it doesn't work that way.

> **The money connection remains a driving force, and so most curricula for engineers and scientists are designed to produce skilled graduates, not educated citizens.**

Traditionally, the university was created to provide a well-rounded education with a religious dimension in the curriculum. Early European and American universities were private and mostly affiliated with a specific religion, and many still are. A university education was originally designed to create autonomous thinkers and good citizens. But times have changed.

The emphasis on skill-building education suggests that corporate America is looking for skills to build larger company profits rather than autonomous individuals with a global sense of moral and social responsibility. Therefore, a lot of the research and skill-building courses are oriented toward the improvement of bottom-line profits for the "Industrial-Military-University Complex."[g]

When you learn how the academic game is played, it becomes apparent why students find it easier to follow a Code than to exercise personal moral and social responsibility. Undergraduates are shortchanged by taking a hodgepodge of courses badly taught by untrained graduate students or "tenured drones," according to the Carnegie Foundation for the Advancement of Teaching.[16]

This corrosive environment in higher education creates constant tension within a university system that some insiders want to call a "family." The university is only a family to this extent: Technologists at the university have similar backgrounds

---

[g] I first mentioned this triad in Chapter One. I am not saying that a partnership shouldn't exist, but the motives and intent of the university should be examined and altered to promote higher-quality reasons for a university education—self-improvement and moral and social responsibility. In other words, an active concern for basic human rights and the fragile environment should be paramount.

and allow "dirty little secrets" to be transmitted to the next generation.

The Code of Silence has become a game in academe. John Bradshaw, in his book *On the Family*, believes that a dysfunctional traditional family unit exhibits this game-playing as one of its distinguishing traits. The university family can exhibit the same characteristics of a dysfunctional family unit, as I argue in the next chapter.

Bradshaw describes this type of destructive behavior this way: "They are playing a game. They are playing at not playing a game. If I show them that I see they are playing a game, I shall break the rules and they will punish me. I must play the game of not seeing that I play the game."[17] I experienced this game more in academia than I ever imagined possible.

Bibliography, Notes & Further Reading

[1] For a good start into the world of business in general and business ethics in particular, see Henderson, *What's Ethical in Business?* For a look at the business of construction and engineering, see Laton McCartney, *Friends in High Places.*

[2] For a layman's explanation of the ethical theories, see Martin and Schinzinger, *Ethics in Engineering*, 51-60. If you want a detailed explanation of the Utilitarian Theory, see John Stuart Mill, *On Liberty* (Bungay, Great Britain: Penguin Books, Pelican Pub., 1987) and John Stuart Mill, *Utilitarianism, with Critical Essays*, ed. Samuel Gorovitz (Indianapolis: Bobbs-Merrill, 1971).

[3] This information was taken from "Pentagon Says Corps of Engineers Rigged Data," *Omaha World Herald* (Associated Press), 6 December 2000.

[4] Design firms, architects, and engineers typically work on a percentage basis, but sometimes under a lump-sum contract with the project owner. For example, the architect in charge of a building project hires his own subcontractors—the specialized engineers—to design the structure's frame and systems and to estimate the costs. The architect working on a percentage basis will typically bill the owner the amount of the fee percentage, usually 5% to 10%, multiplied by the total cost of the project, including his own design subcontractors' fees. The higher the cost of the project, the more the designers will earn. Contractors who physically build the projects usually prefer these types of contracts, because they reduce the overall risk for the contractor and shift the risk to the owner.

[5] Bruce Wilshire, *The Moral Collapse of the University* (Albany, N.Y.: State University of New York Press, 1990). Wilshire writes that the university causes alienation in the educating act, which leads to a crisis of authority and of identity in the profession. He wants the university to reorganize itself, to reintegrate the self with the world, and form a humane foundation for knowledge. Other well-known authors have written similar books: e.g., Allan Bloom, Charles Sykes, and Ernest Boyer. Please refer to this Chapter's Notes for their contributions.

[6] Hoffer, *True Believer,* 85.

[7] Allan Bloom, *The Closing of the American Mind* (New York: Simon & Schuster, Inc., 1987).

[8] I am only one of many insiders in higher education who find the academic rhetoric does not match the reality in universities' hallowed halls. Charles J. Sykes, an investigative journalist, has provided a short "bill of indictment for the professors' crimes against higher education." Sykes says that professors

are "overpaid, under-worked, architects of waste; they have abandoned their teaching responsibilities, distorted university curricula, justified research of little value, written about trivial research, unaccountable to anyone, mortgaged the nation's scientific future, committed academic fraud, and have turned universities into vast factories of junkthink." Refer to his book, *ProfScam: Professors and the Demise of Higher Education* (Washington, D.C.: Regnery Gateway, 1988), 5-7.

[9] For an examination of the university-industry connections, see Raymond Spier, "Ethical Aspects of the University-Industry Interface," *Science and Engineering Ethics*, 1 (1995).

[10] A warning recently came from some educators about the increasing role of research money in the face of a slowing economy. In a recent article in a major journal on engineering education, sources cite "less time to devote to students" as a problem. The article also says, "You mess around with the public-education system, and you are messing around with the whole future of the country." I agree, but the article implies the economy is at stake. It is symptomatic of the university's mission to help corporations at the expense of autonomous-thinking, good citizens. See Alvin P. Sanoff, "Feeding the Squeeze," *Prism*, May-June 2001, 26-28.

[11] Robert L. Cook, "The Dilemma of Teaching Ethics in Engineering and Technology," Paper presented at the Midwest Regional American Society for Engineering Education (ASEE) Conference, Kansas State University, 22-24 March 1989. Another source is Sykes, *ProfScam*.

[12] In my field of specializations, civil engineering and construction technology, professors who are labeled good teachers are often considered second-class academics. Good teaching requires time away from the profitable research activities, and thus many times the universities' administrators will not promote or tenure these professors, even when they win teaching awards from their own colleges. It happened at the University of Nebraska, and it is a well-documented problem across the United States. For a good primer on teaching and research requirements for professors, see Ernest L. Boyer, *Scholarship Reconsidered: Priorities of the Professoriate* (Princeton, N.J.: The Carnegie Foundation for the Advancement of Teaching, 1990).

[13] Two authors have presented considerable and convincing evidence that reinforces my experiences at the University of Nebraska. They are (1) Sykes, *ProfScam*, and (2) Lewis, *Poisoning the Ivy*.

[14] Sykes, 33-50. Sykes, a journalist, details the flight from teaching to research.

[15] Stephen Budinsky, "The Ivory Sweatshop?" *U.S. News & World Report*, 29 March 1999, 102-103. A second article, Ben Wildavsky, "Grad Students, the Sorest Apprentices," *U.S. News & World Report*, 20 March 2000, 66, underscores the problems in academia in the United States.

---

[16] This information was found in "Cutting Classes," *U.S. News & World Report*, 4 May 1998.

[17] John Bradshaw, *Bradshaw On: The Family* (Deerfield Beach, Fla: Health Communications, Inc., 1988), 61. I am using Bradshaw's information; the actual quotation is by R.D. Laing.

Chapter 8
Dirty Little Secrets in Universities

Dysfunctional University "Families"

Human beings want to belong to a group or family unit. Sociologists and psychologists have established this trait among technologists in particular. The purpose and support many of us gain from professional organizations, business groups, and other associations can be fulfilling and good for us. But dysfunctional families, teams, groups, and organizations also exist, in part because their members try to hide "dirty little secrets" to protect themselves and their organizations from public scrutiny—and accountability.

The medical profession and university medical schools appear to have similar destructive secrets. In his book *Blind Eye*, James B. Stewart presents a well-documented account of doctor-professors who typically cover up for other doctors' mistakes, university administrators who fear litigation and thus will not cooperate with investigations, and medical regulatory agencies and professional societies that become part of the cover-up.[1]

According to Stewart, the Southern Illinois University (SIU) medical school graduated Dr. Michael Swango in spite of his apparent incompetence and bad evaluations by the teaching staff. A number of mysterious deaths were linked to Swango, but half-hearted, incomplete investigations by SIU officials cleared him. A group of Swango's fellow students took the extraordinary step of submitting a letter to University administrators calling for his expulsion.[2] However, medical professors and SIU officials ignored or rejected students' and nurses' repeated complaints about "Dr. Mike," as he would later become known in Africa.

Swango graduated from SIU and moved to Ohio State University, to veterans' hospitals, and eventually to foreign countries where any doctor was thought to be better than none.[3] But in this case, they were wrong: Swango would later become a convicted psychopathic serial killer of patients and staff, primarily within university hospitals.[a]

Whether they are doctors or technologists, the "family" members in corporations, government agencies, universities, and professional societies tend to protect one another from accountability. You have already read about technologists who helped cover up gross negligence, even murder.

> **The analogy of a dysfunctional family, in which one or more members have acted in ways incongruent with society's norms, can help explain the underlying cause of man-made disasters.**

The family analogy also helps explain the destructive desire to keep the problems in academia hidden. This conspiracy of silence is similar to the secrecy of families in which a parent has done something that could shame the entire family if it became known. According to mental health professionals, members of neglectful and abusive families often exhibit "unrealistic expectations, denial, indirect communication patterns, rigidity, and isolation"[4]—traits also found in many business and university workplaces.

When a child is abused, or when some family member commits a shameful act, everyone in the family—the abused as well as the abuser—may try to hide the events from public

---

[a] Swango was thought to have murdered more than 60 people during the 1980s and 1990s. He poisoned his victims with arsenic, nicotine, and other substances that usually left no detectable traces. He was sentenced in September 2000 to three life terms in prison without parole.

awareness. The abused child can be both traumatized for life and afraid to tell anyone what has happened.[5]

Why? While there may be other reasons, the need for security and acceptance certainly influences the choices of the victim and perpetrator and affects the family's stability. The fear of public exposure causes family members to behave irrationally. The abused child may fear abandonment or more attacks. The shamed person may fear removal or isolation from the family. And, of course, the abuser wants his or her actions hidden from public view for obvious reasons.

Perpetrators and victims not only want to keep secrets from the public and from other family members; often they also want to remain in the same dysfunctional family or organization. So the family attempts to protect itself from outside publicity at any cost, playing a game whose goal is self-preservation but whose effect is ultimately destructive. This scenario is all too familiar to therapists and psychologists.[6]

> **The conspiracy of silence to hide the damaging secrets is very real in traditional families, in corporate "families," and in university "families."**

The parallels between a dysfunctional family and a dysfunctional professional group are disturbing. Technologists demonstrated this irrational behavior during the Holocaust. The university practices its own form of self-preservation at the expense of the public and its customers—the students and their parents. Dysfunctional members of a university can harm students' perceptions of right and wrong, sometimes for life.

The Rat Syndrome

Students in colleges of engineering and technology learn early in their education about the game played within academe. One aspect of this game is what I call the "Rat Syndrome"[7]— another part of the Code of Silence.[8]

The standard excuse for cheating—"everyone's doing it"—may be closer to reality than we want to believe. A 1999 poll conducted by a major news organization turned up these discouraging statistics:[9]

- **"84% of college students believe they need to cheat to get ahead in the world today."**
- **"90% of college students say cheaters never pay the price."**
- **"90% of college students say when people see someone cheating, they don't turn him in."**
- **"90% of college students say politicians, the media, and high schoolers cheat often."**
- **"1 in 4 adults believes he has to lie and cheat to get ahead."**

I came to recognize while teaching that the problem was not limited to students who were actually cheating. Those who were not cheating were reluctant to disclose or even to discuss the problem. These honest students, as well as professors who knew about the cheating, refused to get involved. They simply remained silent. The honest students said that they did not want to "rat" on their fellow students or on their professors who allowed the cheating to continue. "Ratting" is the students' word for the academic equivalent of whistle-blowing. It is an essential part of the Code: Do not tell on me and I will not tell on you. And it is a growing problem on college campuses.

The Rat Syndrome is a problem among professors as well as students. I have observed some professors pretending not to see unethical behavior by a colleague. This syndrome reminded me of what I had read about technologists' roles in the Holocaust. Many German technologists pretended not to see some of their colleagues' monstrous acts. And many of them remained silent even when some of their own professionals, who happened to be Jews, were falsely accused, fired, and many times, executed. Most technologists during the Nazi domination of Germany remained silent about the persecution of Jewish technologists, as discussed in Chapter 1.

Other writers have found that a significant number of professors and administrators have retaliated against students who called attention to unethical teachers. The emotional abuse of students can include discrimination, harassment, and outright threats[10]—actions that mimic the behavior of dysfunctional families. This abuse by unethical teachers bent on keeping secrets is a growing problem in academia, one that creates a toxic environment for everyone.

The "don't ask, don't tell, don't get involved" Rat Syndrome in higher education is a prelude to disasters like the Hyatt Regency and the Challenger. Most likely, this syndrome was a primary factor in the use of efficient technology to kill during the Holocaust. The Industrial-Military-University Complex can have widespread repercussions.

Poison in the University

Insider Michael Lewis asserts in *Poisoning the Ivy* that academics are afraid to confront their colleagues about suspected unethical activities. It is true. Each professor knows that he or she may later need the other's support, especially when it comes to the vote on tenure. Lewis also believes that the system of governance in universities is flawed. He calls the university life of a professor "a fine place to do nothing."[11] There *is* something going on, however, the keeping of "dirty little secrets," as Lewis calls the conspiracy in academia. I call it the Code of Silence.

Lewis identifies seven "sins" of teaching, among which are many of the same problems that I believe contribute to the Code. Lewis estimates that about 30% of all professors are guilty of one or more of these "seven sins" of higher education.[12] I believe his estimate too conservative.

The number-one sin on Lewis's list is abandonment of teaching responsibilities.[13] He believes that scholarship and research are the "bad joke" of academia. But while many professors do abandon teaching in their flight to conduct research and to publish, this problem is just a small part of a troubled system. Misrepresentation and fraud by researchers in academia are often in the news.[14] In addition, trivia and drivel in "scholarly" papers or journal articles pass for quality scholarship.[15]

Ernest Boyer of the Carnegie Foundation has lectured widely on the priorities of academics in higher education. Boyer researched the history of the professoriate and called on universities to enlarge the scope of scholarly activity to include discovery, integration, application, and teaching. He says universities have "a crisis of purpose."[16] It can be argued that they do have a purpose: business as usual.

The notion that fellow academics work and play well together in most universities is a myth. Some universities have openly turned to psychologists to help dysfunctional departments with problems that include "resentment, professional jealousy, and sniping about perks."[17] University faculties are entangled in a type of low-level warfare that eventually leads to inferior educational opportunities for all students, including future technologists.

Higher education, with its disturbing secrets, transmits the Code to the next generation. Universities, as large bureaucracies, have many problems. But the problems begin when they deny that their systems are dysfunctional. This poison affects the very foundations of higher education, because its hallowed halls and ivory towers promise the search for truth. Furthermore, those academics involved understand that denying the existence of the Code is part of the game.

> One way universities perpetuate the denial and the Code is by discrediting and removing anyone who wants to talk about the family secrets.

Earlier, I compared a dysfunctional professional group to a dysfunctional family. These behaviors begin in higher education and then continue into the business of technology. A medical doctor, Catherine McKegney, has observed that medical students typically learn similar behaviors:

> As with neglectful (and abusive) families, it is important to recognize that the system's coping style has been its best in the medical family. Because membership substitutes for

intimacy in this family, appearing different is too painful to be risked. Physicians internalize this family's and society's unrealistic expectations and learn to deny the pain of their training and the clues to their ongoing stress, paying the consequences later in their careers.[18]

Later in the doctors' careers, the patients may also pay dearly.

McKegney could just as well have been describing an engineer or scientist's education. Like dangerous medical doctors who continue to practice, engineers can often cross state boundaries to work in their profession again. This behavior has a direct connection to disasters, and when members of a dysfunctional organization want to question it, they may find themselves the victims of intimidation. This intimidation can be open or very subtle, but the result is the same—conformity and silence in the face of injustice.

Mobbing in the Workplace

Typically, a member of an organization, company, or agency wants to stay within his peer group for the protection and benefits it offers. To be an outcast is to know deep insecurity. As you have read, sociological studies confirm that job security and money are two of the primary desires of technologists. But the same group dynamics that can provide protection and other benefits can also turn the workplace into a nightmare for those few individuals who try to speak against the Code.

> **Coercive behavior by members of a group to force others to comply with the group's demand is called "mobbing."**

Noa Davenport, Ruth Schwartz, and Gail Elliott define mobbing as "emotional abuse in the American workplace."[19] Their book builds on the pioneering work of Dr. Heinz Leymann of Sweden, who first named and investigated the phenomenon in Europe. Mobbing is also the treatment that real or perceived whistle-blowers receive in this country from their companies, professional organizations, and co-workers.

Dr. Leymann first used the term "mobbing" in the 1980s, after discovering that violence in the workplace resembled the kind of violence found on children's playgrounds. He investigated people labeled "difficult" by their organizations and found that "their behavior was not a character flaw, but rather the work structure and culture created the circumstances that marked these people as difficult ... and once identified as difficult, the company created further reasons for terminating them."[20]

Dr. Leymann first defined mobbing as "psychological terror" involving "hostile and unethical communications directed in a systematic way by one or a few individuals mainly towards one individual."[21] A large public awareness campaign in Scandinavia and in German-speaking countries forced organizations to examine how "difficult" employees are treated and led to protection for these people. This protection does not exist in the United States.

The accepted definition of mobbing today closely resembles the process of ridding an organization of a whistle-blower, although whistle-blowers are not the only targets. Differences of opinion between workers can also lead to mobbing. "The mobbing syndrome is a malicious attempt to force a person out of the workplace through unjustified accusations, humiliations, general harassment, emotional abuse, and/or terror," according to Davenport, Schwartz, and Elliott.[22]

I raise the issue of mobbing in order to show (1) how to recognize the problem and (2) how it is connected with the Code. The authors of *Mobbing* identify four reasons why individuals engage in the practice. These four reasons also shed light on the dysfunctional behavior of some members of professions responsible for the public's health and safety.

"Mobbers" want to do one or more of the following: (1) force someone to adapt to a group norm, (2) revel in animosity and eliminate those they dislike, (3) gain sadistic pleasure stemming from boredom, or (4) reinforce prejudices. More than one "mobber" can participate in destroying a fellow employee's career and health, often with upper management's tacit or active approval.

> **The first reason for mobbing—to force someone to adapt to a group norm—was well illustrated in the Challenger disaster.**

The true believers at NASA were convinced that the organization could "only be cohesive and strong if a certain uniformity exists."[23]

The typical methods used in mobbing are (1) hostile communications from others and limits on self-expression, (2) attacks on one's social relations, (3) attacks on one's reputation, (4) attacks on the quality of one's professional and life situation, and (5) direct attacks on one's physical and mental health.[24] Technologists who want to tell the truth may have to deal with such tactics in the workplace.

Technologists are highly specialized individuals who sometimes are educated in dysfunctional universities and then may work within dysfunctional organizations. While this does not mean that all individuals within the organizations must also be dysfunctional, an individual will have to make a decision to remain in the group or to fight the collective irresponsibility.

Tunnel Vision in Academe

Most engineering and science curricula focus on building the technical skills educators believe their students need for the profession. It is very focused learning, and unfortunately, a significant number of technologists and educators believe that this narrow concentration on the technical aspects is the way it should be. This type of curriculum secures for technologists a degree prized in a bureaucratic work environment, which in turn leads to many rewards for the team effort in creating technology. But this specialization also has a dark side.

According to Allan Bloom in *The Closing of the American Mind*, the slide toward more specialization with less emphasis on personal morality has been increasing since the 1960s.[25] Bloom believes that educators have a blind side that affects our ability to recognize or to admit to ourselves the problems in education. He attributes this blindness to the teaching of "cultural relativism," or only the knowledge specific to one's own group or society.[26] Bloom believes that we are "closing our minds" to the purpose of education and that we should not teach the "values of our culture" without exposing students to a liberal education.[27]

According to Bloom, the purpose of education is "avoiding prejudices and trying to know what is good and bad." The re-connection of the study of science with the systematic study of the humanities is Bloom's central theme.[28] More emphasis on the humanities, including traditional subjects in history, art, literature, and the classics, could provide a path to personal moral and social responsibility.

The literature in engineering and technology contains a growing number of calls from within the professions to allow students more time for the humanities in the curricula. During the last two decades, nothing much has changed from the specialized education that, at best, tolerates dabbling in the great ideas. For instance, in the Civil Engineering curriculum at the University of Nebraska, of the 130 credit hours required for graduation, only 18 are in the humanities and social sciences.[b] That's only 14% of the total. And technology students whose department and advisors emphasize skill-building technical courses typically take the introductory courses to fulfill this requirement. Sadly, the instructors of many of these courses are graduate students, not the seasoned professors.

Bloom doesn't call merely for these subjects to be emphasized in the curriculum, but for the ideas to be taught in a way that leads students to place more value on autonomous thinking. The ability to value goodness, justice, and equality for all

---

[b] *UNOmaha Undergraduate Catalog*, 1999-2000.

persons requires self-awareness and a deep appreciation of the interrelatedness of all life—values that have traditionally been central to the humanities.

Although humanities courses are available to technology students, most technology professors have little enthusiasm for them. Rarely do faculty members advise their students to take courses beyond the entry level.[c] During my teaching career, I have seen this attitude change little among most engineering and technology faculty—or among students. Two common questions from students are "How many humanities do I have to take over there?" and "What are the easiest courses over there?" Note the words "over there": Engineering students tend to view the humanities as a separate world that has little or nothing to do with their lives or careers. I believe they learn this attitude from a few of their professors who practice the Code of Silence.

Many faculty as well as students in technology tend to think in terms of "them" and "us." An invisible boundary line has been drawn, and we do not want to venture "over there" with "those people." If we did, we might have to think about what we do to earn a living. These great ideas of humankind should have no such boundaries, but the Code makes it difficult to overcome them.

We can and should learn about the richness of life from world literature, art, history, philosophy, and other disciplines in the humanities. Renowned philosopher and writer Mortimer Adler listed 103 great books that he believed met the requirements for his Paideia Project.[29] Topping his list are Homer's *Iliad* and *Odyssey*, the Old Testament of the Bible, Plato's Dialogues, and Aristotle's Works.[30] Bloom's first choice was Plato's *Republic*.[31]

---

[c] My teaching experiences in engineering and technology began in 1985. During this period, I estimate that over 95% of my student advisees wanted to take the "easiest" humanities courses available to them. I discouraged the practice and worked to end it, but I had little success among most of the other faculty members.

In my experience, most technology students know little, if anything, about these and other great books.

> **It is extremely rare for technology students to read any book outside of their technical education during their student careers.**

This avoidance of ideas that impact the technologist's work creates a narrowly focused individual and, in the final analysis, is part of the Code of Silence.

Emphasis on Specialization

The ideas found in the humanities persuade us to contemplate our "selves," to look critically at the society in which we live, and to acknowledge our interdependency with one another. Specialization does not encourage these ideas. In fact, the events of the 20th century suggest that it has the opposite effect.

The specialization of a technologist's education is not confined to the U.S. or this generation. The technologists during the Nazi regime were highly specialized, as were those in the former Soviet Union. Loren R. Graham's *The Ghost of the Executed Engineer*[32] is based on the life and death of a Russian engineer, Palchinsky, who died trying to change the horrible working conditions and to stop the degradation of the environment. Soviet engineers operated in conditions that constantly produced fear. According to Graham, most technologists stopped raising questions about safety and other ethical issues for their own self-preservation. Today, it is widely recognized that the Soviets decimated and poisoned their environment to keep up with the United States in the arms race.

Most alarming are the similarities between U.S. trends in professional schools for technology education and the extreme specialization in the old Soviet Union. In the decades after 1930, according to Graham, the Soviet Union trained more engineers than any other country in the world. The technologists were told to produce more and to neglect all factors that might slow production of goods. The U.S. economy was also in a frenzy of mass production. The assembly lines were designed to make people work as machines, without thought of the emotional distress it might cause them. Smokestack industries flourished, largely unregulated.

A quick look at everyday corporate and government terminology will illustrate the point that human concerns are often secondary. The "personnel department" has been replaced by "human resources." The value of an individual worker is seen as just another resource, like material, equipment, money, and other things that can be manipulated and controlled for the good of the company.

Palchinsky, the executed Russian engineer from Graham's book, had long advocated the need for humane working conditions and technology projects that would help people instead of hurting them. He believed that efficiency in business and justice for human beings must always be linked. It was a rare view in most of the Western world as well as in the Soviet Union at the time. In essence, Palchinsky was questioning the value of the cost-benefit ratio analysis, which the technologists of today learn in their specialized education. He was murdered for his beliefs.

According to Nicholas Dewitt, the leading authority on Soviet education in the 1960s, the intense focus on specific skills by professional schools produced "ball-bearings-for-paper-mills engineers."[33] It is commonly accepted that the fall of the Soviet Union was linked to its total neglect of human beings and their individual welfare.

Today's over-specialization and the neglect of the humanities in the training of technologists should sound an alarm. Palchinsky should be remembered for giving his life for something very important. He lived and died for the great ideas that remind us of the sacredness of all human beings and bind us together.

The current specialized educational environment and licensing system in the United States continues to grow at an alarming pace. In May of 2001, Arthur Schwartz, an attorney and general counsel for a prominent engineering organization exclusively for licensed engineers, asked engineers to take a "fresh look" at their profession.[34] As a non-engineer and observer of engineers for almost twenty years, he believes that the profession is headed toward more "fragmentation," not less specialization.

The current licensing system for engineers is flawed and may not be in the best interests for the public's health and safety. Schwartz suggests that the engineering profession consider a broader licensing system to include more engineers. He is right in challenging the current system, because the vast majority of technologists work in areas exempt from the current requirements for a license. He writes that the public would be better protected if all engineers were licensed by the state. He has a valid point, and yet the engineering and technology college curricula grow more specialized each year.

M. Scott Peck wrote in *People of the Lie* that three general principles are true of specialized groups.[35] First, they develop a self-reinforcing group character. Second, they are prone to narcissism, experiencing themselves as uniquely right and superior to other groups. And third, through a self-selection process,[d] the society employs group members who have particular characteristics—e.g., aggressive police officers and soldiers.

****

As you have read in Part Two, engineers, technology professors, architects, and many other technologists are members of specialized groups that fit Peck's profile. The arguments in this book for preventing the spread of the Code coincide with my understanding of Peck's view of the *Lie*: The prevailing acceptance of self-regulating, specialized groups often serves the interests of the members more than the public's safety. The

---

[d] The self-selection process has two components. First, the person with certain traits selects for herself the specific career that fits her needs and characteristics. Second, a group of the same type of individuals tests and selects persons with the highest degree of desired traits for entry into the "club."

traditions and true beliefs of these specialized groups perpetuate dangerous myths, particularly in higher education, where future generations of technologists first experience them.

Writing this book has been a major factor in my journey to understand my *self* and responsibilities to my profession and to the public. Preventing the spread of the Code requires more than just possessing knowledge; it requires individual and collective action. To be a compliant and obedient participant or an apathetic witness to a preventable disaster is to be an accomplice in the evil. Passivity is not a virtue.

As the famous psychologist Carl Jung said, our logic is not enough: "We should not pretend to understand the world only by the intellect; we apprehend it just as much by feeling. Therefore the judgment of the intellect is, at best, only the half of truth, and must, if it be honest, also come to an understanding of its inadequacy."[e] Part Three of this book is about ethics in the workplace that can help prevent the spread of the Code of Silence. It is about our rational self and its struggle to experience the emotional self.

---

[e] C. G. Jung, *Psychological Types*, 1923.

Bibliography, Notes & Further Reading

[1] James B. Stewart, *Blind Eye* (New York: Simon & Schuster, 1999).

[2] Ibid., 50.

[3] Ibid., 305-306. Swango had apparently poisoned people while a doctor in Zimbabwe, Zambia, and South Africa, and was headed to Saudi Arabia before he was apprehended in Chicago in 1997. In addition, an article appeared in the April 2001 issue of the *Reader's Digest* magazine about Swango's guilty plea to avoid the death penalty. The magazine article pointed out "that two university teaching hospitals had hired him after he was convicted of poisoning."

[4] Catherine P. McKegney, M.D., "Medical Education: A Neglectful and Abusive Family System," *Family Medicine*, November-December 1989, 452-456.

[5] Many, many books explore the problems of child abuse. Three of them are (1) Steven Farmer, *Adult Children of Abusive Parents*; (2) Harold Bloomfield, *Making Peace with your Parents*; and (3) Stephen D. Grubman-Black, *Broken Boys/Mending Men*.

[6] John Bradshaw, in *Bradshaw On: The Family*, 84-85, provides a summary of a dysfunctional family's characteristics. Bradshaw's detailed description of a dysfunctional family is found on pages 61-85.

[7] Cook, "Dilemma."

[8] I first used the term in an engineering conference article on student ethics in higher education and the role that teachers play. My investigation and survey research showed that cheating by students on tests, reports, papers, etc., was a serious and widespread problem at most colleges and universities, including the University of Nebraska. My findings were reported in Conference Proceedings that I presented for the American Society for Engineering Education: "Ethical Dilemmas in the Classroom and in Construction: A Classroom Case Study with Survey Results," American Society for Engineering Education Annual Conference, Toronto, Ontario, 24-28 June 1990. The survey instrument was administered to about 1,200 engineering and technology students at the University of Nebraska, where I was teaching at the time. Cheating on college campuses is common knowledge, and the extent of the problem is often reported in newspapers and journals and on the Web.

[9] Carolyn Kliener and Mary Lord, "The Cheating Game," *U.S. News & World Report*, 22 November 1999, pp. 55-66.

[10] For a detailed account of this problem, start with Dan H. Wishnietsky, ed., *Sexual Harassment in the Educational Environment,* Center for Evaluation,

Development and Research, Hot Topic Series (Phi Delta Kappa, 1992).

[11] Lewis, 56. Many well-known authors echo the same thoughts about higher education's lack of concern about inferior teaching and unethical professors. Charles Sykes, Ernest Boyer, Allan Bloom, and Mortimer Adler have presented their own versions of the disorder of moral and social irresponsibility and the conspiracy that hides the problems. Bloom in *The Closing of the American Mind* (New York: Simon & Schuster, 1987) provides a detailed history of the problems in higher education. He believes that much of the blame rests with professors and administrators who pay little more than lip service to the need for more humanities and great books in curricula. The great modern-day philosopher and writer Mortimer J. Adler (*Reforming Education: The Opening of the American Mind*, New York: Macmillan Publishing Company, 1988) worked hard to reform education, with limited success. Adler is well known for promoting the Great Books series, especially works by Aristotle.

[12] Ibid., 105.

[13] Ibid., 58-104.

[14] Daniel Greenberg, "Publish or Perish—or Fake It," *U.S. News & World Report*, 8 June 1987. There are many more sources, but this one sums up the problem of academic fraud rather well.

[15] Sykes presents these conclusions in summary form in *ProfScam*, 6. More information can be found on pages 33-50.

[16] Ernest L. Boyer, *Scholarship Reconsidered: Priorities of the Professoriate* (Princeton, N.J.: The Carnegie Foundation for the Advancement of Teaching, 1990), 55.

[17] "Universities Turn to Psychologists to Help Dysfunctional Departments," *Chronicle of Higher Education*, 1 August 1997, A10-A11. This article was given to all departments in the College of Engineering & Technology at the University of Nebraska during an attempt to force students to remain silent about unethical professors.

[18] McKegney, 452-54.

[19] Davenport, Schwartz, and Elliott, 14.

[20] Ibid., 22-23.

[21] Ibid., 22.

[22] Ibid., 40.

[23] Ibid., 58-59.

[24] Ibid., 36-37.

[25] Bloom writes eloquently about these changes. I would encourage you to read his entire book; however, the following sections are especially relevant: "The

Sixties (313-335); and "The Student and the University" (336-382).

[26] Ibid., 37-39

[27] Ibid.

[28] I wrote a conference paper on this subject and at the time, I relied heavily on Bloom's book. See also Cook, "Ethical Dilemmas."

[29] For more information on Adler's proposal about the future of public schools, see Mortimer J. Adler, *The Paideia Proposal: An Educational Manifesto* (New York: Collier Books, Macmillan Publishing Co., 1982).

[30] Ibid., 335.

[31] Bloom, 381.

[32] Loren R. Graham, *The Ghost of the Executed Engineer* (Cambridge, Mass.: Harvard University Press, 1993).

[33] Ibid., 70.

[34] Arthur Schwartz, "Time to Take a Fresh Look at the Engineering Profession," Viewpoint, *Engineering Times*, May 2001, 5. *Engineering Times* is a publication of the National Society of Professional Engineers. I have been a licensed engineer and a member of the Society since the mid-1970s.

[35] Peck, 228.

Part 3: The Search for Workplace Ethics

*****

"No man, for any considerable period, can wear one face to himself, and another to the multitude, without finally getting bewildered as to which may be the true."

Nathaniel Hawthorne, The Scarlet Letter, 1850

Chapter 9

The Great Ideas of Humankind

Truth or Consequences

The value in searching for truths in the great ideas of humankind should be self-evident.[a] They are called "great ideas" because philosophers, educators, and historians generally agree that they have withstood the test of time and scrutiny. They are the ideas that have been found to contain at least a thread of eternal truth that helps human beings live a life worth living.

I tell my students to develop moral autonomy, and this admonition may seem incongruent with my advocating authors who write with authority about the truth. But it is not. In my Socratic method of teaching ethics, I try to ask the right questions to lead the students through the process of thinking rationally and emotionally, developing autonomous moral reasoning, and then making an informed decision. So, the place of great books and great ideas in the curriculum is straightforward: They can provide the framework for inquiring minds to *ask the right questions*.

A rational person, as defined earlier,[b] can become increasingly aware of the value of these classic and timeless "truths,"[1] but she must first begin two ongoing processes: (1) a journey deep inside her internal self to find the genuine or true

---

[a] Philosophers seldom use the term "self-evident," because self-evident truths are difficult to prove. Yet, the founding fathers of the United States used the term in our Declaration of Independence when they wrote that the universal right to "Life, Liberty and the pursuit of Happiness" is a self-evident truth.

[b] See Chapter 1.

self,[c] and (2) a quest to understand the available external wisdom, not just knowledge, from any source in which she can find the truths.

Wisdom and knowledge are not the same. Some gifted people can retain an enormous amount of what usually passes for wisdom in college classrooms—knowledge, facts, data, information, etc.—and do very well on college exams. But when they have to apply concepts, theories, and common sense to everyday situations, they may fail to solve the problem or to recognize that a problem or ethical dilemma even exists. Many cultures say that old people are wise from experience, and many are. Yet, solving a problem using only personal experience in a specific culture may only perpetuate a wrong solution or a myth.

It is unwise to know only information and facts. Awareness of a self-evident truth, or any truth for that matter, is a late phase of real understanding, or wisdom, which can lead to appropriate morally and socially responsible action congruent with genuine understanding. But this can occur only when a person employs both intelligence and emotion in making decisions.

Internal truths, or those inside our minds and our hearts, are always available when we have the desire and the will to access them. External wisdom or truths, on the other hand, are revealed in philosophy, in its close cousin ethical theory, in the classical writings, in world religions, in great minds of today, and in many other common sources of great ideas. A thread of truth runs through all these sources.

> This self-evident truth is simple yet profound: that all life is interrelated and interdependent.

This inescapable truth of interdependency obligates us to find ways to live our private lives in congruence with our conduct

---

[c] Some readers may interpret my concept of "self" in a religious sense and may prefer the word "soul"; others may read it as the Freudian "id, ego, superego."

in the workplace. When these two aspects of our existence are at odds, we are living a lie—a false self is controlling our actions. The consequence is disorder in our inner selves and the outer world that can lead to tragedies both personal and public.

In an old television program called "Truth or Consequences," contestants had to determine who was lying. There were no consequences for the liars themselves, only for those who could not see through their stories. The TV audience was always told who was lying and who was telling the truth, but in the real world, most of us do not really know for certain. The disasters of the 20th century confirm that terrible consequences await those of us who cannot determine who is lying—or telling us only part of the truth.

The path to the discovery of truths is not the same for everyone. For some people, the discovery of the wisdom in the great ideas may come before the discovery of their true selves. The two interrelated searches for truth can and often do occur simultaneously. However, the important thing is to begin the search for truth, and to do that, we need to be informed and knowledgeable—and to empathize with those we serve as creators of technology. The public should be informed and empowered to make its own decisions about its health, safety, and welfare.

Informed Consent

Scientists and engineers sometimes do not tell the whole truth and nothing but the truth. Technologists walk a thin line between good and evil when they create, because their work often involves life-and-death decisions. If we knew who was dissembling, we might not cross a particular bridge, or enter a building, or buy a particular make of automobile, or vote for a political candidate. Perhaps if we really knew all the facts, we might elect not to use a medicine, a pesticide, or a specific food additive.

Would it not be appropriate for an expert to inform consumers of technology about the real risks that we may face?

Yes, it is appropriate, and it is the law of this country in most situations. Experts and corporate leaders have a moral and legal duty to provide all information to those affected by their technology so they can decide whether they want to participate in these experiments. The creator of a technology should tell what she knows for sure and what she does not know for sure about the expected outcomes in the use of the technology.

> **This concept of telling the truth about the real impact of a project, process, or system before a person becomes a subject of the experiment is known as "informed consent."**

In other words, creators of technologies should ask those of us affected by the technology for our informed consent before the experiment begins. This individual approach is not always easy in our fast-paced society. It may be foolish to require a bridge design engineer to stop each traveler and inform him of the risk of crossing the bridge. But it is not foolish to expect the bridge design engineer to do his or her legal, professional, and honorable duty to protect every person who uses the creation. Is this practical? If it were not, all of us would risk death every minute of every day—a possibility that conjures up a picture of cave dwellers sitting around a campfire, afraid to go out at night.

Often, it is both practical and morally necessary to secure each individual's informed consent. In order to apply this simple ethical concept, technologists must recognize the principles that underpin it. The subject of the experiment should be able to understand, intellectually and emotionally, the request to participate in the experiment. It is also very important to the concept of informed consent that the subject be a rational human being. As you will recall from Chapter 1, a rational human being may be defined as one who desires to avoid death, pain, and loss of opportunity, and to acquire the basic needs of life (food, water, shelter, clothing, etc.). These things are widely recognized as logical and reasonable for human beings to desire.[2] A rational person neither seeks pain nor gives up food—nor, I believe, does a rational person inflict pain on or deny food to another human being.[d]

> **Genuine informed consent can occur only when a rational person is not under any duress or pressure to obey an authority.**

For instance, the pressure to keep a job in order to support one's family can be undue duress. Probably the technologists involved with the Hyatt Regency and Challenger disasters were under this type of indirect duress—or, at least, they may have thought so.

Most of us are under indirect duress when we choose to participate in "experimental" technologies. People living downstream of a dam or downwind of a nuclear power plant usually have no real concept of the inherent dangers. These people may not be able to move elsewhere for a variety of economic and cultural reasons. Indirect duress can take many forms; there is always pressure to forget about the things that should trouble us at night.

Is the duress indirect or direct when we eat genetically altered foods? Would it make a difference if we knew the food was altered before we ate it? Would it be morally and socially responsible to provide our new, under-tested, experimental, genetically altered foods to starving populations in Africa or elsewhere? Questions like these are not easily answered. But asking the troubling questions is a necessary first step for technologists to discern right from wrong.

The public trusts technologists, corporate America, and government leaders to do the right thing. Why? Because most people believe the experts would not place them at risk for

---

[d] I realize that this statement has possible exceptions: The issues of assisted suicide and mercy killings of the terminally ill come to mind. I, too, have a living will. But under normal circumstances, where the person wants to live, the definition remains essentially accurate.

preventable man-made disasters. Thousands and thousands of people have been dead wrong.

Many technologists and community leaders convince themselves that it is not possible to provide full disclosure about potentially life-threatening products. They may even hide the troubling truth or their own doubts from themselves. There is an alternative, of course: Creators of technology could simply stop the development and application of potentially dangerous creations until they have been fully tested. However, we usually do not want to place our careers in jeopardy, or abandon the enjoyment of the act of creation, or accept responsibility for a decline in the value of our company's stock. These rationalizations are the essence of the Code.

The fine print about potential hazards on a manufacturer's label is not adequate for informed consent. The person reading the fine print may not be able to understand it for a variety of reasons. If you have ever tried to read the extremely technical and very small print on disclosure sheets placed in some medicine bottles, you know what I mean. If we stopped to read those things, most of us would not dare consume the pills.

The awareness of the problem of informed consent has led governments to try to protect us with regulatory agencies like the Environmental Protection Agency (EPA), the Occupational Safety and Health Administration (OSHA), and the Federal Aviation Administration (FAA). Before OSHA came into existence, the number of deaths and injuries per person-work-hour was much higher in my profession of engineering and construction.[3]

The work environments during the industrial age have placed human beings in contact with toxic materials and with unsafe machines. Predictable deaths and injuries have resulted. The truth can be painful and costly for creators, but the denial of the truth can be catastrophic for other human beings and for our planet.

The Truth in Great Ideas

A general familiarity with the great ideas will help us understand the concept and application of ethical theories in the workplace. They will help an open-minded person ask the right questions. Philosopher Mortimer Adler writes, "Philosophy is everybody's business."[4] Technologists during the 20th century did not always live up to Adler's expectations and appeals to rational thought.

Even without realizing it, we often use the language of the great ideas—words like *good, bad, right, wrong, unjust, evil, ethical, moral*—to discuss and evaluate the human condition.

> **Great ideas are not the property of philosophers and theologians. Technologists should get to know them.**

These ideas contain the basic concepts that attempt to describe the world in which we live and to provide insights into how to live a good life. The concepts can help us understand ourselves, our society or culture, and our diverse world.

Most of us have heard the succinct assertion that "life is a process." It is not easy to fully grasp the significance of this little nugget of truth. A normal person desires to live a life worth living and, amidst the constant change, to give this right to everyone. Our ancestors have provided the building blocks with which to accomplish this goal by better understanding our world and our place in it.

 Adler, like many other philosophers, dedicated much of his life to identifying and sharing the richness of great ideas. In his popular book *Six Great Ideas*, Adler writes in everyday language about truth, goodness, beauty, liberty, equality, and justice. Understanding the meaning of each idea often leads us to identify new issues and ideas that we

should confront, especially in this technological era. Adler believed that before one can understand and truly want justice, equality, and liberty for others, one must understand the concept of truth. The truth we find in great ideas can also lead to the discovery of the truth about our selves.

No one can know all truths. In the process of living, wise persons pursue knowledge, truth, and wisdom as much as possible. They then make judgments based on this limited knowledge. You and I make these judgments every day. Most of us settle for knowledge or information that supports an idea well enough to persuade other rational persons to accept it as true.

The journey toward genuine self may involve aspects of spirituality, religion, philosophy, and psychology, but the crucial component is the personal courage to explore one's own thoughts, beliefs, and reasons for individual actions. It is a difficult road, and yet it is a necessary journey if a person wants to live a life worth living.

I cannot, in this short space, provide the wealth of knowledge, truths, and wisdom found in the great ideas.

> But I can challenge technologists and others to look deep inside themselves and beyond their world of specialized knowledge.

In our democratic republic, the great ideas of liberty, equality, and justice for others should not be just words in a book. These ideas should inform the way we live our day-to-day lives and perform in our occupations or professions. Not to do so makes a citizen of this country a hypocrite, at best. If you have not begun this wonderful journey, I encourage you to discover for yourself this wealth of knowledge and wisdom. The references and endnotes in this book are only one place to begin.[5]

The discovery of our true, authentic selves, coupled with our recognition of external truths about the world in which we live, can provide us technologists with the impetus to accept individual moral and social responsibility for our actions. The search for the truth about our genuine selves persuades and lures each of us to reflect—about our individual experiences and about the real feelings connected with those experiences.

Success in this self-discovery process requires a desire to do it; coercion by others will not work. The journey toward discovery of genuine self is often the first step for many of us, and it helps us to understand the deep truths about the interrelatedness of all life on Earth and possibly beyond. These things are the essence of the great ideas that Adler and others have cherished. The search for truth at the most basic level of the human condition is an endless road, a journey toward personal moral and social responsibility.

Repression of the Truth

Recall for a moment the role of technologists who were responsible for the design and construction of the killing machines of Nazi Germany. They suppressed and then repressed their awareness of the terrible events around them in order to be able to continue. They were living a lie about their roles in the genocide.

Sigmund Freud and others have written extensively about the concepts of suppression and repression. Sometimes, these coping mechanisms can be useful; at other times, they can be deadly. The Nazi designers of death who were not sociopaths[e] must have used these mechanisms in order to justify and commit the horrible crimes against humanity. They simply tried not to think about what they were doing until, finally, the suppression gave way to complete repression—no conscious awareness of doing anything immoral.[6]

As you read in Chapter 1, the Nazis' chief engineer was afraid of losing his job and his status in society if he did not work for the Nazi German government. He proceeded to use his creative

---

[e] If a person has the capacity to distinguish right from wrong actions, then he can choose. If a person does not have this ability, mental health experts call the individual a sociopath.

energy, and that of many others, to design and to build an efficient, cost-effective infrastructure for the infamous death camps. The technologists responsible for the Hyatt Regency Hotel collapse and the Challenger explosion tried to shift blame to others, and, much like the Nazi designers of death, many of them would not accept responsibility for their actions. These are classic examples of suppression and repression, mechanisms that lie at the core of the Code of Silence.

> **A person who suppresses simply tries not to think about some thing or event that continues to trouble him.**

When we suppress troubling thoughts long enough, they move deeper into our psyches, so that we do not have to think about them anymore. When we suppress thoughts and memories long enough, they fall through a kind of trap door in our minds.

Active suppression consumes a lot of energy, so repression can close the mind with this trap door. However, under the right circumstance, repressed memories can return from time to time. The troubling thoughts may haunt a person until, somehow, the trap door opens ever so slightly, and he is forced to relive the past. The repressed memories again become active, and the troubling thoughts return.

Many people can experience recurring cycles of suppression and repression if they do not find effective treatment. Combat veterans, abused children, victims of violent crimes, some creators of man-made disasters, and even the rescuers at these disasters often use suppression and repression to cope with trauma. They may not understand the terms or consciously recognize the process, but it can keep them alive until they can effectively deal with the underlying problems in their inner selves.

Some technologists say that it is always someone else's responsibility to confront the evil person, organization, or government that misuses technology. At least, many professionals seem to want to believe this myth. From the Titanic disaster forward, many technologists and other professionals have repressed their genuine selves and denied their empathetic human feelings. They have chosen to go about their daily lives and jobs seemingly blind to the reality around them.

> **A person whose true self is repressed is characteristically unwilling to accept personal responsibility for his or her actions.**

Hiding troubling thoughts from conscious awareness leads some people to trample on the rights of others. To paraphrase President John F. Kennedy, "When the rights of one individual are diminished, the rights of everyone are diminished."

Most survivors and rescuers at man-made disasters have one thing in common: a Post Traumatic Stress Disorder (PTSD). One could argue that our whole profession, in repressing the truth about its faulty doctrines and its role in preventable disasters, suffers from a kind of PTSD. For a while, this repression works to keep troubling thoughts away, but an innate or inborn desire in most of us to be treated fairly and to treat others fairly intercedes to awaken some of us. It would be difficult to explain how the human species has continued to exist in this technological society without this instinct to be moral.

Bibliography, Notes & Further Reading

[1] For more details about the great ideas, see William S. and Mabel L. Sahakian, *Ideas of the Great Philosophers*. Mortimer Adler, a well-known philosopher in our time, wrote extensively about great ideas derived from the ancient writers and philosophers such as Aristotle and Plato. Allan Bloom and other humanities educators and writers have called for the great ideas to be taught *with enthusiasm* across the curricula in universities.

[2] This definition was presented during a seminar and workshop on "Ethics Across the Curriculum" taught by Michael Davis in July 1997 (Center for the Study of Ethics in the Professions, Illinois Institute of Technology, Chicago, Illinois).

[3] While finishing this book, I lived in Omaha, Nebraska, the home of one of the largest conglomerates in the world, Peter Kiewit, Inc. Kiewit Construction Company, part of the conglomerate, was profiled in January 2001 in the local newspaper, the *Omaha World Herald* (28 January 2001). The tallest building in Nebraska, First National Center Tower, is under construction by Kiewit, and after 662 days of work, no reportable injuries or deaths have occurred. This is indeed a good record for a 40-story building. When skyscraper mania was rapidly growing in the 1920s and 1930s, the engineers were predicting one death per floor. Hundreds of deaths per building were forecast, expected, and condoned as "the price we pay for progress."

[4] Mortimer J. Adler, *Six Great Ideas* (New York: Collier Books, Macmillan Publishing Co., 1981), 3.

[5] Adler's hundreds of books are well respected and easy to read, but many other authors may provide a good place to begin the search for great ideas. You may want to review the references at the end of each chapter for additional sources. Another good place to start is a search in your public library or on the WorldWideWeb under philosophy, religion, psychology, etc.

[6] For a full discussion of repression and related areas, also see Calvin S. Hall, *A Primer of Freudian Psychology* (New York: A Mentor Book, Penguin Books, 1954).

Chapter 10
The Instinct to Be Moral

Why Be Moral?

Why be moral? This question lies at the heart of the human condition, and searching minds over thousands of years have struggled with the quandary that it poses. Many of my engineering and construction students helped me to focus attention on this important question.

This chapter is about the lessons I have learned from experience and education and, most importantly of all, from my students. I discovered from teaching engineering ethics for a decade that the most pressing question on the students' minds was—Why be moral? To answer that question to their satisfaction, I soon discovered that I needed to know *why I should be moral.* Not my students, not someone else, but *me.*

So, I began my own search for answers to the question by trying to understand the nature of evil and by questioning my level of moral development. This process took me down a road less traveled, a quest for the truth about my "self." I wanted to know what my true beliefs were and what roles family history, genetics, education, and other factors had played in those true beliefs. In other words, I needed to know my self, even the stuff that I did not want to think about.

The connections among all these factors and many more have highlighted, at least for me, the dichotomy between professional success as an ambitious engineer, businessperson, lawyer, or member of any other occupation and potential personal failure as a husband, father, or human being. Eventually, this path of discovery made much clearer to me the connection between workplace ethics and the question that had begun my search— Why should I be moral? Determining right from wrong depends on answering honestly this troubling question.

I have outlined for you my continuing journey to know the truth about my self because the process convinced me that human beings have an instinct to be moral. Exploring the social sciences, acquiring knowledge about psychology and world religions, and searching through the great books and great ideas helped me immensely on this journey. So, I have taken the time and space in this book to try to explain the connections among these aspects of my view of reality. If, in the following pages, the arguments seem hurried or incomplete, it is because my ongoing journey to know the truth—as best I can at any given moment—is also incomplete.

Let's begin this discovery process with the ability to know the difference between right and wrong, good and evil. If a person has the capacity to distinguish right from wrong actions, then he can choose to do either. If a person does not have this ability, mental health experts call the individual a sociopath. A rational person, as defined earlier, recognizes the value of personal morality—whether or not he always acts in ways that are congruent with this knowledge.

> **At least, a rational person should know the difference between good and bad, right and wrong actions.**

Non-human life forms appear to operate primarily on the basis of instincts.[a] Their actions seem to be based only on self-preservation, or the will to survive, and it is widely accepted that this instinct dwells in all living organisms, including human beings.

We seem to be programmed genetically to fight for survival. But humans, with our large brains, have evolved to use

---

[a] Later, I will discuss that these "appearances" can be deceiving because many animals including some primates, dogs, and elephants have emotions and reasoning abilities similar to human beings.

reasoning to help make decisions about competing ideas and actions. This ability is what most people call innate and learned intelligence, purportedly indicated in the Intelligence Quotient (IQ) number derived from standardized tests.

Psychologists, educators, and medical doctors are becoming increasingly aware of a different but equally important way to measure intelligence. Emotional Intelligence, or EQ, also helps us choose among alternatives.[1] We can think and reason about life and death, about our relationship to others, and about the future—in other words, about the components of the human condition. Rational and morally autonomous human beings know instinctively that anyone who harms another person places his or her own life in jeopardy. If I have a right to injure someone for my personal gain, what prevents my victim from injuring me for the same reason? Logically, nothing does.

One way of thinking about the word "moral" makes more sense to me than all the others combined. Recall for a moment the genuine evil found in the horrors and destruction of the Holocaust. Technologists made it possible and made the process work efficiently. The consequences of the negligence of the Hyatt Regency engineers and the silence of some technologists at Challenger's launch define the word "immoral" better than any philosopher's or theologian's definition.

No definition, philosophical discourse, or religious argument can better convey the sense of the word "moral" than the terror and injustice in these types of events. EQ enables a normal person to understand intuitively and to empathize, and thus to recognize the immorality and be repulsed by both the active and passive forms of evil.

Fully evolved and rational human beings search for satisfactory answers about standards of honorable conduct that we ought to follow. In Part One, I defined morality as the ability to determine, and to act in accordance with, what is right and wrong based on standards common to all societies. The classical thinkers over the centuries have argued that we ought to be concerned with right and wrong and to act consistently on the principles of conduct that promote virtuous behavior.

According to modern-day philosopher Michael Davis, "morality is the standard of conduct that every rational person wants everyone else to follow, even if it means also having to follow the same standard."[2] This definition at first sounds self-serving, but if we did not have this standard of conduct, societies would not be possible.

The basic question "Why be moral?" generates two related and more specific questions: "Why should *we* be moral?" and "Why should *I* be moral?"[3] Rational human beings know intuitively why we, as a society, should do what is right. If people in a society were not moral most of the time, there would be constant chaos and anarchy. Affairs in business require honesty and fairness among participants.

Imagine a world where you expected that everyone was lying all the time. Business and commerce would stop. Can you also imagine a society in which it was acceptable to commit murder without question or punishment? Constant fear would paralyze people, and we would revert to the premise "kill or be killed." For civilization to exist, our collective interests require moral conduct most of the time from most citizens. Moral conduct for survival seems to be a truth transcending cultural and national boundaries.

We *should* be moral for collective reasons so that society can exist and improve the human condition. But what should convince us as individuals to be moral? Are there not benefits to being a thief when everyone else is honest? Crime will pay sometimes, right? In other words, why should *I* be moral?

> **An individual accrues more long-term benefits from being moral than from not being moral.**

They include an increase in true personal happiness, less psychic pain (internal suffering of the self), and less social ostracism. To reiterate, a rational person does not want to face these problems that could threaten his individual survival. A normal person desires to avoid pain.

The two engineers found to be negligent for the Hyatt Regency collapse lost their personal reputations, their company's reputation, and even their professional livelihoods. Hundreds of employees probably became unemployed because of these engineers' negligence. Some Hyatt contractors lost their businesses, and their suppliers lost revenue. Large out-of-court monetary settlements reflected the agony for all involved. The actions and lack of appropriate actions by a few men to fulfill professional responsibilities have a devastating effect on the lives of many innocent people. The human suffering after such tragedies is immense.

> **The point is this: If only the technologists would stop their hurried work long enough to consider the consequences of carelessness, of negligence, of an unexamined inner self, perhaps fewer disasters would occur.**

The shame and dishonor also remain with individual technologists like those involved in the Challenger's explosion. Family members and business partners must have suffered from the ordeal. Loss of respect from peers and family members is a large personal cost. The immoral, *rational* person cannot be happy in any sense of the word, and this internal struggle and tension, called psychic suffering, can literally become a struggle for physical survival. The literature is full of examples from many walks of life that show this cause-and-effect relationship.

The personal reasons to be moral may still sound self-serving, yet they complement the reasons that we as a group should be moral. The life of an organization or society depends upon the behavior of its individual members. If only one or two team members are immoral, the whole team suffers. The organization may survive for a while, but when a key employee or a threshold total number of employees are dishonorable, man-made tragedies and disasters can occur.

The society as a whole suffers when these catastrophes continue to plague us. And the Enron Corporation's financial collapse in 2001 and 2002, in which thousands of employees and investors lost their life savings and retirement benefits because of a few corporate officers, demonstrated that it is not just physical disasters that cause great harm.

I will go one step further in this theory of morality and ethics. Perhaps, in addition to the personal benefits for the individual, we have a primal or innate human need to be moral.

> **The willingness to be moral may be more than a choice. It could be instinctual.**

To love and to be loved by another person seems to be instinctive for rational human beings. The drive to exist and to survive also appears primal and instinctive because of its intensity within all living things. Otherwise, our human condition might drive most of us to the absurdity of suicide.

If we combine only these two human needs, love and self-preservation, which are widely assumed to be intrinsic to the human species, perhaps a reasonable answer to the age-old question is possible. The underlying reason why each of us should be moral relates directly to the love of life itself. To be moral is logical and not narcissistic at all. To love life and to love others as we should love our own life is rational. Our personal need to be moral is crucially connected with our ability to understand the interrelatedness of all human beings.

My knowledge, experiences, observations, and soul strongly suggest that normal humans have an inborn, primal need or drive to be moral. Can I prove this instinctual need exists? Of course not. But I hope it does. We humans cannot prove a lot of things, and yet we continue to act in ways congruent with their existence, which in turn helps us make sense of the world around us.

Perhaps my view that humans have an instinct to be moral is idealistic. Yet, I would rather err on the side of optimism than assume evil is innate. Students were consistently more honest and empathetic when I assumed them to be. This observation also rings true for those of us who raise children. So, why should we be moral?

> **Because the alternative—not being moral—degrades the value of human life and of all life forms, and can result in anarchy and chaos in societies.**

The failure to be moral could lead to the death of our species. Why should *I* be moral? Because not to do so would harm my own "self," which can lead to destructive behaviors. Thus, persons in touch with their feelings desire to be morally responsible for good and logical reasons. They include (1) a stable society where equality, liberty, and justice are available to everyone, and (2) less pain in our own souls, bodies, and minds.

Continued progress toward a just and good society depends upon individuals' sense of moral responsibility to their genuine selves and to others who share this planet. All life is interrelated and interdependent—this is what I have come to understand as the basis of the human condition. The search for answers to troubling questions should be recognized as necessary for our growth and for our survival as a species.

In the sections that follow, I discuss the interdependence of all life and its connection with ethics in the workplace. To better explain this concept, I will again tread softly into the philosopher's domain to examine the idea of genuine evil. Thousands of books try to explain evil in all contexts, and that is beyond the scope of this book—and my abilities. Instead, I will limit my discussion to the context of man-made disasters and technologists' roles in them.

Genuine Evil and Interrelatedness

A paradigm for the human condition that does not include genuine evil does not have a foundation in reality. Therefore, the following ideas form the foundation of my current philosophical understanding about life and its meaning. It may not be your understanding, but that is okay. My insights continue to mature as I search for answers to another question that has plagued objective human beings: Why is there so much evil in the world?

Evil is real. As I wrote earlier, it can be active or passive—intentional acts or the lack of action to stop evil when it appears. In other words, genuine evil happens because human beings cause or allow it to happen. No one and nothing can force a person to commit evil; it is a personal choice made by everyone but a sociopath. One may have to be prepared to die to resist forces of evil; but a person at his or her rational best may choose to be killed rather than submit.[b]

Help does exist to recognize and to resist genuine evil. This help is available to every person who wants it, and it resides within each of us—within a person's deepest being, the inner self.[c] It is a persuasive, non-coercive "life-force"[d] that resides within us, and this life-force can help us search for answers to troubling questions about the human condition.

This eternal life-force allows us to connect our self-discovery to our relationship with the rest of the world. The life force is also external to each individual, because it resides in all human beings, and perhaps in other species as well. Both the

---

[b] This statement may seem to contradict my definition of a rational person, but as you will read later in this chapter, the conscious awareness of an instinct to be moral occurs in three stages of development. In the last stage of moral development, self-sacrifice can be a rational act when confronting evil.

[c] I defined this earlier, but for your convenience, here it is again. The word "self" is the word I prefer in the context of this book. Others may recognize my concept in the religious word "soul," while others may recognize it as "ego, superego, and id" in the Freudian psychological sense.

[d] I will use the phrase "life-force" to describe a transcendent essence. Others may be more comfortable using a more common term such as "God," "Yahweh," etc. I apologize for any misunderstanding that may arise from my choice of terminology. My desire is to create an awareness of a source of strength and knowledge beyond our own selves and yet within us, and at the same time, not to become involved in organized religions' semantics.

internal and external manifestations of the life-force can lure a person to extend his or her appreciation, acceptance, promotion, and protection of the basic human rights of others.

Those who are in touch with their true selves discover that they should also act toward others in ways congruent with this understanding of their selves and of the life-force. These discoveries also cause us to view in a much different perspective our beliefs and our actions in our private and our working lives. We learn to view them as interdependent and inseparable. At this level of understanding, we become conscious of a self-evident truth—the need for personal moral and social responsibility in our daily lives, no matter where we may be.

> **Congruence between personal beliefs and professional actions can mean harmony of mind, body, and soul.**

This natural process of self-discovery is intrinsic to human beings, because it is rational to want life, health, shelter, absence of pain, and so forth. And it follows that a rational human being's sense of right and wrong is intuitive and inborn. To believe otherwise would mean accepting a doctrine of humankind that is contrary to most theological and philosophical positions.

The only doctrine of humankind that is logical and intuitive for me is this: Human beings are born good and learn evil, not born evil and then learning good.[e] As I wrote earlier, to be moral is an act of self-preservation, which is perhaps built into our genes through instincts. We stray from this instinctual behavior for a host of reasons that psychologists, the clergy, philosophers, and many others have tried for centuries to explain.

The Code of Silence is one symptom of this departure from our moral true self. The practice of this Code, with its

---

[e] This position is congruent with the concept that human beings were created in the "image of God." If God is good, as most people assert, then all human beings are born with a knowledge of what is good, just, etc., for themselves and others.

characteristic internal and external silence, with its passive and active forms of evil, diminishes opportunities for the non-coercive life-force to have a positive effect. Novel ideas for solutions to today's problems can come from this life-force, but each individual human being should be ready and willing to listen for new insights—and then to implement novel solutions.

Life is an adventurous process where we should learn from the past, take into account the present situation, listen to the life-force, and then make a rational and intuitive decision. This decision, in a specific knowledge domain like technology, should be a result of four steps:[f]

1. Gather appropriate past knowledge.
2. Study the written discourse about that past knowledge.
3. Study current discourse about all appropriate and related existing knowledge.
4. Listen for and use novel possibilities found within one's true self with the help of the life-force.

Technologists' decisions about life and death should be based on knowledge that we think and feel is right for all life. We should feel what others feel and put ourselves into their shoes—this is called empathy before the fact, not sympathy after the fact. Then we might not be so willing to experiment on others in such a callous and indifferent manner as history has shown is possible.

People trust technologists to do the right thing. My privilege as an engineer to create should be grounded in and based upon your guaranteed right to survive—and to thrive. Anything short of this premise is inherently flawed and destructive for all life forms.

My concept of the interrelatedness of all life and the effect of this innate, persuasive life-force comes from many sources and experiences. One primary source is my understanding of *Process*

---

[f] This four-pronged approach is not new, just worded a bit differently. For instance, the United Methodist Church embraces a similar four-step process, called the "Quadrilateral," to discover truth.

Thought.[4] Process Thought provides for the possibility of novel ideas from within us with the help of a transcendent source that is in all human beings. Process philosophy and theology can motivate us to examine our own existence in relation to the rest of the world, and these concepts confront us with the distinct possibility that the universe does not revolve around human beings and our creations.

> **All life forms are interdependent, and human beings possess the same survival instincts as other species. In addition, our related instinct to be moral spawns the rights of life, liberty, and the pursuit of happiness for all human beings.**

Obviously, some people do not want to examine their cherished beliefs and myths, and as a result, they follow other true believers into a spectrum of evil. Man-made disasters prove that many technologists and their accomplices have ignored available wisdom from the past, suppressed or hidden from their "selves" disturbing information, and denied or ignored any possibility of transcendent truth. The interrelatedness of all life requires each of us to break free of the narcissistic early childhood stages of moral development.

The Process of Moral Development

Well-known scientist Lawrence Kohlberg conducted research on moral behavior and found that humans exhibit

different levels of moral development as they grow older.[5] Kohlberg's research showed three levels of moral development that he labeled pre-conventional, conventional, and post-conventional. Later researchers have suggested that Kohlberg's research had a male bias, but the levels of development have been confirmed.[6] Figure 9 illustrates the three levels of behavioral development first proposed by Kohlberg. I have added my concept of true self to the mix.

Post-Conventional Level

- True self in process
- Golden Rule is standard
- Autonomous and universal thinking
- Chooses to be moral

Conventional or Social Level

- False self often in control
- Group norm is standard
- Obedient/loyal to authority
- Pleases others for personal gain

Pre-Conventional Level

- Developing a sense of "self"
- Obeys authority to avoid pain
- No concept of empathy for others
- Narcissistic state to survive

Figure 9: Levels of Moral Development

At the pre-conventional level, a person acts in ways that directly benefit him without regard to others. The child learns to cry when hungry or to get attention. And a child quickly learns how to avoid pain. Children learn to behave in ways in which authority figures or parents want them to behave. They avoid knocking the clock from the table, for example, to avoid getting punished. These acts are rational for a young child, who does not think about the long-term consequences of his actions but instinctively wants to survive.

If an adult continues to behave at this earliest level of moral development, he will defer to authority to achieve personal gain without regard to the welfare of others. It is a narcissistic state of being, and while some people remain in it throughout adulthood, it is irrational for adults to do so.

When a child matures to the point that he develops a sense of "self" and of the world around him, he becomes conscious of the innate and instinctual need to be moral, both collectively and individually. He or she now has the ability to choose a course of action. To choose not to be moral, as I discussed earlier, is irrational.

Kohlberg's second level of moral development, or the conventional level, is one step higher than the child-like behavior of the first level. At this conventional or social level, a person wants to follow the norms of family, groups, and professional societies. The standards of these groups are the final standards for behavior at this conventional level, and the group standards are accepted without much thought as to their moral implications or long-term consequences. The person remains obedient to authority, with a heightened desire to please others and to be loyal to them. As a result, his self-identity is closely tied to those authority figures in the organization, company, or university.

At this conventional level, we can choose to live a false self, a self that is controlled by someone's expectation of us. Freud called this effect the superego, or the part of the mind influenced by others.[7] We can choose to ignore and to suppress our genuine self at this level of moral development. Some of us manage to get beyond this stage, but often technologists acquiesce to authority, as the Challenger disaster demonstrated.

The last level of moral development, the post-conventional stage, involves a search for our genuine self or true self. According to Kohlberg, we choose to be moral because it is the right thing to do. His view appears to coincide with my theory that human beings have an instinctual need to be moral. Kohlberg says that we arrive at this autonomous level of thinking through acceptance of others' rights.

At this last level, Kohlberg believes that we recognize the general good from this position of acceptance. Our choice to do what is good is not reducible to the self-interest of level one or the social conventions of level two. The Golden Rule is thought to be universal truth at this level of moral development.

Psychologists and others may disagree about the exact stages of moral development through which human beings travel, but there is general agreement that most people strive to reach stage three. It is an internal need to be an authentic human being.

So, why don't more of us reach this level of understanding? The answer lies deep within us, in our understanding of authentic, genuine, or true self. Normal human beings search for the truth about themselves and the world around them. It is instinctual to do so.

The Quest for Truth about Our "Self"

Earlier, I linked a human being's instinctual need to be moral with the self-evident truth of the interrelatedness and interdependence of all life. These two things are directly connected to an instinctual need to know one's genuine or true self. Without this self-knowledge and the ability to use it, bad things can and do happen—both privately within our individual psyches and publicly within our workplaces. For many of us, the desire and will to "know thyself" is the first step toward understanding the great ideas of liberty, equality, and justice for others.

A technologist hides from her genuine self when she pretends not to recognize the harm that she is doing to others—and to her inner self. It is a technologist's moral and social responsibility and duty to protect the lives of other people, even those she does not know or may never meet. Previously, I have described the state in which technologists pretend to be somebody or something they are not—the false self. This false self is a primary symptom of the Code of Silence and of the man-made disasters described in Part One. A very different road exists that can lead a rational person toward an understanding of his or her genuine self.

What is a true or genuine self? The concept may be easier to describe than to define. However, we need a working definition of genuine self to continue our search for the truth about man-made disasters.

> **A genuine self can be defined as a rational person who is conscious of the instinctual need to be an authentic human being.**

This awareness of need has both internal and external manifestations. An individual does not have to be conscious of these instinctual needs for them to be present. A genuine self will desire (1) to search for inner self-knowledge, (2) to live a life worth living, and (3) to act congruently with these truths in private and in public. It is not enough just to believe these things to be true; a genuine self desires and acts to live these truths every day—at home and at work.

The opposite of being genuine is pretending to be something we are not. A false self may pretend that he has no control over evil around him or within him. He may pretend it is not his responsibility to try to change things, or he may even pretend that evil simply does not exist. Pretending can be disastrous, both personally and collectively within society.

When a technologist thinks about the unethical things happening around him and in him, he has started down the road toward genuine self and to a life worth living. At the time, he may not have questioned the problems publicly, and perhaps he may have suppressed the troubling thoughts for a while. But the search for personal authenticity has begun when a person recognizes that an ethical dilemma exists.

> **Personal authenticity or genuineness is a journey, not a destination.**

The quest for the true self has been part of the human condition even before the time of Plato. The ways in which we choose to conduct our public lives as expressed in our work or profession affect our internal self and, of course, affect those around us in profound ways.

I wrote earlier about my concept of part of the human condition—we are emotional as well as rational beings.[g] Daniel Goleman argues convincingly in *Emotional Intelligence* that feelings are indispensable for good decision-making.[8] Goleman presents persuasive evidence that we have two distinct brains or minds, and our emotional intelligence (EQ) may be more important than our IQ for living a good life. He says, "Reason is not freed from emotion."[9] Recognizing these connections can lead to better decisions in all aspects of one's life.

Those who claim that the scientific method is the only way to make good decisions fail to realize that reason or logic is not so pure and infallible as many would have us believe. A rational person intuitively knows and desires to use both measures of intelligence to make decisions. A person may block the process for a time. But it is a natural process that maturing children seem to unlearn and adults have to relearn.

The journey toward genuine self is fraught with pitfalls. Mental health professionals have told us that we put many barriers in place to limit our knowledge of our distinct, genuine self. Our tendency to hide from conscious awareness our past experiences (not necessarily just from childhood) often contribute to destructive behaviors.

The destructive behavior can be directed outward toward others or inward toward our own inner self. Either way, what we fail to acknowledge as destructive behaviors will persist. This suppression can lead to severe mental stress, to mental disorders,

---

[g] We have two measures of human intelligence, the intelligence quotient or IQ and our emotional intelligence quotient or EQ.

to physical diseases, and even to an early death.[h] The inability to acknowledge the past and its influence on the present and the future can lead technologists to make bad decisions.

John Bradshaw writes in his book *On The Family*, "To live and never know who I really am is the greatest tragedy of all."[10] The discovery of our genuine self can bring moral autonomy and independence from the pressures of society and from authoritarian leaders who want us to conform to their true beliefs. According to Bradshaw, "It was total obedience without *critical judgment and inner freedom* (my emphasis) which led to black Nazism, Jonestown, and My Lai."[11]

The process of looking inside one's own belief system can be painful, but it is necessary in order to live—and to let others live—a life worth living. It becomes much easier to follow anyone who promises to take away our personal responsibility and the pain that accompanies suppression and repression. "Avoiding pain is the basis of mental illness," according to M. Scott Peck.[12]

> **We should accept responsibility for our actions, according to Peck, because "neuroses and character disorders are disorders of responsibility."[13]**

The desire to travel the road toward personal authenticity can foster the growth of our natural and innate need to be ethical in our actions. As Peck observes, "Love is a willingness to extend one's self for the purpose of nurturing one's own or others' spiritual growth."[14] The love of one's genuine self (not the harmful narcissistic selfish love) is directly connected to our well-being and to the well-being of those around us.

When we cannot love our own self, we cannot love and protect the lives of others. This individual spiritual growth and the acceptance of personal moral and social responsibility are

---

[h] These effects have been amply documented in the literature of psychology from Freud and his followers onward.

necessary to stop the conspiracy to hide the Code of Silence and its connections to man-man disasters.

The lack of acceptance of personal responsibility can be described as "soul murder, if we lose contact with our own feelings," according to Bradshaw.[15] When we journey toward genuine self, we become more aware of our interdependence in the world. The old saying "live and let live" rings true. This process of discovery can bring elasticity and resilience to adverse change, which can help us to recover.[16] We are at less risk of becoming blind followers of an evil system when we have resilience.

When we can develop an active concern for others, we have moved away from an obsession with our narcissistic selves. We are then able to accept the genuine importance of all life as a truth worthy of implementation in our private and public lives. The path to personal authenticity is a difficult journey to undertake while trying to compete in our workplaces, but it can lead to a life of value and worth.

Professional Success and Personal Failure

Sam Keene in *Fire in the Belly* identifies "warfare, conquest, and competition" as the path most traveled, and he used those terms as they apply to our business environment in the United States.[17] All too often, university students upon graduation head into large corporations or large government agencies where personal identity is lost, where 60- to 70-hour workweeks are common, and where frequently moving from one job to another disrupts family life.

> The business world of technological advancement is a game of conquest and competition, and this game is learned at our universities that specialize in skill-building curricula.

The obsession to fit into corporate life and to be one of the team can lead to job burnout. We try to live up to the expectations of society without questioning the value of those demands on us and on our family. Keene adds "rustout" to burnout as a problem within corporate America, which includes the business of technology. He writes that rustout is a type of combat fatigue caused by a lack of passion in what we do.[18] This lack of passion to "do it right the first time" seems to increase as people's careers wind down during their forties and fifties.

Boredom and depression caused by the competition to succeed and to make a living cause rustout and burnout, according to Keene. The hurried life seldom allows time for any true enjoyment of life that goes beyond bottom-line profits. Unfortunately, human beings tend to adapt, at least for a time, to conditions that allow little time for the search for genuine self. We are driven by the desire to keep our jobs and status in the community.

Keene's observations about the high price of success in the business world[19] describe a symptom of the Code of Silence that exists in the creation and application of technology:

> If the competition is always pressing you to produce more and faster, if life is a battle, if winning is the only thing, sooner or later you are going to come down with battle fatigue. They become disillusioned and numb to ethical issues; they think only of survival and grow insensitive to pain.

Business warriors and workaholics resemble substance abusers in many ways. Both obsess about the next fix or the next project or the next creation when they become disillusioned and numb to the reality of their own condition and the plight of others affected by their fixations. The workaholic has repressed the truth about the troubling question: What of value am I creating—and destroying—in the way that I am living and working? Both types of abusers of mind, body, and true self try to escape the instinct to be moral, the internal and external lure to discern right from wrong. In time, these behaviors can destroy other human values needed for an authentic and genuine life.[20]

Today more than ever, the true believers in our super-competitive worldwide corporate culture demand that their employees (warriors) obey the ethics, the priorities, and the goals of the "company." And this policy usually means attention is focused on short-term, bottom-line profits for the corporation. Our work, where we earn our living, has become "The" life of many technologists.

The corporations that employ most of the technologists constantly bombard their employees with this theme. Corporate leaders cultivate the delusion that happiness comes only from work. Of course, they mean only work at their company. It becomes an oppressive family environment, a culture that defines right and wrong for the employee.

When the technologist moves to another company family with different values, or works in a foreign country, she can become confused about good and evil. Decisions about right and wrong begin to look relative: Those who make the rules dictate right and wrong. And for some technologists who want to give up autonomous thinking and moral reasoning, this corporate "family" can become a safe haven: "I was only following orders" is their battle cry.

While I was writing this chapter, a publication by my university caught my eye. The Career Center at the University of Nebraska in Omaha illustrated in its newsletter the misplaced priorities for a life worth living. The center offered students the following prescription for happiness:[21]

If You Want To Be Happy:

For a minute.........eat a peach

For an hour..........watch a sunset

For a day............go fishing

For six months.....get married

For a year...........inherit a fortune

For a lifetime.......**enjoy your work**

Based on this university publication, leaders in higher education in effect tell students that work is the most important thing in life. My experiences in industry and in the universities confirm that this Career Center in Nebraska echoes the prevailing attitude. According to its newsletter, marriage is far down the list of priorities.

It is sad and troubling when universities and corporations promote the value of work over that of committed relationships and marriage. Even if the Career Center's managers were trying to express their views about the trends in real life, they reinforced in many students the belief that their jobs should be everything. Taken literally, the statements suggest putting work before marriage and before raising a family.

This obsession with happiness at work promised by the "company" does not lead to the discovery of the genuine self or the beauty of interdependence of all life. Instead, it leads to the death of self and often results in the early death of one's physical body—and certainly contributes to the high divorce rate. A well-known proverb underscores the problem:

> **Do not think you are on the right road just because it is a well-beaten path.**

In our society, we learn to play the game of pleasing others to get what we want. Technologists, particularly engineers and scientists, play the game well in their professions, and this behavior is consistent with their common characteristics and college education.

Ralph Waldo Emerson is credited with saying, "A foolish consistency is the hobgoblin of little minds." When technologists or others believe their job is the most important thing in life, then families will be diminished and societies will be damaged. Emerson was right about the foolishness of destructive repeated behaviors. The blue- or white-collar worker may bring home the suppressed anger and become violent or simply withdraw from family and social life. Examples of the tragic consequences of these types of behavior are in the news every day. The phrase "going postal" is familiar to most of us because of so many workplace shootings during the 1990s. This symptom of disorder within the self is a cry for help.

The importance of the interrelatedness among our work world, our private family life, and our selves cannot be overstated. The real hobgoblin, the Code of Silence, continues to infect many technologists, making ethics in the workplace a battleground.

The Connection with Ethics

Personal and business values and the actions based on these values must be congruent for one's genuine self to emerge and to flourish. If they are not, the chaos in one's life will result in much personal psychic pain and even mental illness. The Code of Silence reflects this chaos, and preventable disasters illustrate the disorder's effect on the public.

To begin the journey to be moral is an act of our will—the will to go beyond what others tell us that we are or ought to be. The journey creates in each person a desire to be genuine—to be free of false pretenses, deceit, and charades.

A technologist can become a morally autonomous person. This journey gives us a world-view that can lead us to ethical awareness and to the application of ethics in the workplace. It is as if a veil has been lifted from our eyes. Shakespeare recognized this truth when he wrote, "This above all—To thine own self be true and it must follow as the night the day, thou can'st not then be false to any man."

The importance of the interrelatedness of all life on this planet and our place in the process becomes an obvious truth when we seek to understand our genuine self. Ethics in the workplace then makes sense, from both a logical and emotional framework of understanding. Our IQ and EQ have become one.

The acceptance of personal moral and social responsibility for our actions inhibits the growth of the fail-safe mentality and the conspiracy to hide the underlying truth about disasters. The process can begin within each of us with a journey toward genuine self. Ethics and morality, individually and collectively, are indeed entwined.

Bibliography, Notes & Further Reading

[1] This realization grows among professionals who study emotional intelligence. Daniel Goleman wrote one of the first well-written books on the physiological implications of the subject. See Goleman, *Emotional Intelligence* (New York: Bantam Doubleday Dell Publishing Group, Inc., 1995), 28.

[2] I attended a seminar and workshop on "Ethics Across the Curriculum," taught by Michael Davis, in July 1997 (Center for the Study of Ethics in the Professions, Illinois Institute of Technology, Chicago, Illinois). This definition of morality came from Davis's workshop.

[3] These two questions have plagued humankind for a very long time. One of the best books that I have discovered is Kai Nielsen, *Why Be Moral?* (New York: Prometheus Books, 1989).

[4] Alfred North Whitehead, a well-known mathematician of the early 20th century, developed process thought or philosophy into a formal structure. His book *Adventures of Ideas* was first published in 1933 and re-issued in 1961. John B. Cobb and David Ray Griffin expanded Whitehead's ideas into a theology-based concept in *Process Theology: An Introductory Exposition* (Philadelphia: The Westminster Press, 1976). A later book by C. Robert Mesle, *Process Theology* (St. Louis: Chalice Press, 1993), is a good introduction to the subject. However, Cobb's book is more detailed and based more closely on Whitehead's original work. The reality expressed by Whitehead, Cobb, and Mesle about existence and the constant change in our world is far different from the traditional Judeo-Christian concepts about God and the world. Process theology rejects the following five traditional views of God and the world: (1) God as Cosmic Moralist; (2) God as the Unchanging and Passionless Absolute; (3) God as Controlling Power; (4) God as "Sanctioner" of the Status Quo; and (5) God as Male. For more details, see Cobb and Griffin.

[5] Lawrence Kohlberg, *The Philosophy of Moral Development*, Vol. 1 (New York: Harper & Row, 1971).

[6] Martin and Schinzinger, 9-21.

[7] For a widely respected layman's discussion of Freud's constructs of the mind and how we think and act, see Calvin S. Hall, *A Primer of Freudian Psychology* (New York: A Mentor Book, Penguin Books, 1954).

[8] Goleman, 28.

[9] Ibid., 29.

[10] Bradshaw, 20.

[11] Ibid., 19.

[12] M. Scott Peck, *The Road Less Traveled* (New York: A Touchstone Book, Simon & Schuster, 1978), 16.

[13] Ibid., 35.

[14] Ibid., 18.

[15] Bradshaw, 20.

[16] "Bouncing Back from Bad Times," *Harvard Women's Health Watch*, Harvard Health Publications Group, February 1998, 2-3.

[17] Sam Keen, *Fire in the Belly: On Being a Man* (New York: Bantam Books, 1991).

[18] Ibid., 61.

[19] Ibid., 61.

[20] Ibid., 55.

[21] "If You Want to Be Happy," *Career Center Herald*, University of Nebraska at Omaha, Omaha, Nebraska, March/April 1998.

Chapter 11

The Journey Toward Ethics

The Meaning of Ethics

The concepts of ethics are derivatives of philosophical ideas. The pursuit of truth about the human condition and how human beings ought to live is generally thought to be the domain of philosophy. But I have come to understand ethics as philosophy in action, particularly in the workplace—and the desire for ethics in the workplace is a journey, not a destination. In this sense, ethics is the same as the search for genuine or true self that I discussed in the preceding chapter.

Generally, people who are not academics tend to think of ethics as it relates to workplaces. Most of my engineering and technology students had this preconceived notion about the meaning of ethics. For example, professional organizations may have a code of ethical conduct, but they do not have philosophical codes. Various philosophical theories about the human condition exist, each with a limited number of proponents and followers who believe that they have the best theory.

Some academic people in the field of philosophy think of moral philosophy as the foundation for workplace ethics, especially in its use of a common language for ethics. Later in this chapter, I will present an ethics checklist for decision-making, but for now, I want to offer some ethics terminology to use for the remainder of this book. This will not be an extensive discussion of philosophical or ethical models but an introduction to autonomous ethical thinking with the help of the classical great ideas. A common language about ethics helps us to recognize and to solve everyday moral dilemmas in our workplace. This understanding plays a crucial role in preventing disasters and stopping the Code of Silence.

Three primary senses of the word "ethics" are generally accepted among academics.[1] The word can describe a branch of philosophy that deals with moral theories that can be used to pursue the truth regarding some thing or idea. The discerning of truth is not exclusively the domain of scientists and other technologists.

> **Modern-day true believers in the infallibility of the scientific method exhibit the same dangerous egotism as the religious establishment in Galileo's time.**

Different fields of study, including the natural sciences, psychology, theology, and other "ologies," can contribute much to the pursuit of truth about the human condition. So this sense of ethics as a field of philosophy with merit in discovering truth should be included for its contribution to ethical decision-making.

The second sense of the word "ethics" attaches itself to the special standards or codes of conduct for members of certain groups or professions. Ethical standards or codes have value in solving moral dilemmas in the workplace because they can provide a starting point for technologists and others who are unaccustomed to the process. The codes also can be part of a checklist for those who are experienced or inexperienced in ethical decision-making.

Codes of ethical conduct for technologists also can be used to teach technology students and to inform businesspeople about ethics, but codes have limitations, as I will explain later. This sense of the word is perhaps why most people think of the workplace when they think of ethics. For now, the contributions of this sense of the word will be included in the process of solving ethical dilemmas.

The third sense relates to codes of personal behavior, but it comes closer to the meaning many people use when wrestling with the concept of ethics in private life. In the classical sense, "ethics" means ordinary morality of the kind discussed in the last chapter. According to the classical approach to morality, to be moral is to be concerned with right and wrong actions. Aristotle taught that this concept of ethics could be used to describe a good or virtuous person.

This third sense of "ethics" may come closer to the central meaning found in most codes of professional conduct and in most codes of behavior in world religions. This sense of "ethics" as Aristotle might have understood it is included for its contributions to determining right and wrong in the workplace. Workplace actions should be a reflection of ordinary morality for individuals in their private lives.

Understanding all three senses adds a dimension not found in any one particular concept. However, I want to add this vital idea to the three senses of "ethics": A person should also have an *active* concern for right and wrong. This means action, not just word games. Philosophers, ethicists, and religious leaders have been accused of talking at length about right and wrong, but then stopping short of acting on their beliefs to stop genuine evil from spreading in their own backyard. Nazi Germany was a prime example.

Right and Wrong Actions

What makes an action right or wrong, good or bad, moral or immoral? This question directly relates to the senses of the word "ethics." The maze of philosophical definitions can be circular and confusing to many, especially those of us in technology. So, I will try to condense volumes of information to a more manageable size, trusting that philosophers will give me some leeway. Technologists can better apply the codes of professional conduct to everyday ethical dilemmas if we can better understand philosophers' jargon. This was true of the engineering and technology students in my classroom.

In general, "right actions" refers to acceptable good behaviors, or conduct that is ethical. Someone is said to be a good person when his or her behavior is permitted by an *appropriate, permissible standard of conduct.*[2] There is ambiguity and risk in this definition. The permissible standard of conduct can be confused with actions that are deemed good by a specific society but that might not be moral for all human beings.

In other words, some people believe that each society may set its own standards of morality independent of any other group. This belief is what I call the theory of relativity of ethics. This theory should be rejected outright as self-evidently false because of the actions of Nazis, Stalinists, and other evil governments. This relativity is contrary to the two reasons discussed in the preceding chapter for a person and a society to be moral.

 Another ethical theory, pragmatism, is often used to justify harming some people if the majority receive more good. As a metaphor of this theory, which is closely related to utilitarianism, think of the legal profession's symbol of justice, the balance scale. It represents the balancing of claims to the truth. If one side of the scale is heavier and thus tilts downward, that side of the argument is considered better.

Lawyers and judges talk in terms of the preponderance of evidence or proof beyond a reasonable doubt. And preponderance is considered the lower standard, similar to a majority rule. So, our legal system and laws contain the traits of utilitarianism, pragmatism, and other moral philosophies.

At about this point, students sometimes become overwhelmed with definitions. In the classroom, I could be part educator and part performer to help them, and concrete examples were quite useful. For instance, a huge dam creates electrical power, recreation areas, and flood control, and therefore it is said to be good because more people will benefit from the dam than will be harmed. These are valid considerations, but they should not be the only ones.

I would then ask the students this question: Besides the obvious majority-rules problem, what other considerations should be discussed? They would raise the issues of bird habitats, fish protection, pollution by tourists, jobs created and lost, long-term agricultural effects of flood control, and other more pressing social needs for the money. These are also valid considerations. Yet, their omission of one very important consideration added a great deal to my understanding of the Code of Silence.

Usually, the last thing the students would consider was the safety issue for those who live in the river basin below the dam. Dams have failed more than once, as noted in the short list in Appendix A. Suppressing the thought of the worst that could happen in the application of technology is a problem in my profession, and when the worst is considered, it is often discounted through the cost-benefit analysis discussed earlier. For instance, nuclear waste removal, transport, storage, and security remain daunting problems for those who advocate more nuclear power production.

Applying the ethics theories and terminology to these questions was fun at first for my students. But after a while, the seriousness of what they were discussing dawned on them. I could see the transformation in their body language. They began to debate the dam project using such terms as "pragmatism," "informed consent," "justice," "good," and "evil." For example, the realization came to them that the theory of pragmatism discounts the cost attributed to the dislocation of thousands of inhabitants or to the change of a whole ecological system imbalance.

This effect in the classroom of autonomous thinking is one primary reason that I enjoyed teaching—and learning from the students. We were actually wrestling with truth in ideas and how they apply to the real world. This process of questioning true beliefs and accepted practices is the beginning of the end of the Code's influence in engineering and technology.

Mabel and William Sahakian, in their book *Ideas of the Great Philosophers*, provide a nonprofessional's account of criteria of truth and the fallacies of reasoning. These myths have helped to justify unethical actions by the majority—or an act of suppression among technologists. It is little known that pragmatism, or the philosophy of practical consequences, is predominantly American in origin. The theory holds that "if an idea works, it is true" and that anything that is true must have "cash value."[3]

In Chapter 1, I quoted the Accrediting Board for Engineering and Technology for the definition of engineering.[a] The technology professions maintain a keen interest in designing and building things *economically*. The point is this: My profession has too often emphasized economics more than safety. It has not done the right thing for long-term public welfare and safety.

> **This way of doing business is rational neither in terms of ethics nor in terms of survival for life on a small planet.**

A rational human being determines, and acts in accordance with, what is right and wrong on the basis of morally justifiable standards of conduct." I believe these standards must be common to all societies. The person who follows these standards is then said to be moral because of this right action. Some philosophers believe that an appropriate, "permissible standard of conduct" can exist only when all rational human beings of the world want everyone else to follow such a standard, even if it means they also have to follow the same standard.[4]

I agree with this academic definition with one qualification: The use of the word "permissible" in this definition should not be confused with the minimum expectations of some members of an organization that has a written code of ethics. As I write in the next section, one inherent problem with an

---

[a] "Engineering is the profession in which a knowledge of the mathematical and natural sciences gained by study, experience and practice is applied with judgment to develop ways to utilize, *economically*, the materials and forces of nature for the benefit of mankind."

organization's code of ethics could be called the least effort syndrome.

Most codes that I have reviewed over the years contain minimum standards designed to satisfy governmental regulators and consumer watchdog groups. The codes can become stale, irrelevant, outdated, and ignored almost as quickly as they are written if upper management does not fully understand and implement the codes. Unethical technologists find loopholes in codes, and then, they use the code to justify their actions because the code did not specifically prohibit the harmful actions. Other members may not follow the intent of the code because, among other reasons, the code is badly written. The code becomes the least that one *must* do instead of the most effort that one *could* do. On the other hand, a "permissible" standard of conduct for all human beings is maximum effort by individuals who desire to be at Lawrence Kohlberg's highest stage of moral development discussed in the last chapter.

Is such a worldwide standard possible? Yes, it is. The Nuremberg trials, the United Nations, and the World Court[b] have moved humankind closer to this possibility. Standards of permissible conduct common to all societies exist, whether or not we consciously recognize or acknowledge them. For instance, indiscriminate murder is wrong in any society. Any action or lack of action that leads to murder cannot be part of a morally permissible standard of conduct. The value of protecting and nurturing our children is another commonly accepted standard that crosses all boundaries and cultures. It would lead to cultural and

---

[b] In early 2002, the administration of President George W. Bush said that the United States would not be bound by former President Bill Clinton's decision to be part of the World Court. In effect, the United States will not agree to global standards to prosecute suspected war criminals. It is my understanding that President Bush did not want our soldiers and government leaders subject to any court but an American court. However, the World Court was to prosecute only if a country would not or could not bring the accused to trial. It seems an incongruent position.

species suicide if we did not act in accordance with these standards of conduct.

Entwined with moral acts are ethical acts. In the context of the workplace, ethical acts are those right actions that result from following a set of standards of morally permissible conduct *of a specific group*.[5] These standards are those right actions that each member of some particular group wants every other member of the group to follow, even if it means having to follow them, too. Again, I want to qualify this accepted academic definition. These right, moral, or ethical actions must transcend *all cultural boundaries* before being placed in the category of truth, and they should not to be confused with the least effort syndrome. The Nazi rules did not meet these criteria.

The working knowledge and vocabulary of ethics allow us to explore the ingredients of a morally permissible standard or code. Codes help us define, recognize, and solve ethical problems about personal moral and ethical responsibility in the workplace.

Good checklists containing the universal standards for ethical decision-making by technologists include the codes and standards as part of the process to determine right from wrong actions and good from bad things. If this system sounds circular, it can be to some degree; yet, the process needs to be reiterative if we are to determine the best possible course of action when faced with an ethical dilemma. The ethics checklist in Chapter 12 will demonstrate this reiterative process.

Codes of Ethics for Professionals

Codes of conduct have a long history dating back to early world religions.[c] Codes of conduct are found within most religions, and the three great world religions of Judaism, Islam, and Christianity have done much to spread them. Engineers,

---

[c] For more information on codes for professionals, please refer to the endnotes at the end of this chapter.

lawyers, doctors, architects, contractors, and many other professionals have their separate codes of ethical conduct. And many occupations not generally considered professions—manufacturing, sales, and journalism, for example—have their own standards of conduct.

Many different codes exist within the myriad different specialized branches in professions.[6] Civil engineers have their own code, electrical engineers theirs, and so on. The roles of codes of conduct in the professions are similar in many respects to their roles in many world religions. The most common roles of ethical codes are[7]

- inspiration and guidance for the members;
- support for decision-making by members;
- deterrence and discipline within the organization;
- education and mutual understanding;
- public image of the organization;
- protection of the status quo; and
- promoting the organization's business interests or survival of the organization itself.

What should be the emphasis of ethical codes of conduct in the workplace? What are the limitations of codes? The answers depend upon a person's or an organization's intentions and motives. A person with the intent to circumvent a code will look for, and find, loopholes in it. The less content in a written code, the more loopholes can be found. If the organization wants to prevent outside interference or scrutiny, the code can be used to protect its members from publicity. This protection often diminishes the value and acceptance of personal moral and social responsibility by its members.

> **History has shown little correlation between the existence of a code and any punishment by the organization of its unethical members.**

Members are reluctant to punish other members. To do so would bring bad publicity and possible government regulation to the organizations and professions. Medical doctors, lawyers, engineers, and architects are examples of self-regulating groups. Other limitations of these codes include vague wording and sections that conflict with one another, as the analysis of the ethical dilemma in Chapter 12 will illustrate.

Codes should not serve as final moral authority for conduct because of ethical conventionalism and relativism.[d] These concepts of relativism are tied closely to customs and traditions of a specific group of people. Ethical relativism has long been argued to be an acceptable standard of conduct, as reflected in the admonition "When in Rome, do as the Romans do." It is the dangerous theory of relativity of ethics that I described earlier.

Using this theory, American corporations could conduct business in foreign countries in ways that are legal there but not in America: bribing a government official, for example, which is accepted practice in a number of Third World countries. This fallacy of logic comes under many names that are related to ethical relativism, including the self-interest of ethical egoism, customs, traditions, religion, and pragmatism.

The laws and codes used by the Nazi technologists were written for all the wrong reasons and were specific to their immoral desires. A code is not morally justifiable simply because the members of the group say it is. Yet, even with all these reservations and limitations, codes can be helpful. The codes can provide a threshold of ethical behavior that is considered a good starting point. Most technologists believe that the emphasis of the codes should call on them to[8]

- support responsible conduct of members, which in turn protects the public and the members of the organization;
- set general guidelines for members that make it easier to resist workplace pressures to act unethically;
- promote understanding within the organization and the general public; and

---

[d] For more about these theories, see Mabel and William Sahakian's *Ideas of the Great Philosophers*.

- punish members who don't follow the intent of the codes, creating an obligation for all engineers to act in accordance with the same standards.

A code should be a living thing or a process whereby the rights of all people are protected from harmful acts. In the case of the Hyatt Regency skywalk collapse in Kansas City, the process worked only to the extent that the engineers lost their licenses to practice engineering—at least in Missouri. The codes neither prevented the disaster nor stopped the technologists from practicing engineering in other states after the disaster.

Typically, engineers, doctors, and other professionals who lose their licenses can work for the government or under the supervision of another licensed professional—or move to another state or nation to continue their practice. It is time for the state licensing boards and professional societies to examine that standard to see whether it protects the public or simply protects the members of those professions.

One major engineering organization of which I am a long-time member, the National Society of Professional Engineers (NSPE), publishes a code of ethics for engineers. The NSPE Code and a sample code for the training of technology students are found in Appendix C. The NSPE Code of Ethics contains about 2,000 words and is divided into three main sections—long by most standards, but even so, it is inherently unable to cover every situation. And the NSPE Code has conflicting sections, confusing language, and gaps that cause more problems.

NSPE Code Sections II-1 and II-4 are examples of passages that cause conflict and dilemmas. Section II-1 says, "Engineers shall hold paramount the safety, health and welfare of the public in the performance of their professional duties." Section II-4 says, "Engineers shall act in professional matters for each employer or client as faithful agents or trustees." Can an engineer do both at the same time? Perhaps, in certain situations, but it is difficult, and the conflict often leads to problems.

In particular, these two sections of the NSPE Code cause problems for engineering students. Is the company or the client more or less important than the safety, health, or welfare of others who are impacted by the creations? Can one be ethical and succeed in business? I hope future generations of technologists recognize that the answer is yes. Codes are a form of an ethics checklist that can provide guidance for the tough questions. There are no simple or absolute answers to these questions, but good answers can be found.

Checklists for Ethical Conduct

This checklist, Figure 10, incorporates the ideas in this book into a process for ethical decision-making. It also incorporates more than 30 years of my experiences in private practice, in governmental service, and in the academic world, as well as my understanding of the ideas and experiences of a number of authors.[9] It would be foolish to claim that this checklist is absolute truth, but it can provide a good method to analyze moral dilemmas. It can be a beginning of moral autonomy.

The **FAIL-SAFE** checklist can help technologists analyze workplace dilemmas, including those in higher education.[e] A moral dilemma of a recent college graduate will be analyzed in the next chapter, and the checklist will be used to demonstrate a process of ethical decision-making.

The dilemma focuses on the business world but has its roots in classrooms across our country. The **FAIL-SAFE** checklist will be applied only to the main character, Joe, although other participants' actions in the situation could be analyzed as well.

---

[e] I named this checklist **FAIL-SAFE** to remind users of this process that all designs and creations can fail and that to think otherwise will only create more Titanics and Challengers. Therefore, this checklist is neither absolutely true nor "*fool*-proof."

Find the legal duties and moral dilemmas.

Assess all possible facts available within your organization.

Identify all possible options and their consequences.

Learn the intent of the applicable code of ethics.

Study and apply moral and ethical concepts.

Ask for help from experts outside your organization.

Face the publicity test.

Empathize with those affected by your decisions.

Figure 10: The Fail-Safe Checklist for Ethical Decision-Making

The quandary that Joe faces is a composite of situations that I have seen or experienced or that have been related to me. Joe's story is true to the extent these things have happened in the everyday lives of engineers and other technology professionals.[f] Joe is a civil engineer because I am one, and as a civil engineer and educator, I am an insider who wants my profession to progress.

---

[f] Any similarity between his situation or him as an individual and any specific situation, person or persons, company, or university is purely coincidental.

Bibliography, Notes & Further Reading

[1] Credit should be given for the three senses of the word "ethics" used in this section to (1) Michael Davis, *Thinking Like an Engineer* (New York: Oxford University Press, 1998), vii-ix; and (2) Martin and Schinzinger, *Ethics in Engineering,* 3rd ed. (New York: McGraw-Hill Co., 1996), 3-5. I added my thoughts to their explanations to form a composite picture of the meaning of ethics used in this book.

[2] Some of this discussion is from a seven-day workshop in which I participated on "Ethics Across the Curriculum," taught by Michael Davis in July 1997 (Center for the Study of Ethics in the Professions, Illinois Institute of Technology, Chicago, Illinois). A small group of professionals representing a variety of professions from across the United States were invited by the National Science Foundation to learn how to teach other professionals to teach ethics in their classrooms.

[3] Sahakian and Sahakian, 151-52.

[4] Davis, *Thinking Like an Engineer.*

[5] Ibid.

[6] A number of references are available and helpful. A few notable ones are (1) Martin and Schinzinger, 105-109; (2) Charles E. Harris, Michael S. Pritchard, and Michael J. Rabins, *Engineering Ethics: Concepts and Cases* (New York: Wadsworth Publishing Co., 1995), 25-41; (3) Deborah G. Johnson, *Ethical Issues in Engineering* (Englewood Cliffs, N.J.: Prentice Hall, 1991), 93-155; (4) Charles B. Fleddermann, *Engineering Ethics* (Upper Saddle River, N.J.: Prentice Hall, 1999), 16-33; and (5) Carl Mitcham and Shannon R. Duval, *Engineering Ethics* (Upper Saddle River, N.J.: Prentice Hall, 2000).

[7] Martin and Schinzinger, 106-108.

[8] This list of common roles for codes relies extensively upon my experiences, the work of Michael Davis in *Thinking Like an Engineer*, and upon the work of Martin and Schinzinger in *Ethics in Engineering.*

[9] Three sources were used as references for my checklist: a checklist containing seven items presented by Davis, "Ethics Across the Curriculum"; a six-step checklist in Martin and Schinzinger, 16; and a three-step checklist in Kenneth Blanchard and Norman Vincent Peale, *The Power of Ethical Management* (New York: William Morrow & Co., Inc., 1988), 27.

Chapter 12

The Process Toward Ethical Decisions

Joe's Moral Dilemma

The analysis of Joe's dilemma will illustrate the process of ethical decision-making using the Fail-Safe Checklist presented in the last chapter. The unfolding of the details of his dilemma will also demonstrate the ease with which a young, ambitious engineer can fall prey to accepted industry practices and to authority figures. After Joe's dilemma is analyzed, the Fail-Safe Checklist will be applied briefly to the Hyatt and Challenger facts as we know them.

The following checklist method is intended to stimulate thought and dialogue. The analysis is brief and limited in some areas, and it may even contain deficiencies, but my objective is to demonstrate the potential for a rational and empathetic decision-making process.

> The purpose of the three analyses is not to suggest or provide any absolute answers, but rather to stimulate autonomous moral reasoning and to show the need for a process to discover alternatives.

The Moral Dilemma: Incompetent Managers

Joe is a motivated young civil engineering graduate from a typical American college of engineering and technology. Even though his degree requirements did not include an engineering ethics course, he took a business ethics course in another college. He graduated with top honors about a year ago and was immediately hired by a well-known design/build engineering firm specializing in roadway bridges.

The international corporation of 1,500 employees, Goodfast Inc., in which Joe works has a cost-plus-percentage contract to design and construct a four-lane steel-plate-girder bridge across a river in a major metropolitan area. He is one of four team members assigned to the project, which is on a fast-track schedule. The old bridge was condemned and closed to traffic six months ago, and the public has pressured politicians to complete this project as soon as possible. The State Department of Transportation (DOT) awarded the project to Goodfast primarily because time was of the essence.

During the design phase, Joe reviews the structural design of the four steel girders, which support the concrete deck of the bridge. He believes the girders too small, and he asks his team member, Mary, who designed them, to explain her reasoning to him. After Mary's explanation, Joe is still unconvinced that the safety factor applied to the design is correct. He meets with his team leader, who dismisses his concerns because Mary has been designing bridges for ten years. The team leader tells Joe to back off because the project is already behind schedule and because they have fifteen more projects waiting to begin.

In spite of his team leader's admonition, he meets with the head of the department, Rob, about the situation. Joe has learned through the water cooler crowd that Rob has lost touch with real structural design calculations over the years because he has concentrated on managing about 350 employees. Several designers have told Joe that they think Rob is incompetent to seal the new design as the engineer of record. Joe wants to see for himself.

Rob defends his team leader and tells Joe to forget about it and get back to work. Rob performs the final safety check within the company before the design is presented to the State DOT for final approval. Joe still feels he is right about the low safety factor of this bridge and believes that the bridge will be unsafe.

Joe is now asking himself these two questions:
What actions could I take?
What actions should I take?

F-A-I-L S-A-F-E Ethics Checklist for Joe

Step 1: Find the legal duties and moral dilemmas.

Joe is asking the right questions. And he realizes he has an ethical dilemma, but he is unsure whether he has a legal duty as well. At this point, he could back off and protect his job opportunities with his firm, or he could resign and forget about the situation. In the classroom, my students immediately debated only these two possibilities. At first, most of them could not see alternatives. I believe many technologists involved in disasters look at only these two options, with tragic results. Sometimes, engineers are simply lucky, and the normal safety factors of routine design protect the public from catastrophes.

But Joe took a business ethics course, and he wants to pursue a solution to the dilemma that will protect the public and allow him to sleep at night. He locates an ethics checklist given to him by a college professor and begins this process.[a]

Since Joe is not a lawyer, he decides to seek a legal opinion from a lawyer within his firm who is also his friend. He believes the friend would keep the situation confidential. He is worried about being fired because he has not followed the advice to forget and to move on.

Assume Joe's attorney friend determines that he does not have a company duty to pursue the problems. Joe, however, has more than one problem: A moral dilemma exists in his relationship to Mary, to his team leader, to Rob the department head, to his company, to his profession, and to himself. But while Joe's lawyer friend agrees that Joe has an important ethical and professional dilemma to solve, since no crime has been committed, and since

---

[a] If employees like Joe could have the opportunity to take an engineering ethics course within their own department, they would be more likely to recognize their industry-specific moral dilemmas and what should be done.

no company policy covers the issues, he feels he does not have a duty to help Joe.

With the legal duties separated from the ethical issues, Joe moves to Step 2. In Step 1, Joe was seeking facts from an expert; now he turns his attention to relevant facts about his dilemma.

Step 2: Assess all possible facts available within your organization.

Asking appropriate questions is a good way to begin Step 2 of the process. Unless the dilemma is an immediate life-and-death situation, Joe should gather information primarily from within his organization at this early stage.[b] Step 6 will require Joe to consult with outside sources.

What facts would help Joe make a good and justifiable decision? In Step 1, he asked a lawyer for more information. Now Joe could talk to other members in the firm, such as a trusted friend in his department or someone outside his department, to gather more facts.

What facts might be relevant to this situation? First, he should determine whether the design safety factors that Mary used are actually too low. He would need to do more research about the company's procedures and policies, ask other team members about normal design criteria, and possibly ask his professors from his college days. At this time, Joe would not need to tell people the

---

[b] If the moral dilemma contained an immediate life-and-death situation, the time to make a rational decision would be reduced to a time frame not unlike that in which police officers, paramedics, doctors, and other emergency workers must operate. You may not even have time to use any written form of a checklist, but must simply react to save a life regardless of the consequences to your career. A worker in a deep, unshored trench may be in immediate danger of a cave-in and thus of being buried alive. A rational genuine person will act to save this worker. The technologists at the Challenger space shuttle launch had to face this issue.

specific problem, only that he is researching for his own benefit—which is true.

The second group of facts would be the accusations about Rob, the department head. Is he incompetent to seal drawings and specifications? This search could be more problematic for Joe. He certainly could talk discreetly with other company employees or listen to more water cooler talk, but he has to be very careful, prudent, and ethical in his approach. Joe wants to rely upon Rob to catch the error, but Rob has indicated no interest in doing so. And the team leader is probably getting pressure from Rob to speed up production. This would help explain why the team leader wants Joe to forget about his concerns. Because the company has a large backlog of work waiting to start, there is yet more pressure. So, the stress is intense and comes from several directions within the company. This hurried work life of a design engineer is quite common.

Joe needs to determine whether Rob can—and will—catch the wrong safety factor or seal and approve the dangerous design. Joe is experienced enough to suspect that once the design is sent to the state DOT, specific design details will not be thoroughly checked. And any city authority will only check for general conformity to the local politicians' requirements for architectural features, overall project schedule and budget, and other general factors.

Let's suppose that Joe is convinced from the facts that he is right about the unsafe design. A four-lane, four-main-girder bridge is rarely designed with significant redundancy. Without that redundancy, the structure can fail catastrophically if only one critical member fails. Chapter 2 presented several cases in which structures failed because of this problem. The old-style bridge design with hundreds of steel members, the truss bridge, did not have this critical problem, as today's more economical designs do. The following graphic shows the difference. If one of the two girders shown below on the right failed, the structure would likely fail.

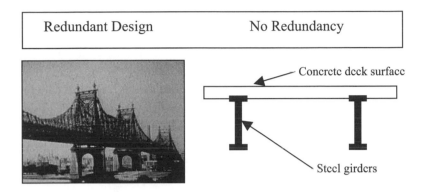

| Redundant Design | No Redundancy |

After gathering available facts, Joe must now assess and analyze the information for accuracy. Sometimes the information simply is not sufficient to make an honorable decision, and the questioner needs to find a way to get the needed data. Joe would need to determine beyond a reasonable doubt that the safety factor was dangerous. Of course, the issue of Rob's competence would remain. The immediate pressure on Joe might be reduced, but other critical projects will be on Rob's desk. Joe believes he should continue to seek the facts about Rob, but he moves ahead with the checklist because of the immediate safety issue.

Assume Joe feels and thinks that he is right about the safety factor on his project, and that he has gathered all knowable and relevant facts. Joe keeps looking for facts throughout the process, and as he finds new information, he may need to return to Step 1. He decides to move to Step 3.

Step 3: Identify all possible options and their consequences.

Joe should make a list of all possible alternatives, placing neither a moral nor a dollar value on any one option. This is an important step: to think new thoughts unrestricted by conventions. It is brainstorming without regard to consequences for any one possibility. Next, he needs to set his options in order, bearing in mind the interests of all those who might be involved.[c] So, at one end of Joe's list, an option might be to consult his company's ombudsman, if it has one. Joe is still concerned about his job, and at this point, he needs the ombudsman to keep this confidential.

The other end of the list might be the option to call a news conference, hoping to expose both the safety problem and the incompetent boss. Many other options lie between these two (please see the endnotes).[1] If Joe were still in this checklist process when construction was to begin, he might feel the public was best served by his talking with an investigative reporter. He would be reasoning that lives were now at immediate risk, and he may have run out of alternatives in his list.

Assume he prioritized all possibilities and then chose the first course of action to be the least harmful to him *and to those affected by this decision.* He will begin an ongoing conversation with the company's ombudsman as he proceeds through the checklist. Such an option is a benefit a large company is more likely to offer Joe; on the other hand, large corporations can provide the cover for employees to blend into the crowd and forget about the problems. Keep quiet and keep your job is the mantra. Many technologists used this approach during the Holocaust.

> **Generally, the best course of action, unless it is an immediate life-and-death issue, is to progress in graduated steps of alternatives.**

For this situation, assume that Joe identified all relevant options and assessed the consequences before his meeting with the

---

[c] Sometimes, the least harmful to one's self is the most harmful to others, which is a moral dilemma that must be reconciled. The engineers with the Hyatt Regency and the Challenger, as well as the technologists in the Holocaust, made choices that harmed many, many people. They kept their jobs, but innocent people died. Many people when faced with a moral dilemma can think of only two options—jump in with both feet or forget the problem. The "fight or flee" response of our primordial and instinctual self is at work, not our rational self.

company's ombudsman. The ombudsman may believe Joe, investigate, and force changes—an idealistic scenario, perhaps, but it can happen. But for the purposes of this process, assume that the ombudsman will not get involved and that Joe feels he has no choice but to proceed with the checklist process—the policies of his profession.

Step 4: Learn the intent of the applicable code of ethics.

Most, if not all, professions like engineering and technology have codes of ethics in place. The accreditation code for curricula of engineering and technology (ABET)[d] is a place Joe could begin, but he wisely decides to use the professional engineer's code (NSPE) because the team leader and department head are registered engineers. The university curriculum code is very similar to the NSPE Code.[2] Joe applies the following NSPE Code sections, which have been paraphrased, to his situation. (You may want to review the actual sections in Appendix C.)

- I. Fundamental Canons
  - o Section 1: Safety is the most important factor
  - o Section 2: You must perform services only in areas of competence
  - o Section 4: Act as faithful agent of employer/client
  - o Section 5: Conduct yourself to enhance honor and reputation of engineering profession
- II. Rules of Practice
  - o Section 1a: Engineer must report unethical activities to authorities
  - o Section 1b: Approve designs that conform to law

---

[d] See Appendix C for the summary version. For the complete ABET Code of Ethics, go to: *http://www.abet.org*

- o Section 1e: If you have knowledge of violations of Code, you must report to professional board and/or public authority
- o Section 2a: Undertake work only in areas of competence
- o Section 2b: Seal and sign only work in which engineer is competent and personally controls the direction of the work
- o Section 2c: Engineers may accept work and responsibility for coordination of entire project, but each technical area must be sealed and signed by qualified engineers
- o Section 4: Engineers must act as faithful agents to their employer or client
- III. Professional Obligations
  - o Section 1a: Engineers shall acknowledge their errors and not distort or alter the facts
  - o Section 2: Engineers shall at all times strive to serve the public interest
  - o Section 2b: Engineers shall not sign or seal nonconforming work and must withdraw from work that does not meet standard practices
  - o Section 7: Engineers shall not injure, maliciously or falsely, directly or indirectly, the professional reputation of other engineers. If you believe others are guilty of unethical or illegal acts, you must present information to proper authorities

After studying the entire code, Joe realizes that he has certain duties and responsibilities. On the one hand, he must hold paramount the safety of the public, and on the other hand, he should not injure without good reason the reputation of fellow engineers. Technologists must realize that this code, as a guide, is imperfect. But the NSPE Code clearly makes these points: know your own technical limits, act honorably, hold paramount the safety of people, and present evidence to authorities when a fellow engineer does not do these things.

So, Joe determines that incompetence cannot be allowed to go unchallenged and that all engineers must place the public's health, safety, and welfare above all.[e] But there is a basic problem with this NSPE Code and most codes. A conflict can exist between one or more sections—a moral dilemma within a dilemma. In this case, engineers who try to protect the safety of the public find in the code that they must also act as faithful agents or trustees for each employer or client. This is an *apparent*, not a real, conflict of sections if taken out of context.

Safety is listed first in the NSPE Canons. And it should be self-evidently true that safety comes before client interests, but the significant disasters of the 20th century illustrate that often it is not. A person who wants to circumvent the intent of this or most other codes can find a loophole when self-interest is placed first.

Joe determines that the department head and the team leader appear to be in violation of the NSPE Code, but this story concentrates on Joe and his relationship to Rob. If the team leader were to seal and sign the work, Rob, the department head, would be operating within the intent of the NSPE Code, Section 2c of Part II. In this case, Rob is the engineer of record. Joe also understands from the code that fellow professionals are required to disclose wrongful acts by their peers to appropriate authorities. It

---

[e] The word "public" is a problem for some technologists. They want to define the public in a specific narrow domain. Some engineers may believe that only their clients and their customers constitute the public. They want to exclude those in other parts of the country, or, for that matter, any other country. This behavior is a deflection of personal moral responsibility, because it implies that acid rain falling on Canadians from America's smokestack industries is not their problem.

would best for Joe if he could find more employees who are concerned and jointly pursue the complaint. For now, assume that Joe will wait until he has completed the checklist and proceeded in graduated steps according to his prioritized list before filing any complaint with the registration board.

The intent and the language of the NSPE Code confirm that Joe's decisions in this process have been appropriate, measured, and ethical. Many professional organizations have ethics boards and ethics newsletters that Joe could consult. He meets with the chairperson of the ethics board and asks general questions to clarify his understanding of the code. Joe does not disclose names or specific events to the chairperson, because he recalls his prioritized list of graduated steps about going public.

Before going to Step 5, one more point needs to made about the NSPE Code of Ethics. Joe could have one more reasonable alternative in Step 3, but the code discourages it. He could be part of a collective bargaining unit within his company. Federal law would allow for a union, but Section 1e of Part 3 states that registered engineers cannot "actively participate in strikes, picket lines, or other collective coercive action." This section effectively prevents engineers from participating in unions with any real power to stop the Code of Silence.

Regardless of what most engineers may think about unions in the construction trades, the history of most unions has illustrated an active concern for the safety, health, and welfare of their members.[f] If collective bargaining with all its federal protections were allowed in engineering, maybe strength in numbers could prevent management from punishing internal and external whistle-blowers. This would be in the public interest. The fear of retaliation by management in the form of isolation,

---

[f] Many engineers consider the unions in the construction trades to be roadblocks to lowering projects costs and to reducing the construction time for completion. Although there is some truth in this position, unions have made major contributions in ensuring safe working conditions for employees and in securing a voice in the discussion of the entire process of construction.

demotion, and arbitrary dismissal prevents employees from questioning authority figures. So, the Code of Silence continues. My experiences and research show that the public good would be better served by ending it.

Step 5: Study and apply moral and ethical concepts.

This is not an easy task for specialized professionals unaccustomed to looking outside their professions for truth or help. Fortunately, Joe took an ethics course last year. Theories on moral development, morality, and ethics are helpful in determining a foundation for moral reasoning and appropriate action.[3] Codes and laws are often derived from these philosophical underpinnings.

Joe remembers the Lawrence Kohlberg stages of moral development and wants to act at the highest level, but he begins to realize his actions might end his career.[4] His desire to do what is right will serve him well. He weighs the loss of his job against the ability to sleep at night if the bridge did collapse and people were killed. He realizes that certain truths are self-evident the right to life comes quickly to mind.[g]

Assume Joe recalls the four classical ethical theories discussed in Part Two of this book. If Joe applies the Utilitarian Theory, the "most good for the most people," he might reason that future team members would have a better work environment if he would settle the problem now. The theory could also justify his actions because he is protecting the public over the interests of a few individuals. He feels that he is protecting the company as a whole, and therefore protecting employees and their families. If Joe applies the Rights Theory, he might reason that he, other employees, and the public have the right to expect ethical and competent leaders. And the public has the right to be safe partly

---

[g] The phrase "right to life," as used in this book, should not be confused with the phrase used by groups advocating the abolishment of abortion in the United States.

because the government can grant or withhold licenses from engineers to protect it.

When Joe applies the Duties Theory, he may learn that he is obligated by laws, codes, and company policy to protect the rights of others from harm. The Virtues Theory might suggest to Joe yet another way to help analyze and solve his dilemma. To be virtuous, a person would have to act at Kohlberg's third level of moral development, and that would require him to place right action and justice for others above self-interest. It is not an easy choice.

An engineering ethics course could have better prepared Joe for these types of dilemmas. I taught students that if all three theories of ethical behavior pointed to a solution also indicated by laws and professional codes of conduct, the proposed solution to the dilemma was probably more viable and right. In Joe's situation, this is true. Joe now feels he must seek help from outside of his company and profession.

Step 6: Ask for help from experts outside your field.

Steps 1 through 5 may have to be revisited because of new information and other possibilities learned along this road less traveled. Joe could now ask for guidance from professors in philosophy, law, ethics, and related fields, and he could be more specific about the problem. He could discuss more details with registration board members—and ethics board members, if any— without filing a complaint. He could visit with fellow technologists in professional organizations that have similar codes of ethics. But an important point to remember when talking specifics with other people is this: Joe must not slander or libel specific people.[h] People are entitled to a fair and public trial in our system of justice.

---

[h] He may want to consult with an attorney to clarify this point. Speaking and writing the truth is a defense against libel and slander, but it is best to consult

It is important to ask for help outside of your profession to counterbalance any biases in your field or organization. At times, professional organizations and registration boards may try to protect their own members from public accountability because of the adverse publicity to the engineering profession or other self-interest issues. The NSPE Code contains a number of sections requiring engineers to protect the honor and prestige of the profession.[i] Even if Joe avoids violating slander or libel laws, he risks violating these sections about reputations. He should visit with the registration and ethics board members about his responsibilities in this area. Usually the law and the board rules agree on this issue.

Let's assume the consensus from outside experts is that Joe should report the ethical problems to higher authorities within his company, the Goodfast corporation. Joe now reviews the list of prioritized alternatives from Step 3 and decides that he will talk with the company vice president after completing the checklist process. The next two steps are crucial for Joe to feel and think that he has done all that is possible and ethical to do.

Step 7: **F**ace the publicity test.

Universities, professional societies, corporations, and other organizations can be closed societies where outside "interference" or public scrutiny is not wanted or tolerated.[j]

---

with an attorney, to ask for confidentiality from the various parties, and to use what-ifs in the discussions with those who will not grant confidentiality.

[i] You may want to review NSPE Code sections: Section 6 of Part I; Section 1f, 2c, and 7 of Part III.

[j] There is an old saying: "If you can look at yourself in the mirror each morning, it must have been okay to do." This is not a reliable way to determine the right course of action, especially when lives are at risk. In addition, it is not a good test of workplace ethics to accept without question what a majority of peers say as the truth. A majority vote can be wrong. Prejudices and biases can hide the truth in a closed organization or society, and the truth can be hidden from our true or genuine self. Nazi Germany was a classic example of a closed society and

Therefore, the publicity test means this: If your decisions were to be published in a newspaper of general circulation, outside your closed part of the world, could you live with yourself when everyone knows what you did? Could you live with the fact that your children and your parents would know what you really did (or did not do)? Joe believes that his decisions, including talking with the vice president, pass this test at this seventh stage of the process.

If Joe had chosen to go immediately to the press with the situation, this publicity test would have been more problematic for him, for the employees in question, for the company, and for others involved. It would have been unjust to everyone if all the facts and issues had not been addressed and company leaders and people outside of the company had not been consulted.

Step 8: **E**mpathize with those affected by your decisions.

The process to Step 8, except for the publicity test, has been primarily rational in its approach. Technologists must also use their emotional intelligence quotient, or EQ, to feel what others feel and to act morally in response to other human beings' feelings and situation. Again, if a person is not a sociopath, this emotional aspect could be called a "gut feeling" or the conscience at work. However, even those of us who are not sociopaths must recognize "true beliefs" and myths and eliminate them from our thought processes. A racist is unable to reason or to feel empathetic about those he or she hates.

When you exercise EQ and IQ, a rational and ethical decision is more likely. Joe, an engineer-to-be,[k] is proud of his

---

persons who suppressed their feelings about the industrialized murder. The Challenger disaster also illustrated a closed group of true believers.

[k] Joe, an engineer-to-be, is technically called an "engineer-in-training" (EIT). Usually, an engineering student will take the EIT one-day exam before graduating. He must then work under the direct supervision of a registered engineer for four years. After this period, he can take the professional engineer's

ability to solve problems in a logical and rational manner, and he has revealed this ability by following this checklist.

Joe thinks and feels that the team leader's and department head's actions are wrong and that he should help prevent this situation from harming the public. Joe has also recognized that Mary, Rob, and the team leader have feelings and rights. Otherwise, Joe might have gone to the press immediately, and that would hardly have been the action that causes the least harm. Most likely, this premature action would have prevented real and long-lasting change within the company.

His feelings and his logic convince him that his decisions have been reasonable, careful, appropriate, and graduated responses to an unethical situation created by his managers. Joe is satisfied with his decisions and now goes to see the vice president to report the problems. If this final step had been a problem for Joe, he might have returned to Step 1 and started the checklist procedure again.

After Joe's Decision: What Next?

What if the company vice president backed his department head and told Joe to forget about it? Joe would have to continue along his list of alternatives from the least harmful. Eventually, he would have to decide about being a whistle-blower and suffering the consequences of this decision.[1] If Joe were married, had a house mortgage, and had a disabled child to support, his decision would be more difficult, but he still would have to decide if he could live with the distinct possibility of a bridge disaster. A technologist who has suppressed thinking about right and wrong may not suffer sleepless nights over this issue (for a while), but

---

one-day exam administered by each state engineering registration board, and if he he passes the exam, he will be registered as a licensed professional engineer.

[1] A whistle-blower is generally described as an insider who goes public with information that could be harmful to the company.

fortunately, Joe has assessed the possibilities and consequences differently.

Students would always ask me what I would do in the situations that I presented to them. I usually told them that I hoped I would have the courage to make the right decision. Of course, the students would not let me off that easy and would ask me whether I would place my family first. Here is the answer I would provide: What alternatives do I have so that I don't have to choose?

Not only does the ethics checklist help in workplace dilemmas, it also can help in our private lives as well. There are alternatives for earning money elsewhere and for securing help from friends, family, church, government agencies, etc. The answer is to think "out of the box." Don't be trapped by those who say you have no choice but to do this or that. We have choices. We just have to be open to new ideas.

What other factors in Joe's situation should be considered in this process? At least five primary factors have set Joe's dilemma in motion:

- Cost-plus-percentage contract
- Design and Build project
- Fast-track project
- Registered engineers as managers
- True beliefs brought from college

A book could be written about each of these factors. Briefly, I will address them and explain how they set the stage for ethical dilemmas for the company and Joe. For example, a cost-plus contract offers no incentive to keep the project budget reasonable. The more money the project costs, the more money his company makes. This situation is tied directly to the next two factors. Cost-plus contracts usually indicate that time is of the essence. If only one company handles both design and construction, quicker completion times are possible, but this savings is not guaranteed. The quality and detail of plans and specifications can suffer.

One more problem with design/build contracts is inadequate checks on safety factors and other design criteria. If separate companies performed the tasks of design and construction, more people would be involved in checking, making it less likely that a dangerous problem would be overlooked.

The issue of fast-track projects parallels the previous two factors when time is of the essence. Fast-track projects are usually those for which construction on one phase will begin before all the design has been completed. For example, the concrete foundations could be built before the structural steel girders have been designed. The possibilities increase for management pressure to work faster, and this pressure can lead to disasters. This rush to completion most likely contributed greatly to the Challenger and the Hyatt disasters.

In the chapter on characteristics of engineers and scientists, the typical engineer was shown not to be a "people person" and a manager of people. The typical young, successful design engineer eventually becomes an older manager with little managerial training. And the typical authoritarian professor in engineering has not been trained to teach effectively but, like a manager, is nonetheless allowed to influence the next generation of technologists. My profession tends to accept these things as the way it is done. We should not assume "accepted industry practices" are good for us and for those we serve.

The application of the FAIL-SAFE checklist to the Hyatt and Challenger disasters will demonstrate that a "Joe" using an ethics checklist would be more likely to prevent these types of tragedies.

Applied Ethics: Hyatt and Challenger

Applying the FAIL-SAFE ethics checklist to the Hyatt and Challenger disasters offers several lessons. I will briefly discuss the primary ones that lend themselves to this process. To set the stage for this checklist process, I will assume the following information in addition to the actual details presented in Chapters 3 and 4:

- o Assume fictitious names for the department managers who were in charge (engineers of record) for each project before the disasters. For Hyatt, her name will be Jill, and for Challenger, his name will be Jack. Both are registered professional engineers.

- o Hyatt: The architect specifically was asking Jill if she had checked the design of the rods holding the skybridges above the lobby floor. She is thinking about what to tell him. The first skybridge was to be installed next week.

- o Challenger: The NASA chief operations officer in charge of launching the shuttle on schedule asked Jack if he had the engineering team's approval to launch.

What should Jack do?   What should Jill do?

F-A-I-L S-A-F-E Ethics Checklist Process
for Hyatt and for Challenger

Step 1: **F**ind the legal duties and moral dilemmas.

In the case of Hyatt, Jill knew or should have known during the design phase that the skybridges had critical elements that had to be designed properly. Her answer to the architect's question was crucial. If she were only the coordinator of the work, the plans had to be signed and sealed by her subordinate registered engineer in charge of the design. The Missouri court documents indicate no written data for this check. If she were the engineer of record, she should have known that she needed to determine whether it was safe. Regardless of whether she is the coordinator or the engineer of record, she should have determined whether her subordinates were competent and honest about the safety of the structure. The point is this: Jack and Jill should first determine their legal and moral duties. She could have said, "I'm not sure, but I will find out"—and it would be good if she really did try to determine the truth.

In the case of the Challenger, legal duties abounded. Under federal laws and regulations, Jack would have or should have known that he had to protect the lives of astronauts and the public. What if the space shuttle had veered back over land and exploded? The public was vulnerable. So, Jack should have told the operations officer, "I don't know yet, but I will find out"—and he could have secured written permission slips from each team member. If you recall, the team did not recommend launching, but management overruled the decision.

Step 2: Assess all possible facts available within your organization.

Both Jack and Jill would have discovered, if they did not already know, that the facts were available to stop the projects from proceeding. Both disasters could have been prevented at this Step 2 if the engineers had followed their instincts and training.

Jill would have discovered that the company had no design calculations for the rods and that the rods' fabricators had not designed them. She would have discovered the accepted industry practices that were unsafe. Someone could have designed the connections with the documentation stored in a secure location.

Jack would have discovered that the team of engineers had strongly recommended not launching in cold weather. Other facts would have been available to support this life-and-death decision. Jack was a registered engineer and manager, but his profession's code of ethics and his duty to the public good should have prevented the launch. He was clearly pressured to "go along, get along."

Step 3: Identify all possible options and their consequences.

If the facts gathered by Jack and Jill were inconclusive, they could have looked at all other options.

For the Hyatt, Jill could have checked with her employees or designed the support rods herself. For the Challenger, the facts were in the record, but management pressured the engineers to acquiesce to authority by the fear tactics discussed in this book. Alternatives existed to stop this duress; for instance, an internal petition could have been circulated among dissenting engineers, and an external whistle-blower could have contacted the press.

Many participants in both disasters should have known the real situation and taken action to stop the process. I suspect many sleepless nights passed for them, which is one consequence of the actions or inactions that many of them chose.

Step 4: Learn the intent of the applicable code of ethics.

In Joe's dilemma, the codes of ethics clearly support safety first. Yet the codes may have been used to support the faulty reasoning that Jack and Jill must be loyal to their employer or client. If either Jack or Jill had waited just one day longer to answer management, and talked with members of the boards of ethics in their professions, the disasters could have been avoided. Hurried work and fast-track schedules lead to these tragedies.

Step 5: **S**tudy and apply moral and ethical concepts.

Joe's ability to study the ethical theories helped him to make the right decisions that protected lives. The concepts supported the codes and the laws. Jack and Jill would have discovered the same thing. Perhaps they knew it already but suppressed the moral duty and put company loyalty first. However, they might have discovered many more alternatives at this step in the process, and the consequences would have been far less deadly.

Step 6: **A**sk for help from experts outside your field.

The hurried pace of both events was no excuse for failing to ask others outside the design firm or outside NASA. Plenty of help was available if they had taken the time. Had they asked, they would have found support to stop the faulty reasoning in both projects.

In Jill's case, she could have pursued the steel fabricator's questions and concerns or talked with the ethics board if management was blocking internal investigations. Jack could have built a consensus among the rocket booster's designers and key politicians to stop the launch. He should have asked more questions and followed his instincts not to launch. Their choices, followed by the relentless publicity after the events, ruined many lives, and these participants should have known this would happen.

Step 7: **F**ace the publicity test.

This step ought to have been the easiest. The reason for this checklist is to make foresight about the consequences of one's actions or inaction top priority. Many Jacks and Jills after both disasters faced huge publicity that helped end many careers.

Step 8: Empathize with those affected by your decisions.

If Jill had put herself in the place of the hundreds of people who were to dance on and under the skybridges, she probably would have made a better decision. If Jack's son or daughter were scheduled to be launched in the Challenger, his decision might have been much different. If they had seen beyond their creative work, hurried schedules, and paychecks, both disasters might have been prevented.

Individual human beings must make the final choice to be moral or not to be moral. This choice is the most important decision technologists can make, because specialized professionals will determine the future of all life on this planet with their vision, or lack of it, for the 21st century.

A Vision for the 21st Century

One meaning of "vision" is a prediction of probable events. History clearly shows us that the continuation of the Code will lead to more tragedies in the 21st century, tragedies that could make the disasters of the last hundred years pale in comparison. I hope that I am wrong, but the World Trade Center disaster on September 11, 2001, may be the tip of the iceberg.

A vision can also be an objective to be achieved in the future. The dangerous ideas, codes, and practices should change within governments and within the business of technology because of humankind's propensity for large-scale man-made disasters. This last chapter contains my recommendations to achieve a safer world and a better environment for all life to thrive. I am fully aware of the idealism expressed in them. I am not naïve about the obstacles we face, but we must dare to think "unthinkable" thoughts, as the founding fathers of this country did for us.

Many American citizens may not remember where they heard it, but most adults recognize the phrase "life, liberty, and the pursuit of happiness." This triad of unalienable rights is essential for a free society.

Because of our education and training, we technologists should recognize a special role and duty to protect these rights for everyone. "Everyone" means the duty is not limited to our immediate family alone. Our duty to uphold the triad of rights should transcend our sense of obligation to our team members, to organizations to which we may belong, and to our particular governments. If anything can be called an absolute truth, this triad can.

At the beginning of each engineering and technology ethics class, I typically placed a five-dollar bill on the desk for anyone who could identify the document that gave us these three rights. I lost only about twenty dollars over the years. Usually, blank stares appeared on my students' faces, and yet by the end of the semester, many of these bright young technologists had begun  to reconnect with their intuitive and emotional selves. Many of them discovered that scientific logic alone would not lead to the best decisions when ethical dilemmas were present. These bright and empathetic students give me hope.

America's Declaration of Independence contains the essence for moral and ethical decision-making by the creators of technology. The Declaration of Independence, in part, says:

> "We hold these truths to be self-evident, that all men are created equal, that they are endowed by their Creator with certain unalienable Rights, that among these are Life, Liberty and the pursuit of Happiness."

Declaration of Independence, July 4, 1776

Some truths are so obvious that they are called self-evident. This is an unfamiliar idea for some people, especially technologists who are not emotive and intuitive in their rational thought processes. I cannot imagine that the philosophers who helped write the Declaration, the U.S. Constitution, and the Bill of Rights were not aware of the need for equality for all. Some of the founding fathers were also slave owners, true. But progress occurs one small step at a time.

A practice does not become right or good just because an individual, a profession, or a nation has held to it for a long time. Liberty or freedom leads to equality in opportunity, which is required for any society to be just. Of course, a person must be alive and healthy to enjoy the freedoms and the right of equality; this is where technologists play a major role in protecting all life.

> The unalienable right to life itself *should* be self-evident. Sadly, human history reminds us it is not.

Unalienable rights are those absolute rights that cannot, and should not, be taken away by others. The "right to life" in the context of this book means the right to defend our self, particularly against an unjust government or any organized effort to interfere with the rights of an individual.[m] I strongly believe that any organization, including professional societies and educational institutions, should reaffirm the truth written by America's founders. Then we should act in ways congruent with this truth.

America's founders declared that everyone has the right to criticize our established authorities without fear of retribution and that we have the right to form institutions and governments to protect these liberties. Governments, businesses, educational institutions, and professional societies of technologists ought to exist only if dedicated to this protection of basic human rights.

> Injustice is injustice, regardless of the lip service or the organization's pretentious mission statement.

---

[m] Again, the phrase "right to life," as used in this book, should not be confused with the phrase used by groups advocating the abolishment of abortion in the United States.

The unalienable rights to own property, to own possessions, and to be safe in the use of these things obligate technologists to protect human beings. This duty is present whether we are officially licensed or not by the government to practice our creative work. Our privilege to receive a specialized education creates this professional duty for technologists for several reasons.

First, it is the moral and ethical thing to do.

Second, our state and federal governments (through citizen taxpayers) subsidize directly and indirectly technologists' education. Many technologists take advantage of student loans, grants, and other sources of support to complete their specialized educations. These educational opportunities oblige a graduate to do what is right regardless of any formal license to practice. A trusting society provides ample rewards for us to be creative in our work; thus, it is our duty to protect it—and our planet and all life—from harm.

Many people believe that the rights to life, liberty, and the pursuit of happiness extend to other species and life forms.[n] Attitudes are slowly changing toward animals, especially higher forms such as chimps, elephants, dogs, and dolphins. Animals are known to experience joy, pleasure, sadness, grief, and other human-like emotions.[5]

> **Perhaps, humans are more of a hypocritical partner in the "law of the jungle" than we want to admit.**

---

[n] Christianity and a few other world religions have typically said that "man" has dominion over the earth and all life on it. This has been characterized over the centuries by the degradation and elimination of many species. This "right" has been disputed and is under attack by many experts and people empathetic with other life forms. For instance, Process philosophy and theology (see *Process Theology* by Cobb and Griffin, Westminster Press, 1976, pp. 63-79) addresses these issues with a world-view that places a duty upon humans to protect all life because of its interrelatedness and interdependency. Governments are beginning to recognize these facts because of issues related to global warming, deforestation, ecological disasters, and related matters.

Technologists from all over the world have tarnished their image because of the damage they do or allow to happen to the ecosystem. Non-technologists often use the contractor's or engineer's safety "hard hat" as a symbol of an uncaring attitude about all life on this planet—an attitude in need of adjustment. A good place to begin to couple hope with action could be a new code of behavior in professions. The wisdom found in our Declaration of Independence would be a great starting point.

Hope: Possibility of a Fail-Safe Institute

We can have a safer and more just society in which advancing technology does not outpace the moral and social responsibility of its creators. Nonprofit and not-for-profit organizations can help accomplish this vision. Funding for establishing and operating such an organization should, and can, come from government grants, from professional societies, and from private sources. The organization must have a structure and constitution that eliminates the Code of Silence from its operations, reports, conclusions, and recommendations. It must be free to tell the truth.

The idea of a Fail-Safe Institute to address the Code first came to my attention in 1999. The idea began to develop within a group of students in one of my ethics classes. The Institute could document man-made failures, determine the human factors and dynamics of these failures, and establish and publish voluntary guidelines for personal moral and social responsibility in the creation and use of technologies.

The Institute could promote voluntary compliance with national quality and ethical standards in education and business. The power of a free press and free speech could be useful in this voluntary compliance system. In addition, the Institute could help create a "safe" environment for individuals to question dangerous creations or actions—in other words, a workable whistle-blower policy and protection system. This is as important in the worlds of academia and government as it is in the private sector.

The Institute could establish a legal referral system for students, for professors, and for industry employees caught in the Code. Mediation and arbitration services could be provided. This type of organization should establish a speaker bureau to train employees, managers, and leaders within industry, government, and institutions of higher education. Above all, the Institute's goals and objectives should be established for the good of all life on this planet.

Perhaps the Institute should be managed and operated by non-technologists for it to be free from pressure to remain silent. Obviously, technologists should play key roles in the Institute, but the overall control of the organization should be in the hands of people outside their specialized domain of influence.

The intent of the organization would not be to punish anyone. Instead, it should be designed to (1) educate technologists and non-technologists about the dangers of the Code and (2) protect people who want to change the status quo. It would require a partnership, a marriage of sorts, between the creators and those people affected by their creations.

Final Reflections on Truth

I am cautiously optimistic about the future of our technology-based culture. Growing numbers of new, empathetic, and bright young technologists provide hope to those of us who have seen too much to be idealistic again. I also find it encouraging that many of the technology graduates I was privileged to have known have an ethical awareness in spite of some professors' attempts to spread the Code of Silence to them.

> My bottom-line optimism for the future is based on the hope that I'm correct about my theory of a rational human being's instinctual need to be moral.

A significant reduction in man-made tragedies that involve experimental technology can begin by exposing the Code of Silence and its tragic legacy. The process of change has started in some circles of power. I hope that leaders in government can foster changes in policies affecting the creation and use of technology during the next several decades. Engineers and scientists should be on the front lines of this war against evil. We the people should demand this progress because our civilization, our children's well-being, and our human species' very existence depend upon a new way of doing business.

In October of 2000, the magazine *Discover* published a list of 20 ways the world could end suddenly.[6] Ten ways were man-made: global epidemics, global warming, an ecosystem collapse, biotech disasters, a particle accelerator mishap, nanotechnology disasters, environmental toxins, global war, robotics gone wild, and mass insanity.[o] It has been mass insanity for technologists to hide behind a Code.

> **It has been mass insanity to develop new technologies without regard to the consequences, and it would be irrational to continue along this path.**

The thoughts presented in this book have been about life or death, about truth or deception, about openness or concealment, about ethics or chaos—and the hope for a better future. These thoughts reflect my philosophy of life, and it is a continuing and evolving process for me. I want to persuade technologists and the public to develop their own personal autonomy about what ought to be.

The importance for each of us of searching for our genuine self cannot be overstated. Asking the tough questions about my life was the beginning of my journey toward genuine

---

[o] The 20 ways are asteroid impact, gamma-ray burst, collapse of the vacuum, rogue black holes, giant solar flares, reversal of earth's magnetic field, flood-basalt volcanism, global epidemics, global warming, ecosystem collapse, biotech disaster, particle accelerator mishap, nanotechnology disaster, environmental toxins, global war, robot takeover, mass insanity, alien invasion, divine intervention, and someone waking up and realizing it was all a dream.

self and toward my understanding of the importance of the interrelatedness of all life. I continue to learn every day.

If I can persuade technologists and non-technologists to ask the right questions and to develop a passion for the process of personal moral and social responsibility, I will have succeeded in a primary objective for this book. Alfred North Whitehead, a 20th-century mathematician and one of the great philosophers of our time, summed it up this way:[7]

> A final reflection ... how shallow, puny, and imperfect are efforts to sound the depths in the nature of things. In philosophy discussion, the merest hint of dogmatic certainty as to finality is an exhibition of folly.

And so it is; business as usual is mass insanity. For all those who sincerely search for answers to troubling questions, and even for those who claim to have all the answers for the rest of us, a reminder: We must remember the folly and the horror of "final solutions." After all, the search for truth is a process of discovery, and it is never finished. It is a mode of traveling.

It is time for progress, not just change. The Code of Silence must be exposed for what it is: *The Big Lie.* Writing this book helped me to understand that each generation of Americans must fight to keep constitutional freedoms alive for our children. I hope this book, in some way, contributes to making the world our children inherit a safer one.

The following admonition attributed to Hippocrates would provide a wonderful and succinct new Code for engineers, for scientists, and for educators in technology in the 21st century and beyond:

"Above all, do no harm."

"We   must   dare   to   think
'unthinkable' thoughts .... We
must learn to welcome and not
to fear the voices of dissent ....
Because when things become
unthinkable, thinking stops and
action becomes mindless."

J.W. Fulbright, speech, U.S. Senate, March 27, 1964

Bibliography, Notes & Further Reading

---

[1] Other options for Joe, in descending order of graduated steps from least harmful: Discuss the issue again with Mary and the team leader, since Joe has more information now; write a memo to team leader copied to Rob; talk to company attorneys about new facts and ask them to investigate; persuade another well-established employee to go with Joe to confront Rob; talk with outside technologists and find an ally to confront Rob; talk with Rob's boss; talk with company CEO; file a complaint with the engineering registration board; go to the press anonymously; and schedule a press conference. You will notice that increasing harm may come to Joe as he moves to the most harmful alternative.

[2] Nearly all universities have a basic code of conduct for students to follow. Yet very few have specific and comprehensive codes of ethical conduct for professors related to interaction with students. An exception to this common problem would be the guidelines for research on humans and animals. It is equally rare to find any requirements or procedures for the students to follow when confronted with unethical faculty or staff of the institution. Sexual harassment is one notable exception. Most codes of professional organizations state that incompetence in their membership is not acceptable.

[3] A good layman's discussion of the concepts of moral reasoning and the usefulness of moral theories can be found in Martin and Schinzinger, 39-79, and James Rachels, *The Elements of Moral Philosophy*, 2nd ed. (New York: McGraw Hill, Inc., 1993).

[4] Kohlberg's three levels of moral development—pre-conventional, conventional, and post-conventional—were discussed in Chapter 10. See Kohlberg, *The Philosophy of Moral Development*, Vol. 1 (New York: Harper & Row, 1971).

[5] Technologists and others have too often believed, erroneously, that other animals do not experience pain, grief, and joy during their lives. A number of books now convincingly suggest that animals do experience emotions similar to humans' in many respects. See Jeffrey Masson, *When Elephants Weep: The Emotional Lives of Animals* (New York: Bantam Doubleday Dell Publishing Group, 1995).

[6] Cory S. Powell, "Twenty Ways the World Could End," *Discover*, October 2000, 51-57.

[7] Whitehead, *Adventures of Ideas* (New York: The Free Press, 1961), 204.

Success, recognition, and conformity are the bywords of the modern world where everyone seems to crave the anesthetizing security of being identified with the majority.

Martin Luther King, Jr., Strength to Love, 1963, p.47.

Appendix A
Significant Disasters
of the 20th Century

The following is a partial list of 20th century disasters compiled by Herring and Schlager. It is sobering to see all of them listed in one place. Many more disasters have occurred since their books were written: Firestone tires on Ford Explorers; the Russian submarine Kursk; passenger plane crashes of United and TWA; and the World Trade Center twin towers.

The three references used in Appendix A and in Chapter 6 are (1) Robert L. Cook, "Incentives for Professional Employees," In partial fulfillment of Master of Science, Civil Engineering, University of Missouri—Columbia, December, 1974; (2) Herring, Susan D. *From the Titanic to the Challenger*. Garland Publishing, Inc. New York, 1989; and, (3) Schlager, Neil. Editor. *When Technology Fails*. Gale Research Inc., Detroit, 1994.

Nuclear Plants

Kyshtym power plant explosion, Sverdlovsk, Russia

Windscale reactor complex fire, England

SL-1 experimental reactor explosion, Idaho

Browns Ferry power plant fire, Decatur, Alabama

Three Mile Island, Middletown, Pennsylvania

Radioactive waste spill, Tsuruga, Japan

Ginna power plant radioactive release, Ontario, N.Y.

Chernobyl accident, Ukraine

Fermi nuclear plant, USA

Boris Kidric Institute

Aircraft and Airships

TWA Constellation crash, Reading, Pennsylvania

Eastern Airlines DC-4 crash, Port Deposit, Maryland

United Airlines DC-6 crash, Bryce Canyon, Utah

BOAC Comet crashes, Mediterranean islands

TWA Super-Constellation and United Airlines DC-7 collision, Grand Canyon, Arizona

Lockheed Electra crashes, Indiana and Texas

United Airlines DC-8 and TWA

Constellation collision, New York

Turkish Airlines DC-10 crash, France

American Airlines DC-10, Chicago

Air Canada DC-9 accident

Japan Airlines Boeing 747 crash, Guma, Japan

Midwest Express Airlines DC-9 crash, Milwaukee

United Airlines Boeing 747 explosion, Hawaii

United Airlines DC-10 crash, Sioux City, Iowa

Lauda Air Boeing 767-300 crash, Thailand

El Al Boeing 747-200 crash, Amsterdam

Military: B-1A, B-52, BAC 111, F-100, F-104, F-111, F-18/F404, F-20, Harriers, Hawker Siddeley 748, Pratt & Whitney JT8D engines, Learjet, Lockheed Electra, Lodestar, L-1011, Sikorsky S-61, S-76A

V/STOL, Chinook helicopter crashes, ZR-2 (r-38) disaster, Hull, England; Roma crash, Langley Field, Virginia; Shenandoah disaster, Ohio; R-101 crash, France; Akron crash

Hindenburg crash, Lakehurst, New Jersey

Automobiles

Chevrolet Corvair
Ford Pinto
Firestone 500 steel-belted tire failures
Audi 5000 sudden acceleration
Volkswagen

Bridges

Quebec Bridge collapse
Tacoma Narrows Bridge collapse, Washington State
Vancouver Second Narrows Bridge collapse, British Columbia
King's Bridge failure, Melbourne, Australia
Point Pleasant Bridge collapse, West Virginia/Ohio
West Gate Bridge collapse, Melbourne, Australia
Sunshine Skyway collapse, Florida
Highway ramp collapse, East Chicago, Indiana
Zilwaukee Bridge failure, Saginaw, Michigan
Mianus River Bridge collapse, Greenwich, Connecticut
Schoharie Creek Bridge collapse, N.Y.
American River Bridge
Big Sioux River Bridge
Elwood, Kansas, Highway Overpass
Hood Canal Pontoon Bridge
Lafayette Street Bridge
Mianus River Bridge
Throgs Neck Bridge

Buildings and other Structures

Molasses spill, Boston
Knickerbocker Theater collapse, Washington, D.C.
Bronx apartment house collapse, N.Y.
Texas Tower radar station collapse, North Atlantic
Ferrybridge cooling towers collapse, Pontefract, England
Ronan Point tower collapse, London
Skyline Plaza collapse, Bailey's Crossroads, Virginia
Hartford Civic Center Coliseum roof collapse
Cooling tower collapse, Willow Island, West Virginia
Kemper Arena roof collapse, Kansas City, Missouri
Alexander Kielland oil-drilling rig collapse, North Sea
MGM Grand Hotel fire, Las Vegas, Nevada
Harbour Cay Condominiums collapse, Cocoa Beach, Florida
Hyatt Regency Hotel walkways collapse, Kansas City, Missouri
Ocean Ranger oil-drilling rig sinking, North Atlantic
L'Ambiance Plaza collapse, Bridgeport, Connecticut
Berlin Congress Hall
Concrete building collapse, Harrisonburg, Virginia
Journal Square PATH station
Louisiana parish hall
Sao Luis Rei apartment
Tullahoma missile silo
Sea Gem offshore drilling rig

Chemical and Environmental Disasters

Ecological disaster, Sudbury, Ontario
Cadmium poisoning, Toyama, Japan
DDT insecticide contamination
Love Canal toxic waste, Niagara Falls, N.Y.
Hanford Reservation radioactive waste, Washington state
Mercury poisoning, Minamata Bay, Japan
Agent Orange contamination, Vietnam
Dioxin contamination, Times Beach, Missouri
Methylmercury seed poisoning, Iraq
Chemical plant explosion, Flixborough, England
Dioxin contamination, Seveso, Italy
Toxic vapor leak, Bhopal, India
Toxic vapor leak, Institute, West Virginia

Ships

World War II Liberty ships sinking
Andrea Doria-Stockholm collision
Amoco Cadiz oil spill, France
Exxon Valdez oil spill, Alaska
Derbyshire sinking
Glomar Java Sea sinking
Titanic
Vestris

Submarines

Squalus sinking, USA
Thetis sinking, England
Thresher sinking, USA
Scorpion sinking, USA

Dams

Austin Dam failure, Austin, Pennsylvania
St. Francis Dam failure, San Francisquito Canyon, California
Malpasset Dam failure, Frejus, France
Vaiont Dam landslide, Longarone, Italy
Baldwin Hills Dam failure, Los Angeles, California
Teton Dam collapse, Upper Snake River Valley, Idaho
Stava Dam failure, Stava, Italy

Spacecraft

Nike missile explosions, USA
Rocket fire, former Soviet Union
Apollo 1 capsule fire, USA
Soyuz 1 crash, Russia
Apollo 13 oxygen tank rupture, USA
Soyuz 11 reentry disaster, Russia
Skylab meteoroid shield failure, USA
Challenger explosion, USA
Ariane, France

Appendix B
Characteristics of Technologists

Table 1[a]
Future Goals of Engineers
(Base: 1146, Ranked in Order of Importance)

1.   Live in a community that is desirable for individual and family.
2.   Help to increase company profits.
3.   Have employment stability.
4.   Work on projects that require learning new technical knowledge.
5.   Work on projects that have a direct impact on business success of company.
6.   Work for a company whose reputation is highly respected.
7.   Gain knowledge of company policies and practices.
8.   Become more involved in company's decision making process.
9.   Become more involved with technical aspects of work.
10.   Become more involved with people.

---

[a] Two references were used: Costigan, Robert R., "The Effective Management of Professional Engineers," A Report Presented to the Faculty of the Department of Civil Engineering, University of Missouri, In Partial Fulfillment of the Degree Requirements for the Degree Master of Science, August 1974, p. 35; Landis, F., "What Makes Technical Men Happy and Productive," *Research Management*, May 1971, pp. 22-42.

Table 2[b]
Career Values of Engineers and Technical Professionals
(Ranked in Order of Importance)

1. Work in a job that is interesting, stimulating, and challenging.
2. Sense of achievement.
3. Professional and organizational recognition for achievement.
4. Ascending degrees of responsibility as a reward for achievement.
5. Steady job and career advancement.
6. Self-realization of potential.

---

[b] Two references were used: (1) Costigan, Robert R., p. 37; (2) Raudsepp, Eugene, *Managing Creative Scientists and Engineers*, New York: Macmillan Co., 1963, pp. 164-165.

Table 3[c]
Most Important Goals of Engineers
as Function of Age
(Ranked in Order of Importance)

Under Age 30

1.   Work on projects requiring new technical learning.
2.   Live in a desirable location.
3.   Become more involved in decision making process.
4.   Work in projects that influence business success of company.
5.   Help increase company profits.

Age 35-39

1.   Live in a desirable location.
2.   Have employment stability.
3.   Work on projects requiring new technical learning.
4.   Work in projects that influence business success of company.
5.   Help increase company profits.

Age 45-49

1.   Help increase company profits.
2.   Live in a desirable location.
3.   Have employment stability.
4.   Work in projects that influence business success of company.
5.   Gain knowledge of company management practice.

---

[c] Two references were used: (1) Costigan, Robert R., p. 39; (2) Landis, F., p. 38.

Table 4[d]

Factors Motivating Engineers "To Do A Good Job"
(Base: 1067, Ranked in Order of Importance)

1.   Achievement needs (need to achieve, pride in doing a good job, personal accomplishment, professional reputation).

2.   Monetary rewards and recognition.

3.   Non-monetary recognition (status, respect, prestige).

4.   Challenging work.

5.   Relations with superior and with management.

6.   Nature of work.

7.   Personal growth.

8.   Responsibility.

9.   Company image.

10. Personal relations with associates.

11. Climate, surroundings, working conditions.

---

[d] Two references were used: (1) Costigan, Robert R., p. 41; (2) Landis, F., p.35.

Table 5[e]

Principal "Bother Factors" Experienced by Engineers

(Base: 1146, Ranked in Order of Importance)

1.   Too little time to keep up with new developments.
2.   Insufficient manpower to do the job.
3.   Scope and responsibility of job not clearly defined.
4.   Too much paperwork.
5.   Insufficient support by other groups in company.
6.   Lack of recognition and encouragement.
7.   Too many different assignments at same time.
8.   Too many conferences.
9.   Poor working conditions (crowded offices, etc.).
10.   Too little guidance.

---

[e] Two references were used: (1) Costigan, Robert R., p. 42; (2) Landis, F., p. 40.

Appendix C
Codes of Ethics

Accreditation Board for Engineering and Technology*

CODE OF ETHICS OF ENGINEERS

THE FUNDAMENTAL PRINCIPLES

Engineers uphold and advance the integrity, honor and dignity of the engineering profession by:

    I.   using their knowledge and skill for the enhancement of human welfare;

    II.   being honest and impartial, and serving with fidelity the public, their employers and clients;

    III.   striving to increase the competence and prestige of the engineering profession; and

    IV.   supporting the professional and technical societies of their disciplines.

THE FUNDAMENTAL CANONS

1.   Engineers shall hold paramount the safety, health and welfare of the public in the performance of their professional duties.

2.   Engineers shall perform services only in the areas of their competence.

3.   Engineers shall issue public statements only in an objective and truthful manner.

4.   Engineers shall act in professional matters for each employer or client as faithful agents or trustees, and shall avoid conflicts of interest.

5.   Engineers shall build their professional reputation on the merit of their services and shall not compete unfairly with others.

6.   Engineers shall act in such a manner as to uphold and enhance the honor, integrity and dignity of the profession.

7.   Engineers shall continue their professional development throughout their careers and shall provide opportunities for the professional development of those engineers under their supervision.

*Formerly Engineers' Council for Professional Development. (Approved by the ECPD Board of Directors, October 5, 1977)

National Society of Professional Engineers®

Code of Ethics For Engineers

Preamble

Engineering is an important and learned profession. As members of this profession, engineers are expected to exhibit the highest standards of honesty and integrity. Engineering has a direct and vital impact on the quality of life for all people. Accordingly, the services provided by engineers require honesty, impartiality, fairness, and equity, and must be dedicated to the protection of the public health, safety, and welfare. Engineers must perform under a standard of professional behavior that requires adherence to the highest principles of ethical conduct.

I. Fundamental Canons

Engineers, in the fulfillment of their professional duties, shall:

1. Hold paramount the safety, health and welfare of the public.
2. Perform services only in areas of their competence.
3. Issue public statements only in an objective and truthful manner.
4. Act for each employer or client as faithful agents or trustees.
5. Avoid deceptive acts.
6. Conduct themselves honorably, responsibly, ethically, and lawfully so as to enhance the honor, reputation, and usefulness of the profession.

II. Rules of Practice

1. Engineers shall hold paramount the safety, health, and welfare of the public.

   a. If engineers' judgment is overruled under circumstances that endanger life or property, they shall notify their employer or client and such other authority as may be appropriate.

   b. Engineers shall approve only those engineering documents that are in conformity with applicable standards.

   c. Engineers shall not reveal facts, data or information without the prior consent of the client or employer except as authorized or required by law or this Code.

   d. Engineers shall not permit the use of their name or associate in business ventures with any person or firm that they believe is engaged in fraudulent or dishonest enterprise.

e. Engineers having knowledge of any alleged violation of this Code shall report thereon to appropriate professional bodies and, when relevant, also to public authorities, and cooperate with the proper authorities in furnishing such information or assistance as may be required.

2. Engineers shall perform services only in the areas of their competence.

a. Engineers shall undertake assignments only when qualified by education or experience in the specific technical fields involved.

b. Engineers shall not affix their signatures to any plans or documents dealing with subject matter in which they lack competence, nor to any plan or document not prepared under their direction and control.

c. Engineers may accept assignments and assume responsibility for coordination of an entire project and sign and seal the engineering documents for the entire project, provided that each technical segment is signed and sealed only by the qualified engineers who prepared the segment.

3. Engineers shall issue public statements only in an objective and truthful manner.

a. Engineers shall be objective and truthful in professional reports, statements, or testimony. They shall include all relevant and pertinent information in such reports, statements, or testimony, which should bear the date indicating when it was current.

b. Engineers may express publicly technical opinions that are founded upon knowledge of the facts and competence in the subject matter.

c. Engineers shall issue no statements, criticisms, or arguments on technical matters that are inspired or paid for by interested parties, unless they have prefaced their comments by explicitly identifying the interested parties on whose behalf they are speaking, and by revealing the existence of any interest the engineers may have in the matters.

4. Engineers shall act for each employer or client as faithful agents or trustees.

a. Engineers shall disclose all known or potential conflicts of interest that could influence or appear to influence their judgment or the quality of their services.

b. Engineers shall not accept compensation, financial or otherwise, from more than one party for services on the same project, or for services pertaining to the same project, unless the circumstances are fully disclosed and agreed to by all interested parties.

c. Engineers shall not solicit or accept financial or other valuable consideration, directly or indirectly, from outside agents in connection with the work for which they are responsible.

d. Engineers in public service as members, advisors, or employees of a governmental or quasi-governmental body or department shall not participate in decisions with respect to services solicited or provided by them or their organizations in private or public engineering practice.

e. Engineers shall not solicit or accept a contract from a governmental body on which a principal or officer of their organization serves as a member.

5. Engineers shall avoid deceptive acts.

a.Engineers shall not falsify their qualifications or permit misrepresentation of their or their associates' qualifications. They shall not misrepresent or exaggerate their responsibility in or for the subject matter of prior assignments. Brochures or other presentations incident to the solicitation of employment shall not misrepresent pertinent facts concerning employers, employees, associates, joint ventures, or past accomplishments.

b.Engineers shall not offer, give, solicit, or receive, either directly or indirectly, any contribution to influence the award of a contract by public authority, or which may be reasonably construed by the public as having the effect or intent of influencing the awarding of a contract. They shall not offer any gift or other valuable consideration in order to secure work. They shall not pay a commission, percentage, or brokerage fee in order to secure work, except to a bona fide employee or bona fide established commercial or marketing agencies retained by them.

III. Professional Obligations

1. Engineers shall be guided in all their relations by the highest standards of honesty and integrity.

a.Engineers shall acknowledge their errors and shall not distort or alter the facts.

b.Engineers shall advise their clients or employers when they believe a project will not be successful.

c.Engineers shall not accept outside employment to the detriment of their regular work or interest. Before accepting any outside engineering employment, they will notify their employers.

d.Engineers shall not attempt to attract an engineer from another employer by false or misleading pretenses.

e.Engineers shall not actively participate in strikes, picket lines, or other collective coercive action.

f.Engineers shall not promote their own interest at the expense of the dignity and integrity of the profession.

2. Engineers shall at all times strive to serve the public interest.

a.Engineers shall seek opportunities to participate in civic affairs; career guidance for youths; and work for the advancement of the safety, health and well-being of their community.

b.Engineers shall not complete, sign, or seal plans and/or specifications that are not in conformity with applicable engineering standards. If the client or employer insists on such unprofessional conduct, they shall notify the proper authorities and withdraw from further service on the project.

c.Engineers shall endeavor to extend public knowledge and appreciation of engineering and its achievements.

3. Engineers shall avoid all conduct or practice that deceives the public.

    a. Engineers shall avoid the use of statements containing a material misrepresentation of fact or omitting a material fact.

    b. Consistent with the foregoing, Engineers may advertise for recruitment of personnel.

    c. Consistent with the foregoing, Engineers may prepare articles for the lay or technical press, but such articles shall not imply credit to the author for work performed by others.

4. Engineers shall not disclose, without consent, confidential information concerning the business affairs or technical processes of any present or former client or employer, or public body on which they serve.

    a. Engineers shall not, without the consent of all interested parties, promote or arrange for new employment or practice in connection with a specific project for which the Engineer has gained particular and specialized knowledge.

    b. Engineers shall not, without the consent of all interested parties, participate in or represent an adversary interest in connection with a specific project or proceeding in which the Engineer has gained particular specialized knowledge on behalf of a former client or employer.

5. Engineers shall not be influenced in their professional duties by conflicting interests.

    a. Engineers shall not accept financial or other considerations, including free engineering designs, from material or equipment suppliers for specifying their product.

    b. Engineers shall not accept commissions or allowances, directly or indirectly, from contractors or other parties dealing with clients or employers of the Engineer in connection with work for which the Engineer is responsible.

6. Engineers shall not attempt to obtain employment or advancement or professional engagements by untruthfully criticizing other engineers, or by other improper or questionable methods.

    a. Engineers shall not request, propose, or accept a commission on a contingent basis under circumstances in which their judgment may be compromised.

    b. Engineers in salaried positions shall accept part-time engineering work only to the extent consistent with policies of the employer and in accordance with ethical considerations.

    c. Engineers shall not, without consent, use equipment, supplies, laboratory, or office facilities of an employer to carry on outside private practice.

7. Engineers shall not attempt to injure, maliciously or falsely, directly or indirectly, the professional reputation, prospects, practice, or employment of other engineers. Engineers who believe others are guilty of unethical or illegal practice shall present such information to the proper authority for action.

a.Engineers in private practice shall not review the work of another engineer for the same client, except with the knowledge of such engineer, or unless the connection of such engineer with the work has been terminated.

b.Engineers in governmental, industrial, or educational employ are entitled to review and evaluate the work of other engineers when so required by their employment duties.

c.Engineers in sales or industrial employ are entitled to make engineering comparisons of represented products with products of other suppliers.

8. Engineers shall accept personal responsibility for their professional activities, provided, however, that Engineers may seek indemnification for services arising out of their practice for other than gross negligence, where the Engineer's interests cannot otherwise be protected.

a.Engineers shall conform with state registration laws in the practice of engineering.

b.Engineers shall not use association with a nonengineer, a corporation, or partnership as a "cloak" for unethical acts.

9. Engineers shall give credit for engineering work to those to whom credit is due, and will recognize the proprietary interests of others.

a.Engineers shall, whenever possible, name the person or persons who may be individually responsible for designs, inventions, writings, or other accomplishments.

b.Engineers using designs supplied by a client recognize that the designs remain the property of the client and may not be duplicated by the Engineer for others without express permission.

c.Engineers, before undertaking work for others in connection with which the Engineer may make improvements, plans, designs, inventions, or other records that may justify copyrights or patents, should enter into a positive agreement regarding ownership.

d.Engineers' designs, data, records, and notes referring exclusively to an employer's work are the employer's property. Employer should indemnify the Engineer for use of the information for any purpose other than the original purpose.

As Revised July 1996

National Society of Professional Engineers
1420 King Street
Alexandria, Virginia 22314-2794
703/684-2800. Fax: 703/836-4875
NSPE World Wide Web site: *http://www.nspe.org*

Publication date as revised: July 1996. Publication #1102

"By order of the United States District Court for the District of Columbia, former Section 11(c) of the NSPE Code of Ethics prohibiting competitive bidding, and all policy statements, opinions, rulings or other guidelines interpreting its scope, have been rescinded as unlawfully interfering with the legal right of engineers, protected under the antitrust laws, to provide price information to prospective clients; accordingly, nothing contained in the NSPE Code of Ethics, policy statements, opinions, rulings or other guidelines prohibits the submission of price quotations or competitive bids for engineering services at any time or in any amount."

Statement by NSPE Executive Committee

In order to correct misunderstandings which have been indicated in some instances since the issuance of the Supreme Court decision and the entry of the Final Judgment, it is noted that in its decision of April 25, 1978, the Supreme Court of the United States declared: "The Sherman Act does not require competitive bidding."

It is further noted that as made clear in the Supreme Court decision:
1. Engineers and firms may individually refuse to bid for engineering services.
2. Clients are not required to seek bids for engineering services.
3. Federal, state, and local laws governing procedures to procure engineering services are not affected, and remain in full force and effect.
4. State societies and local chapters are free to actively and aggressively seek legislation for professional selection and negotiation procedures by public agencies.
5. State registration board rules of professional conduct, including rules prohibiting competitive bidding for engineering services, are not affected and remain in full force and effect. State registration boards with authority to adopt rules of professional conduct may adopt rules governing procedures to obtain engineering services.
6. As noted by the Supreme Court, "nothing in the judgment prevents NSPE and its members from attempting to influence governmental action..."

Note:

In regard to the question of application of the Code to corporations vis-à-vis real persons, business form or type should not negate nor influence conformance of individuals to the Code. The Code deals with professional services, which services must be performed by real persons. Real persons in turn establish and implement policies within business structures. The Code is clearly written to apply to the Engineer, and it is incumbent on members of NSPE to endeavor to live up to its provisions. This applies to all pertinent sections of the Code.

National Society of Professional Engineers
1420 King Street, Alexandria, Virginia 22314-2794

Index

accepted industry practices, 38, 74,76, 81, 89, 108, 129, 130, 132, 149, 150, 157, 232, 249, 251

accident, definition of, 108

active evil, 20,22,92, 103. *See* evil.

Adler, Mortimer, 173, 179, 180, 188, 189, 190, 193

aircraft disasters, xvii, 49, 53

Ammann, O.H., 58

Aristotle, 173, 179, 193, 220

Army Corps of Engineers, 99, 146

atomic bombs, 22, 23, 28, 95, 144

authentic selves, 189

automobile accidents, 54, 184

Bechtel, 126, 127, 128, 129

Berenbaum, Michael, 26

Berkebile, Bob, iv, 68, 69, 70, 71, 76, 78

Bhopal, 48, 50, 51, 267

Billington, David, 58

Bloom, Allan, 160, 172, 173, 179, 180, 193

BLS, Bureau of Labor Statistics, 43

Boesky, Ivan, 128, 129

Bolsjoly, Roger, 18, 19, 82, 83, 90

Boyer, Ernest, 160, 161, 179

Bradley, General Omar, 24, 29

Bradshaw, John, 159, 162, 178, 210, 211, 216, 217

Brown, Nina, 124, 140

building codes, 28, 37, 50, 60, 131

Bureau of Industrial Relations, 122

Bureau of Labor Statistics, 43, 61

Carnegie Foundation for the Advancement of Teaching, 158, 161, 179

Carson, Joe, 18, 19

Challenger, iii, vii, x, xi, xiv, 18, 19, 20, 21, 26, 47, 48, 49, 51, 61, 63, 64, 80, 81, 82, 83, 84, 85, 86, 87, 88, 89, 90, 97, 100, 101, 109, 132, 133, 171, 186, 191, 196, 198, 206, 235, 238, 245, 249, 250, 251, 253, 264, 268

Challenger explosion, lessons learned, 85

Chernobyl, 16, 47, 48, 50, 51, 268

Chunnel, 12

civil engineers, 14, 226

cloning, 11, 23, 47, 96

Code of Silence, definition of, 3, 18

Cold War, 23

Concorde, 49, 52

conflict of interest, 33, 34

conspiracy, xi, 4, 24, 54, 58, 74, 77, 89, 93, 106, 164, 165, 167, 179, 211, 215

cost-benefit analysis, 8, 14, 42, 44, 46, 55, 142, 143, 144, 145, 146, 148, 149, 150, 222

CPIS, California Psychological Inventory System, 124

creative manifest destiny, 18, 95, 97

Danielson, Lee, 121, 122, 123, 139

Darley and Batson, Good Samaritan experiment, 102

Davenport, Noa, 90, 141, 169, 170, 179

Davis, Michael, 7, 60, 121, 123, 124, 136, 139, 193, 197, 216, 231

Dayton, Ken, 128

Declaration of Independence, 115, 182, 254, 255, 257

Defining Issues Test, 116

Design and Build project, 149, 248

Dickerson, Bob, iv, 2, 65, 66, 68, 71, 78

Discover, 18, 119, 259, 262

distancing, 97

DOE, Department of Energy, 18, 19

Dresden, 20, 21

Duncan, Daniel M., 71, 75, 78, 79

Duties Theory, 243

earthquake, 49, 50, 125

Einstein, Albert, 115

Emerson, Ralph Waldo, 214

emotional detachment, 97, 98, 99, 100

Emotional Intelligence, 196, 209, 215, 216, 246

Index

Empire State Building, 12, 42

engineer, definition of, 120

engineering, definition of, 13, 223

engineer-in-training, 246

Enron, 128, 129, 198

EPA, 187

EQ. *See* Emotional Intelligence.

errors in judgment, 108

ethical conventionalism, 227

ethics, senses of, 219

evil

 active, 20

 concept of, 202

 degrees of, 21

 genuine, xii, xiii, xiv, 19, 20, 21, 22, 26, 59, 102, 106, 108, 196, 200, 201, 220

 incarnate, 21

 interrelatedness of, 200

 M. Scott Peck's definition, 107

 nature of, 107, 194

 necessary, 95

 passive, 59, 107, 111, 177

 philosophical concepts, 19

 psychiatrists' definitions, 21

 psychology of, 19

 ultimate, 22

Existentialism, 15, 141

Explorer, Ford, 140

Exxon Valdez, 48, 51, 268

FAA, 187

fail-safe, 10, 46, 47, 63, 81, 83, 84, 111, 112, 113, 114, 125, 215, 229

Fail-Safe, the movie, 112

FAIL-SAFE checklist, 229

false self, 184, 206, 207, 208

fast-track project, 37, 248

Ferguson, Eugene, 57, 58, 59, 62, 109, 110, 112, 119

Feynman, Richard, 82

Final Solution, 19, 22, 25

fixed-price contract, 60, 146, 148, 149

Flemming, Gerald, 25, 26

Florman, Samuel, 15, 16, 28, 135, 136, 137, 14

Frankl, Viktor E., 105. *See* Holocaust.

Freud, Sigmund, 12, 20, 105, 183, 190, 193, 201, 206, 210, 216

Frey, Robert S., 25, 28, 29, 141

Fullbright, J. W., 261

Galileo, xi, 35, 219

genuine self, 20, 189, 190, 206, 207, 208, 209, 210, 211, 212, 214, 215, 245, 260

Gerstl, Joel, 122, 123, 139

Gillum, Jack, 70, 71, 75, 78, 79

Great Books, 157, 179

great ideas, 172, 173, 175, 182, 183, 184, 188, 189, 190, 193, 195, 207, 218

groupthink, 27, 93, 133, 134

Haney, Banks, and Zimbardo

 Prison experiment, 102

Hanford nuclear facility, 46

Hawthorne, Nathaniel, 181

Henan, China, 45, 48

Herring, Susan, 47,49, 264

Hippocrates, 261

Hiroshima, 16, 28, 101

Hoffer, Eric, xi, xiv, 41, 61, 92, 94, 101, 107, 118, 151, 160

Holocaust, 8, 10, 16, 19, 20, 21, 22, 23, 24, 25, 26, 28, 29, 74, 84, 97, 100, 101, 102, 103, 105, 133, 138, 141, 165, 166, 167, 196, 238

Hyatt, Kansas City, iii, iv, vii, x xiv, xvii, 2, 3, 16, 20, 21, 26, 51, 59, 63, 64, 65, 68, 69, 70, 71, 72, 74, 75, 76, 78, 79, 81, 97, 100, 101, 109, 130, 132, 133, 138, 186, 191, 196, 198, 228, 238, 249, 250, 251, 266

Industrial-Military-University Complex, 24, 35, 89, 142, 157, 158, 167

informed consent, vii, ix, xv, 64, 84, 85, 107, 184, 185, 186, 187, 222

Index

instinct, xv, 192, 195, 199, 201, 202, 204, 206, 207, 208, 212, 238, 259

interrelatedness, concept of, 203

intrinsic, 199, 202. *See* instinct.

Jung, Carl, 177

Jurassic Park, the movie, 1

Keene, Sam, 211, 212

Kemper Arena, 40, 51, 61, 266

Kennedy, John F., 91

Kierkegaard, Soren, 15, 141

King, Martin Luther, Jr., 263

Kobe, 50, 125. *See* earthquakes.

Kohlberg, Lawrence, 204, 205, 206, 207, 216, 224, 243, 262

Lewis, Michael, 28, 60, 161, 167, 179

Lickona, Thomas, 104, 105, 118. *See* moral psychology.

low-ball bidding, 147, 148

low-bid process, 147

lowest contract price, 8

lump-sum contract, 60, 146, 148, 160. *See* fixed-price contract.

Manhattan Project, 95

manifest destiny, 95

McAuliffe, Christa, 80, 81, 83

MGM Grand Hotel, 44, 51, 266

Milgram, Stanley

electric shock experiment, 102

Missouri Board for Architects and Engineers, 75

mobbing, viii, 86, 90, 134, 141, 169, 170, 171

moral development, 104, 194, 201, 204, 206, 207, 224, 243, 244, 262. *See* Kohlberg, Lawrence.

moral dilemmas, definition, 30

moral philosophy, 218

moral responsibility, 4

morality, definition of, 197

Morton Thiokol, 18, 82, 83, 84, 86, 90

MSNBC, 83, 90

M-T, 82, 83, 84. *See* Morton Thiokol.

My Lai, 102, 105, 106, 118, 210

myths, 17, 92, 93, 114, 115, 117, 150, 177, 204, 223, 246. *See* true beliefs.

NASA, xvii, 18, 47, 64, 80, 81, 82, 83, 84, 85, 86, 87, 88, 89, 90, 100, 138, 171, 250, 252

Nazi, xii, xiii, 8, 16, 21, 23, 24, 25, 26, 29, 84, 96, 105, 124, 137, 166, 174, 190, 191, 220, 221, 235, 227, 245

National Bureau of Standards, 72, 73, 76

NBS. *See* National Bureau of Standards.

negligence, 2, 59, 61, 63, 72, 74, 75, 76, 103, 115, 164, 196, 198, 278

Nova, 25, 26

National Research Council, 88, 90

NRC. See National Research Council.

NSPE, 228, 239, 240, 241, 242, 244, 245, 278, 279

NSPE Code of Ethics, 228, 242, 279

Nuremberg trials, 224

Oppenheimer, Robert, 95

OSHA, 187

passive evil, xiv, 19, 20, 21, 22, 59, 103. *See* evil.

Peck, M. Scott, 19, 28, 107, 108, 118, 176, 180, 210, 217

permissible standard of conduct, 221, 223, 224

Perrucci, Robert, 121, 122, 123, 139

Petroski, Henry, 113, 119

pragmatism, 221, 222, 223, 227

price, "low-ball," 147

Process Philosophy, 203, 204, 256

Process Thought, 203

Prufer, Kurt, 25. *See* Nazi.

Post-Traumatic Stress Disorder, 71, 192

PTSD. *See* Post-Traumatic Stress Disorder.

Quadrilateral, 203

rational, definition of, xii, xiii, 7, 108, 134

Index

rational human being, xv, 4, 7, 93,185, 203, 223, 259

relativism, 172, 227

repression, 20, 190, 191, 192, 193, 210

right actions, 221

right to life, 243, 255

Russell, Bertrand, xviii

Sahakian, Mabel and William, 193, 222, 227, 231

Schlager, Neil, 47, 61

Schott, Richard L., 123, 124

Schwartz, Arthur, 176, 180

Sears Tower, 12, 16

self, definition of, 20, 201

self-evident, 115, 182, 183, 202, 207, 243, 255

September 11, xi, xiii, xv, 3, 5, 253. *See* 9-11, World Trade Center.

Shimantan and Banqian Dams, China, 45

shop drawings, 38, 73, 74

Simon, William E., 126

skybridges, 2, 65, 74, 249, 250, 253

sociopath, 190, 195, 201, 246

specialization, viii, 171, 172, 174, 175, 176

specialized education, 99, 101, 172, 175, 256

spectrum of evil, xi, xvii, 19, 20, 92, 117, 204. *See* evil, active evil, passive evil.

Spectrum of Genuine Evil, Figure 1, 21

Star Trek, 11

Stewart, James B., 163, 178

suppress, xiv, 93, 99, 191, 206

suppression, xiv, 16, 20, 26, 59, 63, 93, 98, 99, 11, 190, 191, 209, 210, 223

Tacoma, xvii, 51, 56, 57, 58, 76, 81, 84, 265

Tacoma Narrows Bridge, xvii, 51, 56, 57, 76, 81, 84, 265

team approach, 133

team effort, 10, 13, 26, 33, 40, 59, 82, 133, 134, 138, 171

team players, 92, 123, 132

technical imperative, 95, 96, 97

technologists, definition of, 4

tenure, 155, 161, 167

terrorist, xiii, 3, 5, 6, 7, 8, 9, 11, 21, 48, 63

Teton Dam, 45, 267

The Learning Channel, 28, 48, 61

Three Mile Island 16, 47, 51, 267

Time, 14, 61, 78, 79, 96, 118, 140, 180

Tischler, A.O., 87, 88

Titanic, xi, 16, 46, 47, 48, 51, 61, 62, 138, 264, 268

TLC TV, 45

Trinity Project, 22

true belief phenomenon, 92

true beliefs, 14, 59, 76, 89, 92, 93, 94, 111, 114, 115, 117, 150, 152, 177, 194, 210, 222, 245, 248

true believers, 92, 94, 95, 96, 101, 120, 151, 171, 204, 212, 219, 245

true believers, definition of, 92

true self, 183, 192, 202, 203, 205, 206, 207, 209, 212, 218

United Nations, 224

Utilitarian Theory, 143, 144, 145, 160, 221, 243

Vaiont Dam, 267

value engineering, 132

Virtues Theory, 243

whistle-blower, definition of, 247

whistle-blowers, 18, 22, 86, 87, 88, 127, 170, 166, 242

Whitehead, Alfred North, 216, 260, 262

Wigand, Dr. Jeffrey, 18, 19

World Court, 224

World Trade Center, iii, vi, xi, xiii, xv, 2, 3, 5, 6, 7, 9, 20, 21, 46, 48, 63, 72, 132, 253, 264. *See* WTC.

World Wide Web, WWW, 6, 13, 278

WTC, xi, xiii, 5, 6, 8, 9, 10, 16, 19, 21, 64, *See* World Trade Center.

🐎 Quick Order Form

for *Code of Silence: Ethics of Disasters*

- ❑ **Yes**, I want _____copies of the *Code of Silence* (#021005) for **$24.95** each (plus S/H below).

- ❑ **Yes**, I am interested in free information about having Robert Cook speak or present a seminar to my company, association, school, or organization. Please send me information.

- ❑ **Yes,** I am interested in free information about consulting services from AEC Education Consultants. Please send me information.

Include $5.75 for shipping and handling for one book, and $2.50 for each additional book. Quantity discounts available. Canadian orders must include with U.S. funds, an added 7% GST. Missouri residents must include sales tax.

Usually, allow 3-5 days for delivery after receipt of order when paying by credit card or money order. Allow 3-5 weeks for delivery if paying by check; please do not send cash. Payment must accompany orders.

❑   My **Check** or **Money Order** for $_____is enclosed for _____books.

❑   Or, please charge my **MasterCard or Visa** (circle one) for $_____

Card #_____

Name on Card_____

Exp. date _____Signature _____

Name (printed)_____

Address_____

City_____ State_____Zip_____

Telephone (_____)_____Email address_____

Email: *AEC-info@AEC-Education-Consultants.com*   **Fax 573- 374-2021**

www.AEC-Education-Consultants.com

Make your check payable and return to:

Trojan Publishing Co.
200 Madison St., Suite 380, PMB #224
Jefferson City, MO   65101-3280